DR YESHAYAHU (JE
spiritual scientist, philos
founder of the anthropo.....
Harduf, Israel, co-founder of the Global Network for
Social Threefolding, director of Global Event College
and contributor to the School of Spiritual Science. He
is the author of *The Spiritual Event of the Twentieth Century*, *The New
Experience of the Supersensible*, *America's Global Responsibility*, *The
Event in Science, History, Philosophy & Art* and *Spiritual Science in the
21st Century*.

COGNITIVE YOGA

*Making Yourself a New Etheric Body
and Individuality*

Yeshayahu (Jesaiah) Ben-Aharon

TEMPLE LODGE

Temple Lodge Publishing Ltd.
Hillside House, The Square
Forest Row, RH18 5ES

www.templelodge.com

First published by Temple Lodge Publishing, 2016

The Publishers are grateful to Scott Hicks for his editorial work on the text

A CIP catalogue record for this book is available from the British Library

ISBN 978 1 906999 95 7

Cover by Morgan Creative
Typeset by DP Photosetting, Neath, West Glamorgan
Printed and bound by 4Edge Ltd., Essex

Contents

Preface

If anyone in our time publishes the results of spiritual scientific research based on his own experience, he naturally expects to encounter many objections. Let me mention only one that comes in two complementary forms. The first kind of objection is prevalent among those followers of anthroposophy who believe that – Rudolf Steiner's individual example notwithstanding – individual super-sensible experience should not be the source of spiritual science. On the other side stand those who are satisfied with having spiritual experiences, revelations and visions, and regard spiritual science, well, as demanding too much science, because it requires a serious long-term commitment to develop clear, exact and thoughtful forces of spiritual cognition. Now people that raise the first type of objection sincerely believe that only the loyal interpretation of the master's texts and the preservation of the cultural and practical forms he created are the real tasks of spiritual science. It is not difficult to find the contradiction in this belief: since, if spiritual science is supposed to be an authentic science, it must be founded on fresh empirical research of the real world, given in human experience and not merely on the interpretations of texts.* Never-theless, I have encountered this objection repeatedly since I pub-lished my first book in the middle of the 1990s. It is said that because I have grounded my spiritual research in my own supersensible experience, I cannot be considered a loyal follower of Rudolf Steiner and therefore my research should not be taken as a serious con-tribution to the development of spiritual science. On the other hand, no one will deny that many spiritual experiences are misused to justify egotistic desires and to foster a similar belief in external

---

*We could be reminded in this context of Rudolf Steiner's characterization of the disciples of Aristotle as 'a plague of knowledge,' since they became fierce enemies of the new natural science because they tried to dismiss Galileo's individual and original observations of the real physical word by quoting texts from Aristotle written some 2000 years before.

authority. Finding a middle path between these two dogmas, the dogma of tradition and the dogma of experience, is certainly difficult and must be repeatedly discovered.

Now, we shouldn't simply dismiss the first objection out of hand, because its error is based on an important truth which must be fully understood. The loyalty to the authority of traditions, institutions and texts that many people demand is a misrepresentation of the real essence of spiritual loyalty, which should be directed to the *spiritual forces* that bring about the original, creative impulses themselves and not to the external forms in which they are incarnated and preserved. *This loyalty* is, as a matter of fact, absolutely necessary. It is a precondition for advancement in all branches of human knowledge and creation. Progress in human life and knowledge must be grounded in the rich soil cultivated by the founders and developers of each branch of our cultural and social life. If someone wants to present individual research in physics, he must study and assimilate the fundamentals of physics, and indeed much more. He will then demonstrate this knowledge in his whole approach to doing and presenting his individual research. Moreover, when we study the life of scientists and artists who are truly creative and independent, we find that loyalty to their predecessors was the source of their original creations, even when they had to struggle to overcome the outmoded, external forms of the past. What the believers in the dogma of experience maintain, namely, that being free and creative means to receive visions and inspirations out of thin air, is amply contradicted by the fact that the most creative and free people are precisely those rooted in the deepest sources of their fields. The truly great revolutionary gladly acknowledges his indubitable debt to his predecessors, while the creative pioneer and the adventurous discoverer is also the most devoted pupil. For the real pioneers it is a matter of fact that to be 'original' implies the literal meaning of the term: only to the extent that you derive your creative forces from the spiritual origins of your craft, can you aspire to become truly original.

Rudolf Steiner is the greatest example of this, because he founded spiritual science on the best achievements of natural science. Was he loyal to the truth discovered by the founders of natural science?

Most certainly. Was he a free and creative person, who established a wholly new discipline of science? Yes, indeed. Eventually, the freely developed loyalty to the creative founding impulse of your discipline is the same loyalty that you owe to your own true self, since in the spiritual world they both have the same source. However, while in the case of other sciences and arts, the loyalty to the spiritual origins may be conscious in varying degrees, in spiritual science it must become fully conscious. If you want to transform spiritual experience into fully conscious and cognitive supersensible research, you can only find your bearings if you most scrupulously follow the real spiritual steps of your teacher. One can, as a matter of fact, establish, corroborate, and confirm one's individual experiences and insights, only if one grounds each single step in the previously accomplished spiritual work of the masters in this field. (It is important to emphasize that this is not done for external reasons, such as to take pride in one's learning or to gain acceptance in this or that quarter, but purely because of these internal reasons.) One is only honest and conscientious, spiritually speaking, to the extent that one fulfils this requirement. These are the objective laws and conditions in this field of knowledge. And I know full well that it is wholly superfluous to try to convince someone in these matters, as long as that person does not want to experience it for himself. To argue about what spiritual science really is with the believers in the dogmas of tradition and experience is never a productive undertaking. One can only proceed by repeatedly checking one's own inner loyalty and truthfulness in fulfilling the immanent, inherent laws and conditions of spiritual research and then leave it peacefully for the reader to create his or her own individual judgement.

Let me mention briefly in this regard some moments from the formative years of my spiritual work.* My adult spiritual life began in a supersensible experience of the etheric Christ. I immediately started to search for answers and solutions to the innumerable

---

* I have described some aspects of my spiritual biography in an interview with Thomas Stöckli, published in *Das Goetheanum*, January 2001, an enlarged version of which is included in the 2007 reprint of my book, *The New Experience of the Supersensible*, Temple Lodge Publishing.

questions and riddles that this experience brought about. This
search led me directly to anthroposophy. I first studied Rudolf
Steiner's researches concerning the Christ impulse. Next, I moved
on to general anthroposophy, and then a year later, I read Rudolf's
own starting point for spiritual science *The Philosophy of Freedom*.
This happened precisely 40 years ago, in 1976. Alongside a continual and intensive study of anthroposophy, I began to study with
the greatest enthusiasm everything he ever wrote and said about
cognition, philosophy, Goetheanism, natural science and their
transformation into spiritual science. I still remember with the
innermost warmth of soul those short years in my early 20s that I
could devote to assimilating the basics of modern natural science
and biology in Oranim college (a branch of Haifa university where
some 20 years later I received my doctorate in philosophy with my
dissertation on *The Cognition of the 'I' in Husserl's Phenomenology*,
finely supervised by Prof. Michael Strauss). I spent mornings and
afternoons in the classes and labs where one could experience
firsthand the great achievements of present-day physics, chemistry,
biology, physiology and anatomy with all the devotion and enthusiasm of the youthful student forces. Then I worked long evenings
and nights in my little apartment to combine every line of the
natural scientific knowledge with the natural and spiritual scientific
works of Goethe and Steiner. I found out that Rudolf Steiner
demonstrated, in the most concrete, repeatable and testable details,
the practical cognitive art of the creation of a continuous cognitive
bridge, made from the most pure and exact thoughts, that lead from
contemporary natural science and thinking to spiritual science. I felt
that, through the Christ experience I found my earthly home in the
spiritual world closest to the earth, and through Rudolf Steiner's
spiritualized science, thinking and cognition, I could find my
spiritual home on the earth. And the building of a fully conscious
spiritual bridge between the two worlds soon became my daily
spiritual breathing. It became a vital element in my inner life and my
spiritual research that I have been developing and transforming
through the last decades. This became the source of my published
books, lectures and my contributions to the school of spiritual
science, and its application in social life became the source for the

foundation of the community of Harduf. I have published the results of this research in my books, *The Spiritual Event of the 20th Century*, (1993) *The New Experience of the Supersensible*, (1995), *America's Global Responsibility* (2002), *The Event in Science, History, Philosophy & Art* (2011), and *Spiritual Science in the 21st Century* (2013). I consider the present book to be an organic continuation and development of the essential thread that unites my spiritual research throughout the years, based on my main book, *The New Experience of the Supersensible.**

---

* Finally, let me remark that due to recent demands on my time, I had to refrain from referring to Rudolf Steiner's books at every step and turn of the present text. With few exceptions, the grounding of my present research in Rudolf Steiner's corpus will be left to the reader. However, the good news is that the detailed and extensive notes, the references and the bibliography in my fundamental book, *The New Experience of the Supersensible*, can serve you as a useful resource for the present book a well.

Introduction

Rudolf Steiner started from the highest and most recent soul faculties that humanity has developed in the modern age: clear and exact thinking and lucid sense perception. This growing tip of the evolution of human consciousness can be transformed in a twofold way. On the one hand, the clearest and most exact thinking can be spiritualized. This takes place through *The Philosophy of Freedom*. On the other hand, clear and wide-awake sense perception can be spiritualized. This is done by a spiritualization of Goethe's study of the psychological effects of colours. Both can be transformed into new faculties of supersensible research. In relation to this task of spiritual science, Rudolf Steiner introduced the concept of a 'new Yoga will', in the comprehensive context of human and cosmic evolution, in his lecture cycle, The Mission of Michael (GA 194, 1919). He described it as a way to create the 'future culture of Michael' and establish the 'Christ-filled soul relation to nature'.

In the lecture of 30 November he describes it as follows:

> When our sense processes will become ensouled again, we shall have established a crossing point, and in this crossing point ... we shall, at the same time, have the subjective-objective element for which Goethe was longing so very much.... In reality, there takes place a soul process from the outside toward the inside, which is taken hold of by the deeply subconscious, inner soul process, so that the two processes overlap. From outside, cosmic thoughts work into us, from inside, humanity's will works outward. Humanity's will and cosmic thought cross in this crossing point, just as the objective and the subjective element once crossed in the breath. We must learn to feel how our will works through our eyes and how the activity of the senses ... brings about the crossing of cosmic thoughts and humanity's will. We must develop this *new Yoga will*. Then something will be imparted to us that of like nature to that which was imparted to human beings in the breathing process three millennia ago. Our comprehension must become much more soul-like, much more spiritual.... This will be

Michael-culture. (The Ancient Yoga Culture and the New Yoga Will. The Michael Culture of the Future, Lecture from 30 November, 1919, GA 194)

A year later Rudolf Steiner introduced this new yoga practice as a method of spiritual development and spiritual research in the inaugural lecture cycle of the High School of Spiritual Science, entitled The Boundaries of Natural Science (GA 322, 1920), given to anthroposophically oriented academics, scientists, artists, physicians and socially engaged people:

> What, in fact, is the process of perception? It is nothing but a modified process of inhalation. As we breathe in, the air presses upon our diaphragm and upon the whole of our being. Cerebral fluid is forced up through the spinal column into the brain. In this way a connection is established between breathing and cerebral activity. And the part of the breathing that can be discerned as active within the brain works upon our sense activity as perception. Perception is thus a kind of branch of inhalation. In exhalation, on the other hand, cerebral fluid descends and exerts pressure on the circulation of the blood. The descent of cerebral fluid is bound up with the activity of the will and also of exhalation. Anybody who really studies *The Philosophy of Freedom*, however, will discover that when we achieve pure thinking, thinking and willing coincide. Pure thinking is fundamentally an expression of will. Thus pure thinking turns out to be related to what the Oriental experienced in the process of exhalation. Pure thinking is related to exhalation just as perception is related to inhalation. We have to go through the same process as the yogi but in a way that is, so to speak, pushed back more into the inner life. Yoga depends upon a regulation of the breathing, both inhalation and exhalation, and in this way comes into contact with the eternal in man. What can Western man do? He can raise into clear soul experiences perception on the one hand and thinking on the other. He can unite in his inner experience perception and thinking, which are otherwise united only abstractly, formally, and passively, so that inwardly, in his soul-spirit, he has the same experience as he has physically in breathing in and out. Inhalation and exhalation are physical experiences: when they are harmonized, one consciously experiences the eternal. In everyday life we experience thinking and perception. By bringing mobility into the life of the soul, one experiences the pendulum, the rhythm, the continual inter-

penetrating vibration of perception and thinking. A higher reality evolves for the Oriental in the process of inhalation and exhalation; the Westerner achieves a kind of breathing of the soul-spirit in place of the physical breathing of the yogi. He achieves this by developing within himself the living process of modified inhalation in perception and modified exhalation in pure thinking, by weaving together thinking and perceiving. And gradually, by means of this rhythmic pulse, by means of this rhythmic breathing process in perception and thinking, he struggles to rise up to spiritual reality in Imagination, Inspiration, and Intuition. And when I indicated in my book *The Philosophy of Freedom*, at first only philosophically, that reality arises out of the interpenetration of perception and thinking, I intended, because the book was meant as a schooling for the soul, to show what Western man can do in order to enter the spiritual world itself. The Oriental says: systole, diastole; inhalation, exhalation. In place of these the Westerner must put perception and thinking. Where the Oriental speaks of the development of physical breathing, we in the West say: development of a breathing of the soul-spirit within the cognitional process through perception and thinking. (GA 322, 3. 10. 1920)

I introduced the goal of the cognitive yoga practice in Chapter 5 of my book, *The New Experience of the Supersensible*, in a way that is just as relevant to our present study:

Our study of the knowledge drama of the Second Coming will be divided into three major parts:

1. the transformation of thinking, or the opening of the gates of thinking;
2. the transformation of sense-perception, or the opening of the gates of perception;
3. the construction of the bridge of memory and continuation of consciousness over the abyss of spirit-forgetfulness.

When we try to recreate, or recapitulate, the modern Christ experience voluntarily, we are confronted with two major problems, the nature of which is determined by the nature of our daily consciousness, namely, the problem of thinking on the one hand and the problem of sense perception on the other. These two are experienced as the main obstacles, but, at the same time, as the only legitimate gates of entrance into the sought-for land of the Etheric Christ. When a self-conscious bridge is to be built between the normal, wide-awake and rational modern state of consciousness and the inspired and intuited imaginative appearance, speech and acts of the Christ in His Second Coming, so must the consciousness soul itself—which, according to Rudolf Steiner, is the soul of free sense-perception and free Imagination—be our only solid ground of construction. There are, therefore, two closed gates to be opened: the gate of thinking and the gate of sense-perception.

In *The New Experience of the Supersensible* I used cognitive yoga to research deeper aspects of the creation of the cognitive bridge leading to the Christ experience and of the being of Christ. In the present book I have limited the scope of my research to the narrower etheric field. This focus allows me to describe the following in greater detail:

In Chapter one, 'The life cycle of etheric breathing', I use the comparison to the electrolysis of water into two gases, hydrogen and oxygen, to explain the separation and etherization of sense perception and thinking commonly bound together in our representations of the world. This process becomes a life-giving etheric breathing between the human being and the world, and between heaven and earth.

Chapter two, 'The composition of ordinary cognition', shows how ordinary cognition is centred in the mental picture or representation, in which all experiences, including sense perception and thinking, are condensed and downgraded. Stopping this composition and freeing perception and thinking to their original etheric state, necessitates a confrontation with the unconscious forces that bind them to the brain.

Chapter three, 'The pearl of greatest price: Individuation', describes human individuation and freedom as the most significant goal of human and cosmic evolution. This can only be achieved through a physical incarnation on the earth. Only after the human Ego grounds itself in its separate existence, can it use and spiritualize the formative forces that have separated him from the spiritual worlds in order to unite with them again, in full individual consciousness.

In Chapter four, 'Etherization of Sight', I explain, step by step, how colour is detached from the representations of objects, spiritualized and then inhaled directly into the body. This brings about a release of the etheric body from the physical brain. However, the body's resistance increases when we strive to liberate the etheric body from the head downwards, leading us to confront what appears to be an unsurpassable threshold in the lower body.

In Chapter five, 'Etherization of Thinking', it is shown how spiritualized thinking penetrates deeper into the death processes that create ordinary cognition. These forces will join the forces extracted from the etherisation of perception and help them cross the lower bodily threshold.

Chapter six, 'Etherization of Smell', demonstrates, first of all, how the sense of smell is etherized and used to penetrate deeper into the body. Second, we show how to combine the two streams of perception from etherized sight and smell, supported by the forces of etherized thinking, to liberate the etheric body from the head to the heart.

Chapter seven, 'Birth of a new etheric body', describes how the mutual exchange between the etheric world and etheric body liberates the purest and most productive etheric forces preserved and protected since the earliest childhood of humanity. The fructification between the purest etheric forces of the world and the body conceives a new etheric offspring, which becomes the foundation of an independent spiritual life in the etheric world.

In Chapter eight, 'Birth of an etheric individuality', I show how the spiritualized extract of the strongest spiritual activity accomplished through cognitive yoga in the physical world, enables us to conceive and give birth to an independent spiritual individuality in the etheric world.

Chapter nine, 'Early childhood of an etheric individuality', describes how the etheric individuality, once it is born in the etheric world, undergoes its first formative stages of spiritual childhood and develops the spiritual equivalents of the forces that the child develops in the first three years of earthly life.

In Chapter ten, 'Essence exchange with the cosmic source', I describe how the matured spiritual individuality approaches the cosmic source of all creation. It becomes an etheric chalice that receives the forces of the etheric Christ needed for the present and future progress of humanity and the earth.

This progress is endangered from many sides today, and prominent among them is the powerful Ahrimanic vision and practice of the Technological Singularity. In the course of this century countless human bodies and souls will be merged with an infinitely seductive and powerful artificial intelligence and virtual reality. This technology will bind them to a sub-natural and inhuman world, which they will experience more and more not only as a fantastic means of entertainment but also as the magical redemption and healing of all human suffering and mortality. This sub-natural and inhuman world lies, morally speaking, one level below the natural and human physical world. However, through the cognitive yoga practice outlined in what follows, we can consciously rise one level above the physical world to the nearest supersensible world, the etheric. In this etheric world alone can our hearts, minds and deeds be healed and resurrected. And only there, in the deepest forces of our human becoming, can we find the life-giving source of the earth and humanity in the twenty-first century.

1. The life cycle of etheric breathing

We cannot tell from the looks of it that water can be split into hydrogen and oxygen. Though water is liquid and does not burn, hydrogen is a combustible gas – clearly something quite different from water. We can use this as a metaphor for the spiritual process I am about to explain. People are a combination of soul-spiritual and material-physical elements, just as water is a combination of hydrogen and oxygen. In 'spiritual chemistry,' we must separate the soul-spiritual from the material-physical elements just as water can be separated into hydrogen and oxygen. Clearly, just looking at people will tell us little about the nature of the soul-spiritual element.

(26 May 1914, GA 154)

Water is the most common and essential liquid that sustains all the processes of life as well as living beings in the physical world. Like all other physical substances it is not original stuff, but a condensation of etheric and ultimately of spiritual forces. Water is a result of an active process of composition, synthesis and condensation of two very different substances, namely, the gases oxygen and hydrogen.

This can be verified experimentally through electrolysis. The electrolysis decomposes the water (H_2O) into oxygen (O_2) and hydrogen gas (H_2) by passing an electric current through the fluid. When we subject water to an electric current, hydrogen will appear at the cathode (the negatively charged electrode), and oxygen will appear at the anode (the positively charged electrode). Water is thereby decomposed into two gases which are substances with wholly different physical and chemical properties than water.

Now electrolysis is reversible: when we subject oxygen and hydrogen to an electric current, the product will be a wholly new substance, a condensed element, which we call water. But we never could have predicted the properties of the two gases from the properties of water and vice versa. The condensation of water out of oxygen and hydrogen is an actual metamorphosis, creating a real novelty in the world. After all, the fact that two gases produce water when they are put together, should appear as a real wonder, since the properties of water are totally different from its original gaseous components. Similarly we must marvel at the fact that the electrolysis and decomposition of water produces two gases, whose properties are essentially different and even the polar opposite of the properties of water from which they have been separated; for example, hydrogen is actually the most flammable of the gases.

The starting point of cognitive yoga can rightly be compared to an electrolysis process applied to ordinary human cognition, for we let the most energetic cooperation of all of our active soul forces flow into our ordinary cognition to polarize, separate and liberate its basic elements. The soul's electric current is made of a mutually enhancing, reciprocally invigorating synergy of all our soul forces. We must bring our whole human being into activity, by awakening forces that commonly slumber in the deep unconscious will and half-conscious feelings that are covered over by our conscious representations. This synergetic, holistic force is fired by the strongest forces of our innermost will, which is the soul equivalent of electricity in the physical world. It is furthermore charged in the heart by the love of truth, and this love and will stream through the structure and content of our ordinary cognition to break loose its hardening, intellectualized, 'mental water'. When we succeed in this, we electrolyze, decompose and separate it into many soul and mind forces and elements, out of which we choose two: pure sense perception that emerges on one side and pure thinking on the other.

Conversely, the composition and condensation of water out of pure gases can serve as an exact analogy to the coming into being of ordinary human cognition. Once we succeed in the electrolysis of ordinary cognition and experience pure perception and thinking as free etheric forces, we can consciously follow how they are composed and condensed into a mental unity when we represent our experiences and our world. By decomposition and recomposition through mental electrolysis, cognitive yoga brings the two sides of our cognitive process into full consciousness. We discover that, unconsciously, we constantly transform each experience we have into a mental picture which represents it in our consciousness. We are not usually aware of the fact that all experiences and acts of thinking, before they are joined in order to be represented, are essentially free flowing etheric forces that stream in the open etheric world. We condense them together into a mere mental picture (or 'representation') whenever we know something. And in order to know something we must first represent it to ourselves in our conscious minds.

We can use the meaning of the words 'presentation' and 'representation' to help clarify this. 'Presentation' means the full presence of the real thing, while its 'representation' is but a shadowy mental image that we form in our consciousness *after* the real experience. Therefore, for example, while we may experience through our feelings in a half-conscious way, the real presence of the being we encounter, when we bring 'it' to full consciousness and represent 'it' in our mind, we have created only a faint memory picture of the original, fully saturated experience. And this is what we find in our mind after the experience has ebbed away: its mental shadow, empty of its real presence and substance. And this is what we actually mean when we say that we 'know' something when we represent it to ourselves. Paradoxically speaking, we can say that what we experience we don't know, and what we know we don't experience.

As we shall demonstrate in greater detail in Chapter 2, on the composition of ordinary cognition, we are naïve today in regard to how we know the world. We believe that things exist outside in the world exactly as we represent them in our mind and that their separated and condensed state is their real natural state. This amounts to the belief that water is made of water and not of gas and that it was, is and always will remain water. Now, try to convince someone who hasn't witnessed electrolysis that water is the dense product of two gases, a combination and condensate of pure gases that stream freely and invisibly in the atmosphere!

In the cognitive yoga practice, we electrolyze and decompose the condensed result of ordinary knowledge: the mental picture. Mental pictures and their various derivatives (memories, reminiscence, associations, mental patterns and habits, etc.) constitute the basic substance and structure of our minds, the stuff that makes up our common 'mental water'. Their components, once separated from the forces that bind and condense them, become something as different from their properties and appearances in ordinary cognition as the pure gases of oxygen and hydrogen are different from water. This means to extract and liberate the living, light and expansive 'gaseous' essences of all experiences and thinking from their representations and to experience them in their pure, original state. And when we actualize the reverse process, transforming the etherized perception and thinking back to ordinary cognition, we realize that the results of their composition and condensation is indeed a synthetic, new substance, wholly different from both in their original state. This 'mental water' sustains all aspects of our daily consciousness, cognition and knowledge.

The notion that our representations of things are dense compositions made of rarified etheric forces and substances, sounds as ridiculous to the modern mind as the notion that water is a product of hydrogen and oxygen to someone who has never witnessed electrolysis. However, the moment we begin to observe our own cognition, the naïve position begins to shatter, because we discover that we cognize and recognize the world by applying thinking to everything we experience. From the moment we realize that we reflect *about* our experiences when we recognize them, and that we make representations of everything we see, hear and touch, feel and desire, we realize that the real things may not be similar at all to their representations in our consciousness. And we may begin to doubt and agonize, as do many honest philosophers, about the question: what are things in reality, in themselves, outside our representations of them? We realize that as long as we remain in the confines of our ordinary consciousness, we have no 'immediate' or 'direct' knowledge of real things, in their true or spiritual essence, as they exist outside our representation of them. Even ordinary thinking is not experienced in itself as pure thinking, but is known to us as we know all things, by means of representing it to ourselves. Then we realize what many thinkers have realized, that as long as we remain inside the limits of ordinary cognition, there is truly no way out of this dilemma, that our cognition is limited to representation and that direct knowledge about the 'things themselves' is denied to us, as the followers of Kant still maintain today.

The first great natural scientist and artist who protested most strongly and creatively against these Kantian limits of cognition and knowledge was Goethe. Goethe believed that everything is in change and becoming and couldn't accept such an absolute limitation of our cognitive capacities. He studied the creative and transformative forces of nature all his life, and found out that the fundamental dynamic that causes metamorphosis in nature is 'Polarität und Steigerung' (or polarity and intensification). Rudolf Steiner applied Goethe's method to human cognition to create a far-reaching metamorphosis of this cognition. As he described in The Boundaries of Natural Science, we can separate the inhalation of our sense-perceptions from the exhalation of our thinking, just like the yogi of old separated the physical inhalation and physical exhalation that bound him to his body and experienced the immortal, spiritual essence of the soul. In this way we learn, through the cognitive yoga practice, to polarize and separate our ordinary mental constitution as water is electrolyzed. Then we decompose its basic element, the mental picture, separate thinking and sense perception from each other, purify, extract and etherize each one, and intensify each one in its pure etheric becoming. This is the new cognitive breathing of light-filled etheric forces, liberated from the physical body that binds and hardens them together. This is a timely renewal of the ancient yoga method, which was based on the polarization and intensification of the physical breathing, but which we now apply to the more inward soul forces of modern consciousness.

When perception and thinking have been liberated in this way from ordinary consciousness, they are etherized, taking the first step in a long and dramatic process of spiritualization. The cognitive yoga practice consists in this, that we intensify perception and thinking to such an extent that we learn to breathe them in and out, inhale and exhale them according to the needs of our spiritual scientific research. Thus the new will of yoga, that Rudolf Steiner indicated, becomes creative and productive in an individualized way.

Now beside electrolysis there is also a more organic metaphor for cognitive yoga: the natural water cycle in nature. In this cycle, water shows us that it has retained a *potential* of its gaseous origin in its condensed state. It has the inner tendency and capacity to partly escape gravity, become light and gaseous, and transform itself as closely as possible to a pure gaseous state: it evaporates into the atmosphere, gathers itself as clouds and recondenses and reincarnates as life-giving rain and snow. This capacity that water has to transform itself creates a cycle on the earth that nourishes and sustains all life. In this cycle, water is naturally vaporized and rarified, becoming gas-like, and partially escaping the pull of gravity to reach a cosmic circumference and height. There it imbues itself with fresh, life giving, and cosmic forces. Then it re-embodies itself, returns to the earth and endows it with new and fresh life forces gathered from the whole universe.

In the same way, but now as self-conscious, individual human beings, we learn through cognitive yoga breathing how to actualize the whole life cycle of the earth as a life-giving cycle of cognition. Through us, life becomes self-conscious as a free rhythmic and creative cognitive activity working through the whole human being, in which all of the soul forces mutually intensify one another. It flows with the currents and streams of life as they ascend and descend, etherize themselves in us and in the cosmos and embody themselves back on the earth. It is life's cyclic breathing, becoming self-conscious in us, that unites our creative cognitive process with the life cycle of planet earth and all vibrant life streams and cycles in the universe. This conscious life cycle of etherization and recondensation, out-breathing and in-breathing, incarnation and excarnation, becomes a source of a new life- and light-breathing that humanity and the earth contribute to the whole universe.

Through the practice of cognitive yoga, we learn how to co-create consciously with the breathing rhythms of all life on earth and in the universe. In the future humans will be able to breathe cosmic life and light in this way as a natural spiritual breathing, as physical breathing of air is common today. In the cognitive yoga practice we begin, therefore, to actualize human capacities from the future that are still potential in most people today. The external sun's light, life and warmth, cause the exhalation and inhalation of the planetary life cycle in the course of its daily and seasonal rhythms. But the spirit of the sun, the Christ being, has now become the spirit of the earth. Therefore, in reality the practice of cognitive yoga produces intensive new *sun* forces of light, life and warmth through creative cognitive activity. Life becomes self-conscious cognitive creative activity. The forces of spiritual human cognition, streaming from the etherized forces of the will, heart and mind together, unite with the spiritual sun being of the earth itself, to become productive and contribute new and fresh life forces that replace the declining natural earthly resources. This gift of new life intensifies and potentizes the currents and streams of planetary life as they ascend and descend, etherize themselves in the cosmos and condense themselves back on the earth. It adds the contribution of our creative cognition to the life cycle of planet earth and its vibrant new life in the universe. In this way we can speak about the creative, life-giving sun activity of human cognition as a real source of future earthly and cosmic life, light and warmth, not as metaphor but as concrete, actual objective reality.

In this way our new life- and light-breathing also becomes an individualized co-productive activity with the forces of the etheric Christ on the earth. In each moment the Christ embodies, in the earth and in human hearts, the highest spiritual sun forces, the source of all cosmic love, life and light. Since the Mystery of Golgotha, His forces enhance and etherize themselves through all creative human deeds of love, beauty and truth. Rudolf Steiner described the reciprocally circulating etheric life cycle between the Christ, human deeds of love, and the earth like this:

> And here we must ask, what takes place, now that there is always something of the Christ light in human etheric bodies? What occurs in that part of the etheric body in which the Christ light has been received? . . . It is the possibility that was given at that time, as an effect of the Christ light, for something new to appear, something living and breathing and immortal, something that can never perish in death. . . . Ever since that time, then, the human etheric body has held something that is not subject to death, to the death forces of the earth. And this something which does not die with the rest, and which men gradually achieve through the influence of the Christ impulse, now streams back again out into cosmic space; and in proportion to its intensity in

man it generates a certain force that flows out into cosmic space. And this force will in turn create a sphere around our earth that is in the process of becoming a sun: a sort of spiritual sphere is forming around the earth, composed of the etheric bodies that have come alive. The Christ light radiates from the earth, and there is also a kind of reflection of it that encircles the earth. What is here reflected as the Christ light, appearing as a consequence of the Christ event, this is what Christ called the Holy Spirit. Just as the event of Golgotha provided the first impetus for the earth to become a sun, so it is true that beginning with this event the earth began to be creative, surrounding itself with a spiritual ring which, in turn, will in the future develop into a sort of planet circling the earth. (6 July 1909, GA 112)

Since the end of the last century, the above described etheric circulation and breathing between the sun-becoming earth and its etheric sphere, happening through the new Christ forces in human beings, can become fully conscious. Through the spiritual activity described here, it takes place *consciously* during physical earthly life, and not only through the accumulated immortal parts of human etheric bodies after death. Each moment of loving attention, of devoted self-overcoming and truthful transformation, contributes to the sun becoming of the earth and its living, etheric breathing. We learn, gradually and methodically, not in theory, not sentimentally, but in an active and creative way, in every small detail of our daily lives, to become co-creators and partners with the new activity of the etheric Christ, in the etheric breathing between earth and heaven.

2. The composition of ordinary cognition

How would it be with sense-perception if it could only stream into us from outside – stream from the light as colour to the eye, as warmth into our sense of warmth? What would then happen to us? We must make it clear to ourselves: in our waking state we never let this world only stream into us. When we are even only a little active in developing ideas in our thinking, we bring the world of ideas against the instreaming sounds, colours, smells, tastes. . . . You see, if we had been simply given to the world of sense-perceptions, then we would have lived as human beings in our etheric body and with the etheric body in the etheric world, if you were living in an etheric sea as etheric being, you would have never come to that human consistency which you actually have in the world between birth and death. . . . How do you reach this consistency? In that you are organized to suppress and kill this etheric life. And with what do we suppress it? With what do we kill it? Through the counter-thrust of ideas! . . . We would have had an etheric world around us if we had not killed it and brought it down to physical form through the world of ideas.

(GA 198, 10 July 1920)

The basic composition of common cognition: The mental picture

Let us look closer at the structure of our common daily cognition. How do we represent reality to ourselves? Well, to begin with, this is exactly what we don't know, because we take it for granted that we know our world, and that the objects around us, including ourselves, are already known to us because we can represent them to ourselves consciously. So we usually don't ask *how* we know what is known to us. Cognition isn't something we inquire about; we aren't interested to know how we know. The cognitive yoga practice starts, therefore, when we begin to ask this question and lift to consciousness the unconscious processes that prepare and make possible our common knowledge.

If we begin to investigate how knowing and cognizing take place, the first thing we realize is that the moment in which we connect experiences to thoughts and thoughts to experiences in order to represent the world isn't conscious at all. We don't see it. It's invisible and unconscious. This means that the most elementary process, by means of which we know everything that enters into our conscious mind, happens so fast and instinctively that we don't pay any attention to it. It lies outside our daily cognition, which it makes possible in the first place. Therefore, this is the first step in the modern cognitive yoga practice, because here—and only here — can we learn to observe and actually participate in the formative process that brings about our mental pictures and representations of all our knowledge. This takes repeated practice and conscious training, which every person can accomplish because it begins with their most immediate cognitive experiences. And our first discovery is the following.

When we say, 'I know what this thing is, that it is so-and-so', we have already formed a mental picture of this thing. If we are simply satisfied with this mental result, we will not feel a need to inquire further and investigate how cognition really works. But let us observe our reactions to an unknown object, occurrence or experience. When confronted with an unfamiliar object or experience, we begin to think about it. First we will compare it to known representations. We will use our memories and associations in order make analogies and comparisons. We will say: it is similar to this, it reminds me of that. What we are actually doing is searching among our known representations to explain the unknown object of experience. And we test our representations by connecting them with the unknown thing. We try this and that, we look it up in the literature, and continue to study it until we find the concept that will fit the observed object. We find 'what it is' and designate it by its name, or give it a new name. This is the common process of acquiring knowledge that usually escapes our attention. Through the example of trying to figure out what an unknown thing is, we can become conscious of how we do our daily cognitive work. We are constantly composing mental pictures, by combining and synthesizing experiences by means of our thinking, and our thinking mobilizes and applies memories, associations and mental pictures to the object or experience at hand. Because we have done this unconsciously since early childhood, this cognitive process has become as instinctive and embodied as our capacities of speaking and walking upright. Synthesizing and assembling thinking and experiences has become a mental and soul habit, without inquiring about how we do it. As a matter of fact, my speaking and walking functions well enough for my daily needs even if I have no conscious knowledge of their origin, and we treat thinking in the same way. It recognizes and represents the already more or less known environments and routine experiences and tasks of my daily life. And thus we don't inquire further about it, and we usually don't wonder how it is able to organize and explain our inner and outer experiences.

But now we turn our attention to what is left unattended and unaccounted for in daily cognition, and we ask: how exactly does our thinking function? When we observe the daily activity of thinking, we realize that thinking is busy explaining the world. It addresses the question, 'what is this thing?' by answering 'this is what this thing is'. What does our thinking add to our experiences? It tells us *what* we experience. It is thinking that tells us that this is red, this is C sharp, this is sour, warm or cold, and it is thinking that connects very different experiences and sense perceptions together and tells us: this is one unified object: a house, table, person. Each experience — external or internal — becomes a conscious representation in our mind to the extent that it is connected to thinking, because we use thinking to tell us what the thing *is*. Thinking comes to our aid to give the answer to the question we ask when we experience something. Thinking therefore tells us 'what the thing is', and all the answers, that we have received from our earliest childhood up to this very moment determine the content and form of our daily cognition. And our daily cognition always comes with its store of representations and memories, associations and habits, the sum total of everything we know as conscious beings. So we recognize, identify, name and remember the things around us and in the world of our everyday life, and yet, most people would never ask themselves *how* we actually do this. They are simply content with the ability to represent and know things, as long as it works properly, while caring less about the fact that we have no conscious experience and knowledge about the deeper sources of thinking and indeed of experience as well.

The reason for this is discovered by enlarging our daily attention, becoming increasingly aware that the actual activity of thinking and representing is not present in the mental pictures that we are conscious of. We realize then—and this already requires enhanced attention and wakefulness—that the actual activity of thinking, and its source, isn't represented like any other representation, because thinking is doing the work of representing. The work of representing cannot be represented, because it is real spiritual activity and as such part of the real world (and not its image only). This is our first major discovery as *The Philosophy of Freedom* demonstrates. Thinking as living, creative activity already belongs to the real world, and not to the world of mental images. It is a *force*, not an *image*. For our ordinary consciousness, it is hidden 'behind' its own work and veiled by its own products: the mental pictures of which we are conscious and that we use to recognize ourselves and the external sensory world. We are aware only of the end result of a lengthy, unconscious, real process and become conscious only about what has crystallized *out* of this reality, as our finished knowledge of the world. And we remain unaware from where thinking comes and how it gets its remarkable explanatory prowess. This is just taken for granted and used in our daily commerce.

In truth we are always using thinking to construct our mental life, and to represent, name, organize, and explain our inner and external experiences. And we do it all the time, as long as we are awake, while we are not really aware of this constant representation activity that goes on. It is covered constantly by an unstoppable chatter of thought images, memories, associations and habits. We don't realize what experience is in itself, because we are busy talking mentally to ourselves all the time, and this inner talking keeps our mind and our known world intact and stable. However, when we begin to observe how thinking works behind this chatter, we discover that this stable mental state is founded on the unceasing activity of composition. In other words, it is not really stable at all. It is constantly knit together. It is a perpetual result of a constantly active mental representing. This is why we don't fall asleep in daily life: we maintain our wakeful daily consciousness by means of a constant inner speaking while mentally representing the world. The moment we stop this, we fall asleep. The talk that keeps us awake

ends only when we fall asleep, with only a few confused residues
lingering on in our half-conscious dreams. And indeed this is the
reason why we keep this talking-representing on all of the time,
because it keeps our ordinary consciousness and cognition running
and awake in the physical world. The moment we really stop it, our
inner life and our outer world disappear from consciousness altogether and our consciousness disappears with it. But this condition
of sleep is taking place all the time in our unconscious daily life.
Becoming conscious of the activity of thinking, and how we represent the world, is the first step into the normally sleeping, unconscious, state, that accompanies us all the time during our waking
life. When we observe this fact, we realize that this happens because
we don't have a strong enough force of cognition in our daily life
that can bring the transition from wakefulness to sleep into full
consciousness and then make sleep itself into conscious experience.

Training in cognitive yoga creates these intensive cognitive
forces by means of which we can wake up the forces that otherwise are asleep in us all the time, also when we are awake in our
representations. We learn how to consciously experience the real
spiritual forces that work right behind our representations. Then
inside our ordinary state of cognition, which is asleep to the real
formative forces of our consciousness, the new one 'wakes up'
and starts to stand up and walk, speak and think in a higher cognitive world.

The desire for knowledge

The more we practise this attentive observation, we will gradually
realize that our mental pictures of ourselves and of our world are
the constructions that we make in order to become firmly and
physically embodied and awake in a known and secure world. As
was pointed out above, we do this perpetually when we unconsciously and instinctively combine our experiences and thoughts
with each other in order to explain, know and name what we
experience. After this observation becomes a fully conscious cognitive experience, we can take the next step and ask: what would

happen if we stopped connecting our experiences with our thinking in order to answer the question 'what is this?' Well, if we try to do it and merely remain in ordinary consciousness, we will either fail because our mental habits and instincts prove to be too strong, or in the very moment we succeed, we will simply fall asleep. This means that we have to learn to experience something, say, a simple sight or sound, and not react to it mentally at all. We have to let go of the instinctive 'thinking about it' reaction, and all of the other soul reactions that go along with it (such as our vested interests, feelings, emotions, desires, fantasies and associations), in the very moment the simple sight or sound emerges into our field of attention. The more we try to do so, the more we realize that in order to prevent the 'the counter-thrust of ideas' that transforms our experiences to representations, thinking must first of all make itself free from the instinctive *need* to constantly represent all experiences. Then it is transformed into a pure thinking experience, freeing itself from reflecting and explaining all experiences, including the experience of itself. Therefore the lifelong practice of *The Philosophy of Freedom* is indispensable, not as a theoretical explanation of what thinking is, but as a continuous process of the etherization of thinking itself. (This is described in greater detail in Chapter 5 below.)

When this practice is actualized, we find out to what extent our ordinary consciousness and soul life consist in the *desire* to use thinking in order to explain, fix, and possess each and every experience, and we also find out how mighty our hunger is for possessing the world in this manner. Ordinary knowledge is taking hold of the world, making it our own, privatizing it. As we shall presently see, what makes this operation of 'stopping the mental construction of the world' so difficult is really the almost bodily hunger that we feel when we are 'burning' with the desire to explain or name something. It turns out that this desire to know isn't really so different from all our other desires. As we strive to capture, assimilate and possess whatever we desire, bodily, emotionally, and socially, we do the same thing mentally. But while we are much more aware of our basic body and soul desires, hungers, and needs, this desire and need behind our intellectual appetites usually escapes our attention. We don't experience this desire consciously because it remains hidden and covered over behind the acquired knowledge, and because we are existentially much more interested in fulfilling our desire and satisfying our hunger for the knowledge itself. But through the cognitive yoga training, we learn to face this desire directly, and we realize that we crave explaining each experience just as much as we crave physical nourishment and emotional comfort and love.

Therefore, our first task is to slow down this instinctive intellectual desire that motivates the mental feeding process, which functions as fast as any physical instinct. To being with, we will have to struggle to be able to make even the shortest pause in our instinctive rush to gratify our craving for knowledge, but if we persist and intensify the pure, unattached, activity of thinking, we will gradually succeed in expanding and enlarging this delay. First, we can free thinking just enough to open up a tiny interval or gap in time, a momentary flash of spacing, distance, and separation between thinking and experience. Second, with further practise, we will increasingly learn to control this spacing process. We will develop the capacity to bring the continuous composition of thinking and experiences to a halt and command the time of mental composition and synthesis to 'stand still'. In this way we open and enlarge the time interval between experience and the instinctive need to use thinking in order to name, recognize, and represent whatever knowledge we desire. We can stretch time and enlarge this pause until it becomes a veritable, experiential 'virtual duration' or 'pure time' as Bergson would call it. Now we are capable of experiencing whatever we choose without instinctively and compulsorily having to fulfil our desire to think about it. We can practise some short moments of mental fasting, so to speak, giving up the instinctive need to mentally capture, eat, digest and possess our experiences. This short abstention is an intensive and powerful experience, and we feel that our life forces that once served our mental assembly line are invigorated and liberated. The more we can stop the composition process, the more we can liberate living time, otherwise bound to our physical body, in order to experience and observe what emerges and takes shape in, through, and beyond the gap between freed thinking and experience.

Now, when we succeed in stopping this composition, we experience a *fourfold* liberation process. This happens gradually and naturally depends on how strong and long lasting our accomplishment proves to be. Four elements and forces of the soul are liberated here: thinking, perception, feeling and will, around which all the other soul forces group themselves. First, we free thinking and perception and discover that they transform into their enhanced and original gas-like flow. Second, we liberate the invested and captivated feeling and will forces (notice that the will also contains desires and instinctive forces) that motivate the drive to satisfy the mental hunger, causing the composition of each mental picture (the liberation of the feeling and will forces in themselves will be discussed in detail below, as this issue will come increasingly to the fore through the continuous liberation process of perception and thinking). Perception and thinking are both released from the self-seeking powers of instinct, will, desires, needs, emotions and feelings that bind them to each other in each act of representing something that we desire to know, name, fix, possess and command as a private mental asset. This means cancelling the whole cognitive process that rolls on and on in its unconscious, conventional, convenient, habitual manner and freeing the forces and components that it constantly captures and harnesses. Now we discover for the first time to what extent our daily cognition separates our etheric, living, being and becoming from the world's real etheric being and becoming, and isolates us from the real cosmic world of perpetual growth, change and metamorphosis that goes on around and in us all the time. We call both the process and the result of this continuous cosmic-earthly, reversed, becoming: 'individuation'. Thus we break down the otherwise instinctive loop of action and reaction, the sensory-motor mechanism that binds perception and thinking so tightly to each other, and with it we stop and delete the constant formation of both the form and content of our daily cognition. A new form of consciousness and cognition lights up here already when we achieve this first step in our development. And the result of this very first step is already far reaching indeed.

Knowing is killing

The more we achieve this 'stopping of the world' the more we liberate the soul forces invested in its consolidation. These forces sustain the further electrolysis of the mental picture. In this way we discover, step by step, that in the daily process of cognition, when we unconsciously combine our experiences with thinking, we change their essential constitution. We take into our consciousness two subtle and fleeting ethereal or 'gaseous' elements, and compose and condense them together. This composition degrades them both by compressing, contracting and condensing them to a far more solid and less vital level. In each mental picture that we make of *any* experience, be it sense perception, feeling, deed or external object, we enact a remarkable transformation.

For example, the 'red object' that we 'simply perceive' is in reality something we remember, recognize, represent and name 'red' when we look at it and are conscious of it as an object of our perception. What we mean in daily life when we say that we 'simply sense' something is always already known in advance. The red colour we believe that we 'purely' see attached to a piece of cinnabar is already a dead, condensed part of the mental picture of the already known object 'cinnabar', and not at all a pure flowing, living, 'gaseous' sense quality or intensity. It is also objectified in our mind and has become part of a mental representation of an object, which has many other perceptual qualities and modalities, all of which are synthesized and solidified in the same manner. Likewise, a patch of colour or a red beam of light is just our mental representation and not at all 'pure red in itself'. The red we picture to ourselves in our conscious mind is represented and hence not present in its full cosmic vitality and majesty. In short, by the time we have become conscious of anything at all, by the time we have recognized and named any experience, it has already died out in becoming our mental picture. It is actually a leftover corpse of its real and vital cosmic being, just as the human corpse is in comparison with the living and fully incarnated soul-and spiritual human being. It is no longer the thing in itself, independent of our cognition and as long as we remain in the confines of ordinary cognition, we will never know what red is in its true, free floating and streaming, cosmic 'gaseous' state. And if we merely philosophize about this given state of cognitive affairs, we must invariably become loyal Kantians, because Kant was perfectly correct in maintaining and meticulously proving that ordinary cognition can never know from direct experience what the *Ding an sich* (or thing in itself) really is. And the same is true in regard to the experience of 'thinking in itself *(Denken an sich)*'. We have no experience of 'thinking in itself', only its mere intellectual shadow and image, as long as we merely reflect and represent it in our self-conscious mind.

For example, when we consider that act of thinking by which we form the concept of a triangle, we find that the mental object we recognize and name is not pure at all, but rather a fixed object which we must imagine with attributes (like its particular shape, position and size) that we have borrowed from former sense experiences. The mental representations of even the most abstract mathematical and geometrical objects are not essentially different from the representations of any external object. Anything that truly comes to full consciousness, anything we name and 'know' is always only the dead corpse of a real, living thinking and perception that we just don't experience in our ordinary consciousness or cognition. Even the mental picture we make of thinking is not a present, living, active, and streaming experience of thinking *in itself*; it is the dead product of an unconscious past activity. Thinking is never experienced consciously in ordinary cognition as streaming and living cosmic force and neither are sense perceptions. Through our electrolysis, we can get to know that what we call 'thinking' in ordinary cognition is not its true being, but only the corpse left behind after it has completed its daily physical work, unseen and unappreciated like Cinderella. This unrecognized princess connects all of our experiences, naming and recognizing them, so that we can organize and control our daily lives in the physical world. When we say: 'this red object is cinnabar', we have named the finished result of an unconscious cognitive activity that has already been killed, crystallized and condensed. But as long as thinking Cinderella remains unknown, unappreciated, her true spiritual being remains hidden from us. To make her the queen that she truly is, not only in the unconscious night sleep, but in midday, in full consciousness, is the first goal of cognitive yoga.

Decomposition of the mental picture

So we see that in the first stage of the cognitive yoga practice, we experience that ordinary knowing, through forming representations of reality, is a mental killing process. This experience already takes place in a new state of consciousness, which is no longer a consciousness that merely represents things but increasingly experiences them. When we delay and then stop the incessant reactive thinking about our experiences for a second, a new and greatly enhanced state and stage of cognition lights up. Now let us enlarge this gap of time and make some observations while we are in this new state of enhanced consciousness and cognition. The next experience that we have is this: at the moment when thinking and perception are liberated from the mental picture, both are immediately metamorphosed and sublimated; they become gaseous, volatile and vapor-like. Then we begin to experience that each has an etheric life of its own that is killed and therefore can be suppressed, repressed, and hidden in the mental picture. We experience to what extent both thinking and sensation are diverted from the stream of their true spiritual and etheric becoming when we use them to propel our ordinary cognition, and that the moment we stop their composition, we also stop their devitalization and degradation. We stop the continuous killing in our ordinary consciousness.

As if resurrected from the grave of the human mind, thinking and sense perception are then released and liberated to once again unfold their life in their original etheric world. And they show their heartfelt gratitude because they begin to divulge what they really were originally outside our minds, in a jubilation of liberation. To begin with, this is more or less an experience that is only subtly felt, taking place in the fleeting, rapidly fluctuating time gap that we open between them when we decompose the mental picture. But increasingly the cognitive yoga student learns how to focus her full attention separately on each element in its released state, and to let it disclose its true living potentials.

However, before this move is fully undertaken, we feel a need to go back to ordinary cognition from, as it were, 'the other side' and experience once more the lifeless result of this mental composition. The need to experience this dead end again and again from the other, living, side is significant, and the student must learn to pay heed to such subtle inner feelings and intimations, because they will always guide her in the right direction. Spiritual practice, to the extent that it is a real and living process, is never a linear stride forward, but always spiralling and pulsating back and forth. The path of research is always diverging and bifurcating, evolving and then involuting to former stages in order to experience the 'same' place in a different way, and then breaking through to truly new discoveries and dimensions.

Discovering the brain

In ordinary cognition we don't feel our brain when we think and perceive. The brain, floating comfortably in its capsule of the skull, can't feel itself. It is in a fortified citadel, isolated not only from the world it surveys, orders and judges, but also from the living body that carries it, nourishes it and keeps it alive. We only perceive the brain when we are no longer using it for the business of everyday cognition, in other words, when we have progressed far enough in the cognitive yoga to experience free-flowing thinking and perception. Only when we can look back at the brain from the outside, do we begin to experience its real nature with our whole soul.

Let us once again observe the formation process of the mental picture, but now from the outside. When we opened the time gap in between perception and thinking, we actually went outside of our physical brain. This is a real inversion (or *Umstülpung* process, going inside out and outside in), because now our consciousness is really living and weaving outside our ordinary consciousness, in the company of the freed forces that are usually used to construct the mental pictures. This is how we discover the brain as the workshop

in which representations are made, because perception and thinking alike show us that when they are freed from representing, they
are also freed from the brain. When you truly become one with the
stream of pure perception (as shall be described in detail in Chapters 4 and 6 below) you are experiencing yourself *outside* the sense
and nerve system concentrated in the brain. You weave in the real
external light forces, before they have been reduced to a barren
representation of light in the brain. Then from the periphery, from
the perspective of light itself, you look back and see how two
streams, among an infinite number of currents, that you call 'perception and thinking' are flowing and crashing into a central place.
This central place was what you experienced as your 'inner world'
before. This flow of many different currents is strongly pulled in
and sucked into the brain. We *feel* now how forcefully they are
compressed and contracted when we say, 'this is a tree'. The real
life- and light-forces that flow from the real being of the tree, which
in reality is a magnificent flowing together of countless streams of
cosmic-etheric happening and becoming, suffer in our mind an
infinite condensation and degradation. At this place we discover a
remarkably efficient capturing, appropriating, and reversing
machine. It is like a whirlpool, a vortex of physical, mental and
intellectual gravity and attraction, a 'black hole' situated in the
middle of an etheric universe. This reversing device forcefully sucks
in, grabs, captures, dissects and assimilates the freely floating and
streaming world thinking and the fleeting etheric, perceptual
impressions. Every sensation and quality of light, colour, shape,
sound, smell, touch and movement is assimilated. It contracts their
immense cosmic stature into the tiniest chambers of the brain and
meshes them all together into the condensed and lifeless stuff, by
means of which we picture the world. It is the brain that brings to
our full consciousness the finished result: a dead mental picture of a
dead object-like 'tree', a static representation of the real living,
thriving, flowing cosmic tree, now fixed in our mind and memory.
When the representation of the tree in my mind is compared with
the real, living, cosmic being of the tree, it appears infinitely less
alive than a photo is in comparison with the real, living person
photographed. And then we realize that this black hole (or 'satanic

mill' to use Blake's wholly justified and esoterically precise meta-phor) in the etheric world is what we call the brain in the physical world. It is the brain that first captures the freely streaming world forces that we name in our ordinary language 'thinking' and 'experiencing' or 'perceiving', and it is the brain that transforms them into the mentally dead and solid representation of the living and flowing world.

Through our practice of cognitive yoga, we can gain a first hand, empirical and trustworthy demonstration of the creative (because it creates something new in the universe) process of destruction by means of which the modern mind comes into being. It is trust-worthy and scientifically precise because we can recapitulate it at will, experiment with its various aspects and variations, and verify our observations repeatedly. At this stage, we can experience in outmost clarity what Rudolf Steiner described in his words quoted below:

> If you were living in an etheric sea as etheric being, you would have never come to that human consistency which you actually have in the world between birth and death. How do you reach this consistency? In that you are organized to suppress and kill this etheric life. And with what do we suppress it? With what do we kill it? Through the counter-thrust of ideas!

This becomes a fully conscious, etheric experience, of how the cosmic etheric life in which we are unconsciously embedded is killed in the brain. Once we have stopped the incessant production of representations and stepped out of the brain mechanism, we know through direct experience that we would have never devel-oped our clear-cut and wide-awake modern state of self-consciousness without it. We also would have never lived as detached subjects in an objective world populated with material, physical objects, separated from one another in space, if this powerful brain mechanism wasn't working all the time in our unconscious mental background. We experience this for the first time when we stop this brain function, liberate ourselves from its sucking vortex, step out of its centre, and experience the real living world forces that make up our thinking and perceptions before they were captured by the brain. This is the first fully supersensible, etheric, cognitive experience one develops by means of the modern spiritual science. At this stage we can observe and study our whole brain mechanism from the outside, from the perspective of the real, living supersensible world. 'Outside' is naturally meant here qualitatively and not spatially, because conversely, we could just as well say that we actually penetrate much deeper into the 'inside' of our brain. All such physical expressions lose their ordinary meaning in the etheric world. This is a significant spiritual experience of truthful self- and world-knowledge and it only happens through the grace of the brain free thinking and perception, whose spirit eyes we are kindly allowed to use. In the physical world, bodily and mental processes truly converge: the dead brain and the dead mental picture it produces are one and the same process and product, cosmically perceived. Outside the head and brain, thinking and perceptions are free, world open, non-personal and non-representational living and formative streams, which, in the greater cosmic whole, circulate with the ebb and flow of the creative cosmic forces. And we become part of the streaming of this life of the real etheric world the more we join their liberated cosmic flow.

This discovery, therefore, allows us to understand that, by stopping the world and decomposing the mental picture, we have actually begun to become conscious and operative outside the physical brain. Furthermore, we experience for the first time what the real function of the brain from the spiritual point of view actually is. In the physical world we consider the brain to be the instrument that enables us to gather and synthesize our knowledge of the world. In the etheric world we see the reverse side of this picture. We realize that the brain is indeed the most highly evolved and complex instrument of physical knowledge, but it comes with a price tag of which we have no inkling at all in ordinary life. We discover that the brain is an instrument that contracts, narrows, condenses and degrades the forces of our own living body and the living forces of the cosmos, killing and transforming them into a mere mental picture. Furthermore, we discover that in reality the etheric formative forces that create and operate the physical brain are not located 'in' the space and time of the brain's flesh at all, but in its cosmic environment, both close by and very far away.[*]

This is the deeper meaning of discovering that we have a brain: the most sublime divine forces and beings have created the most perfect instrument of earthly knowledge, yet at the same time, it must destroy the very forces that created it, in order to enable human freedom. Thanks to the brain and its attached sense- and nerve system, we are becoming wide awake and free beings in the physical world, which we would have never become if we would have remained forever wholly immersed in the real living super-sensible world. It is shaped and energized by the most beneficial cosmic formative forces, in order that we can excel in producing dead and fixed knowledge about a represented, dead and material world. But this is a divine sacrifice, accomplished for the absolutely fruitful and positive process of human individuation. In this individuation and the positive possibilities that freedom allows, the Gods have invested the best forces of their past, and the highest hopes of their future.

We will understand this from a more evolutionary perspective if we realize that the good Gods didn't want us to remain their eternal babies, no matter how beautiful and sweet we might be. They wanted to raise free co-workers and partners, not children or slaves. The human brain is placed in the universe by the best creative forces as a dam that stops, blocks and kills the living cosmic streams of life in order to make us self-conscious. Only through this stopping and blockage do we awake from our ancient dreamy, childlike, colourful and imaginative cosmic slumber. In the vast and infinitely powerful cosmic fields and forces of the real spiritual universe and real natural forces, humans would have never achieved self-consciousness, independence, free will and moral choice, mental and technical acumen, and all the good things that we value so much as foundations for our modern existence. We would have never been

---

[*] 'It's not what is in the brain that matters, but what the brain is in', as cognitive scientists emphasize today, still from a purely materialistic point of view. For more about this, see the first chapter, 'The Event in Science', in my book, *The Event in Science, History, Philosophy & Art* (VBW Press, 2011).

in the present, modern, position to become—if we so choose—
grown up, creative, free partners of the Gods. It is the brain (as part
of the physical body) that lifts us out of this unconscious existence in
the cosmic whole and makes us into separate individualities. It
individuates us. From the intensely living and real forces of the
cosmic whole, the brain constantly selects the minimum of
impressions, already analyzed and separated from each other by the
various sense organs, and compresses this minimum into the tiny
mental pictures that we make to ourselves in our waking daily
cognition. It is the brain that makes the mind into the 'slayer of the
real' and sets us free. That every morning we wake up in the bright
daylight and self-consciousness, which are the foundations of our
separate, modern personal identify and life, we owe to our brain-
bound intellect. This is the modern cognitive power par excellence
of individuation, which can forcefully experience: 'I think therefore
I am!'

Etheric inhalation and exhalation

As was emphasized above, in cognitive yoga we start from the most
recent stage in the evolution of consciousness: from the wide-awake,
sober and clear thinking and sense perception. This is a significant
distinction, by means of which Rudolf Steiner characterized the
modern spiritual path as a truly modern spiritual science. Only this
starting point is grounded in the latest achievements of modern
consciousness in the age of natural science. Furthermore, we must
be fully conscious of the authentic moral forces that motivate the
new cognitive faculties. True natural science demands an objective
approach to the world, putting aside our personal prejudices,
sympathies and antipathies to the subject of our research. This
should not be underestimated as a positive power to educate and
ennoble the human soul. Also in daily life, we now enjoy a new
measure of clarity and objectivity in perception and to some extent
also in thinking. Although we are only rarely aware of it, it allows us
to represent the external sense world with some measure of objectivity. Obviously this measure is mostly covered over by our desires

and interests, sympathies and antipathies, inclination and habits, but it is still there, and in spiritual science we strengthen it a thousandfold.

Up to this point the whole procedure may have seemed to be a purely 'cognitive' one, detached from the living, feeling soul and body. However, from the beginning this was not really so, because intense forces of will and feeling have already been invested in this cognitive work. We must mobilize the strongest will forces to decompose and transform the hardened ordinary cognition, and this force of will must be thoroughly permeated by feelings of devotion to the deeper truth of being and becoming. Therefore, we have been using our highest and purest forces of feeling and will to support the cognitive process the whole time, and this work tends to bring their opposites into full consciousness. This means that the more efficient we become in decomposing the formation process of each mental picture and learning to stop its composition processes at will, the more the hidden and disturbing forces of opposition, hindrance and temptation surface. On the one hand, we begin to experience consciously what comes to meet us from below, when we descend deeper into our body, from our emotions, desires, inclinations and instinctive bodily forces, and on the other hand we begin to meet what tempts us from above when we go out of our body with the etheric forces of released perception and thinking. This process of soul-spiritual inhalation and exhalation elongates and expands our whole being in both the vertical and horizontal directions. This is what Goethe's concept of 'polarization and intensification' means in practice: a gradual yet dramatic meta-morphosis of the whole human being. This metamorphosis is pro-duced by the simultaneous polarizing pull and tension propelled by the forces of all dimensions, the cosmic highest, the bodily and earthly depths and the expanding circles of the planetary and cos-mic circumference. In this threefold polarized and intensified field the human is transformed. In the physical body this pull and expansion is strongly halted and subdued, but the more we exit our physical body and experience the etheric body the stronger it becomes. Already at this preliminary stage, we will notice new feelings and emotions coming to life that were not conscious before.

But this depends on how much we have experienced this transformative expansion with our whole being, that is, with our body,
heart, feeling and mind. And these feelings and emotional experiences have two distinct, but inwardly related, aspects—the bodily
and cosmic.

Inhalation into the body

As we pointed out above, the first new and intense feelings we
experience through the first stage of the cognitive yoga practice
consist in this, that we experience in a living way how dead, formed,
and finished our ordinary thinking and representing actually is.
This living experience of the dead nature of representation is the
most important experience we undergo at this stage. On the level of
feeling, this experience is encountered as growing pain. We feel that
we take from the world something living, that expresses itself
through flowing sense perceptions and living thinking, and that we
actually kill it by means of our brain and mind. We painfully discover that we are destroying something of the living real world
whenever we form a mental picture, cognize, analyze, order, name
and know the world. The more we feel ourselves to be part of the
world—and the cognitive yoga practice constantly strengthens
this—the more we experience that what is going on inside us is a
real world event. This means that the dead element that we produce
through our ordinary cognition is not only a subjective, personal,
cognitive problem, but a world problem, and now we feel the
world's pain as an intense anguish of soul and heart. This experience lets us deepen and widen our awareness and cognition to the
regions of conscience and heart, where the more advanced stages of
cognitive yoga practice occur. We learn that we need this feeling of
pain, and that we are truly world destroyers, not only when we
build our cities, produce and consume our food, but even more
fundamentally we are already destroying when we 'know' the
world. We now experience with all of our feelings the real cost
exacted from the sentient world and its living beings, and we realize
that this moral debt coming from individuation will have to be fully

paid in the course of all our future evolution. The acceptance of this evolutionary necessity and debt, and the understanding of its positive value, doesn't diminish the pain, but it opens and deepens our mind and heart for the next stages of metamorphosis.

This experience can only be gained through real practice; it cannot be gained through intellectual and theoretical reasoning. Only when we truly stop the incessant intellectual devouring of the world, do we experience to what extent we crave knowledge. It is only when we begin to liberate thinking and perception from the deep desire to know, residing in our soul and body, that we start to feel the pain that always exists behind each act of ordinary, daily cognition. As with physical nourishment, we learn to understand the intensity of our need for food when we practise a little fasting. On the cognitive level, we begin to experience the same deprivation and longing when we begin to delay the fulfillment of the instinctive need to know the meaning of each thing. It becomes clear — paradoxically as this may sound — that knowing is exactly the same as eating, only that in this case it is the brain and not the digestive organs that capture, destroy and assimilate the cognitive foods. It is this feeling that opens the inner pathway to the deeper levels of body and soul: when we have an experience that we cannot immediately explain, our hunger for knowing remains unfulfilled, and an unsettling feeling arises. Something disturbs our peace. Knowing is mastering, but it is also an anesthetic, because it puts us to sleep every time we 'know' what something is. We 'murder to dissect' as Wordsworth said.* And we must kill the spiritual world just as truly as we must first kill the beings that we eat in order to nourish our bodies. In the midst of this unsettling feeling, we intensely crave for the explanation, and we normally would use our old habitual concepts in order to satisfy our need for having the unknown experience 'explained away'. This is the sort of daily 'peace of mind' that we

---

*Sweet is the lore which Nature brings;

Our meddling intellect

Mis-shapes the beauteous forms of things: —

We murder to dissect.

(*The Tables Turned*, William Wordsworth)

crave and continuously satisfy by our cognitive instincts, desires and habits. Therefore, we come to know very well at this stage, that we will have to find the moral courage to confront the sources of these instincts, desires and needs, the deeper we open the gap between experience and thinking. And we know that we will be 'tested' in this regard, and that we will have to demonstrate that we can transform this aspect of our being by our own decision and volition.

We described above the pain that is experienced on realizing that the process composing each mental picture is really a death process, not only in us but also in the real living world. When we observe this experience more closely, we begin to feel the deeper power that causes this composition and this killing. In comparison with this previous pain, what we experience now is a more bodily-soul experience, a more or less conscious sensation that runs through our body and penetrates our cognitive process from below upward. We feel it as a powerful force that can be truly compared to an electric force or current that causes contraction and consolidation; it contracts and meshes together not only pure experience and pure thinking but all the other soul and bodily forces. It is wholly instinctive, and it seizes and controls our brain and sense and nerve system without any conscious cooperation on our side. At this stage, we can only feebly sense this powerful bodily force, which unconsciously rules our conscious life, being, behaviour and cognition.

Now for the first time this unconscious metabolic-bodily process is *felt* through the brain. The brain begins to be experienced consciously as a real extension of the lower bodily digestive organs and processes, which work in our metabolic processes in deep unconsciousness every moment of our life. In daily life we don't feel what's going on in our digestive tract and organs while we kill, dissect and assimilate our physical food, but we do begin to experience this consciously in our cognitive process. The practice of cognitive yoga brings the unconscious working of our stomach and intestines right into our fully etherized cognition, where it is felt and burns inwardly. And this is immensely painful. Yet enduring this pain in the sphere of the head means to begin to experience also the astral-desire forces that control our bodily life, our metabolism, consciously. It is the doorway to the astrally dominated physical and etheric bodies, the password to the strongly guarded 'lower world' which makes us earthly, physically embodied beings in the first place.

The metabolic-emotive-cognitive mechanism

The more we inhale our etherized cognition and consciously descend into the body, the more we discover and experience the true nature of this bodily, instinctive force of capturing, destroying and assimilating. We shall name it the 'metabolic-emotive-cognitive mechanism' (MECM).

Rudolf Steiner described the origin of these forces as follows:

> We have become permeated with desires, longings, sympathies and antipathies, emotions and passions, habits and mistakes, and the reborn ether body which now streams upwards to the brain is darkened, is filled with all this. We send all this upwards from our heart and now, in real self-knowledge, we become aware of it. We become aware that what we received from the gods themselves in the depths of our life-body we are unable to give back to the gods again in the same state in which we received it, but that it has become sullied by our own being. (GA 129, 25 August 1911)

The metabolic-emotive-cognitive mechanism marshals these lower forces from the threefold constitution of the human being and uses them to capture, contract and assimilate all our soul forces. From this point of view, the brain is only an appendage of the digestive system as it eagerly swallows and assimilates them. The MECM makes of the brain an extension of the instinctive-desiring and hungry astral-animal body and soul. In this manner it glues our cognitive processes together with all our bodily-soul forces. The brain as a cognitive digestive organ is constantly reversing the world's perceptions and thoughts while making them into our mental stuff or mental body, exactly as our physical digestion transforms tomatoes and cucumbers into our physical flesh and blood.

The confrontation with this force is a major moral test and pro-bation, because we must be able to demonstrate that we are not going to 'fall in love' with this force of desire. Truthful self-knowledge shows that the other side of this pain consists in the infinite enjoyment of self-gratification, an immense intensification of self-enjoyment and hardening of the ego in itself. The enjoyment of eating and consuming the world in order to become bigger and stronger comes to consciousness most forcefully at this stage of soul inhalation. And if we do not use this moral shock as a cleansing experience of purgatory, it will infinitely tempt us to enjoy the destruction as we revel in the increase in our personal power. Or we can succumb to the other temptation, based on the inability to endure this painful truth and its moral consequences; in that case we could become so frightened by it, that we would seek to escape from the body and stay away from it altogether. This is the essence of the present test. The practice of cognitive yoga, therefore always leads down a narrow middle path, skirting between Scylla and Charybdis, seeking the balance between those two extremes, locating and grounding it anew in each step of the spiritual descent into the body.

Exhalation to the etheric world

When we let ourselves follow the flight of exhalation, of released sense perception and thinking, we open our being to the forces working in the real wide world of becoming, change, and meta-morphosis. This is the real World Wide Web in the external life world. It is a cosmic, sun-lit world, which we enter the more we develop our brain-free perception and thinking. We also feel that the life of the two streams that flow into us through perceptions and thoughts have the same cosmic source (spiritually speaking, feeling comes first, and out of this intensified 'feeling', 'hearing' and 'see-ing' gradually develop). It is only the brain that separates them into two streams, one that flows to us through the sense organs and the other from the brain-bound thinking. Outside the brain, both merge together and lead us in the same direction. Furthermore, we discover that they share a similar, if not identical, rhythm and pulse, whose exact nature at this stage we cannot yet decipher scientifically; but we feel that in the future, if our work continues, we may draw closer to its life-giving and pulsating heart centre. Though still separated from it by many veils, we can feel and also increasingly hear, if we listen to what resounds from afar, that something like a universal life pulse is reverberating through the undulating waves of this living World Wide Web as a whole. It is as if a cosmic 'heart' is beating out there in the distance, which is mysteriously connected to our heart's systole and diastole when experienced outside the body. And we feelingly hear or hear through feeling—again, this is more sensed and felt than actually 'seen' at this stage—that between the rhythms of the human heart and the cosmic heart there is a certain connection, harmony, even synchronicity.

However, while the experiences caused by the MECM have been the source of increasing inner pain, what we experience outside the body can easily become the most intense feelings of unlimited joy, enthusiasm and light-filled ecstasy. The longing may tempt us to expand into the light-filled expanses of the universe and forget all about bodily and earthly limitations and sorrows. Theoretically, perhaps, one might imagine that it would be 'easy' to distinguish between light and light, joy and joy. But in the real supersensible world this is by no means the case. In the final analysis it all depends on the deepest motivations that you carry in your soul from your earthly life that now appear nakedly before you. These motivations strive and lead in this—*or that*, spiritual direction. The more we experience our etheric exhalation, excarnation and expansion in the flowing world of free etheric perception and thinking, the more strongly we are exposed to the temptation to surrender fully to cosmic bliss and forget our earth-bound personality and life. Indeed, we may very well believe that we are actually drawing closer to the real source of cosmic life, while in truth we are only following the most enjoyable escape route that leads away from this source. The attractive power of this temptation must not be underestimated. It must also be seen in the light of the shock that we meet in the deepening experience of pain as we descend deeper into the body. The more painful this descent is, the more blissful will feel the ascent in contrast, and the greater will become our longing and desire to escape the body and abandon ourselves to the ecstatically experienced life- and light-filled cosmic world.

Only if we infinitely enhance and deepen our love and responsibility for the value and beauty of earthly and bodily life, will we be in a position to resist this temptation. In this case we will be able to hear what resounds from the true cosmic spaces that surround the cosmic source of life. And if we manage to listen, we will hear, as it were, resonating through the undulations and harmonies of the cosmic etheric tides, through the rhythmic ebbs flows of universal life, a profound word of admonishment. This voice, which seems to speak and resound through far flung cosmic spaces and times, actually strives to enhance our commitment to the value of our earthly individuality and its karmic obligations and duties. And its voice speaks the very opposite message from the other voice, that constantly spurns us to expand further and further and melt into the infinite light. If we put it in our own words, it says something to this effect: 'Before you continue and actualize the full liberation of modern, present-day cognition and radically metamorphose your present state of consciousness, make sure you fully understand the positive meaning of earthly individuation. Otherwise, as actually happens in misguided spiritual training and one-sided supersensible experiences, you will be tempted to forget and ignore the fact that, inside your intense egoism a precious seed of individual freedom and love germinates secretly, and that this can only happen on the earth. And beware lest you become, when you try to escape earthly egoism, a far greater cosmic egotist, losing the most essential new element that humanity has developed in the modern age of individuation. So, before you venture further into the light-filled worlds, make sure you extract, etherize, and carry with you a concentrated and potent intensity of human freedom and love, that will not be lost when you enter fully into the open living universe.'

And we must be in a position to say 'yes' to this voice of our own free choice, based on our own love for the earth and for the evolving, becoming and free human individuality on the earth.

As we shall see below in greater detail, the gradual inhalation and descent into the body, on the one hand, and the exhalation and expansion outside it, on the other, are two sides of one and the same process of spiritual development. The deeper we go in, the further we can go out, and vice versa. We actualize the spiritualization of thinking and perception as the yoga pupil of old practised the separation of his physical exhalation and inhalation: the deeper and longer we inhale our perceptions and can hold their etherized essence inside our body, the longer we can exhale and expand our thinking outside the body. What is more, we discover that what we find inside the body is but a contracted, condensed, infolded and inversed metamorphosis of what is spread out in the cosmic etheric world—and vice versa.

Such an experience accompanies us from now on in our further stages of the cognitive yoga practice. It becomes a new sort of 'etheric breathing': a breath of becoming, consciously inhaling and incarnating deeper into the body on the one hand, consciously exhaling and excarnating into the spiritual World Wide Web, on the other. And the more this vertical polarization and intensification is actualized, the more does the horizontal expansion into the world's middle, peripheral, etheric spaces. There the reverberating, subtle echo of the world's heart pulsations is beginning to emerge and become ever more perceptible.

3. The pearl of greatest price: Individuation

Thinking, in its own essential nature, certainly contains the real Self or Ego, but it does not contain self-consciousness.... Self-consciousness arises only through the bodily organization.... However, this must not be taken to imply that the self-consciousness, once it has arisen, remains dependent on the bodily organization. Once arisen, it is taken up into thinking and shares henceforth in thinking's spiritual being.
(*The Philosophy of Freedom*, Chapter 9, 'The Idea of Freedom')

The only thing that man can with certainty hold on to [in supersensible experience] is the 'I' thought, the thought: you were an 'I' down there ... to carry the 'I' thought out of the physical world to the consciousness into which man enters is terribly difficult ... this 'I' thought when man enters into the other state of consciousness is as a forgotten dream.... In order to achieve this, help is necessary ... the one who feels himself entering the higher worlds knows something of extraordinary importance, that the Christ-impulse is the only help that does not let us forget the 'I' thought in Earth evolution.
(GA 137, 10 July 1912)

What does our personal freedom and self-consciousness contribute to the universe? In our first journey outside the body, the cosmos itself speaks to us about the objective spiritual meaning of our personal individuality. It reveals to us that everything leading us to live in isolation from the universe for a time, while developing our own independence and freedom is, cosmically speaking, a creative world process of the greatest positive significance. This experience is all the more important because today, any spiritually striving person in her more honest moments, will admit how much she desires to minimize and if possible totally escape from the burdensome duties and responsibilities of earthly life. What is more, many so-called spiritual teachings see the personal ego as the main hindrance to illumination, salvation, happiness, and what not. But the truly conceived spiritual scientific development, in which the cognitive yoga practice is rooted, confirms that the spiritual cosmos has a totally different take on matters of the ego, personality and individuation. The true spiritual world, if we can perceive it without succumbing to the luciferic and ahrimanic temptations, tells us that our human ego consciousness, produced by the process of incarnating in a human physical body, is part of an objective cosmic evolutionary process of cosmic individuation. We learn to experience human individuation as something that the spiritual world as a whole undergoes with and through us. And we feel an immense intensification of the meaning and value of the single human personality in this way. We feel that in each human life a whole cosmic drama plays its course. The human inwardly becomes in this way a co-creative partner in the whole cosmic process of becoming.[*]

Individuation is responsible for the fact that as part of our spiritual human becoming we learn to experience and think of ourselves as a self-conscious 'I' or 'ego'. Here the pros and cons must be studied objectively, because we don't want to lose the greatest prize of cosmic evolution. In the Gnostic Hymn of the Pearl, (or Hymn of the Soul, a variation of which is also found in Jesus's Parable of the Pearl), the evolution of human consciousness is compared to the diver, who leaves behind him the realms of light in order to delve down into the darkness of material existence. He takes this journey to discover a treasure here in earthly life that cannot be found above in the divine worlds from which he came. But what cannot be found in the infinite abundance of light and love of the spiritual-divine worlds? Shouldn't we expect that the divine spiritual worlds would be the place in which, by definition, everything is found in greatest abundance? The answer from spiritual science is that indeed this is the case for everything else ... except self-consciousness and freedom. That is, even in the higher spiritual worlds, among the highest beings of the spiritual hierarchies, you cannot find self-consciousness or freedom as humans can develop on the earth. Nor can it be created there. Subsequently, there is no individually developed capacity for love to be found in the divine worlds, which can only be born out of true freedom.

---

[*]I have also described this process from various points of view in my recent books, *The Event in Science, History, Philosophy & Art* and *Spiritual Science in the 21st Century*.

We find it difficult to comprehend, let alone experience with real feeling, that limitation is necessary for future expansion, that isolation can become the sources of new integration, and that death can become the source of new- and enhanced-life. Individuation is a highly creative process precisely (and this must sound like a paradox at first) because it limits the vastly rich and infinite world — and human becoming to the point of view of a limited 'I'. In return, it gives us the ability to perceive the external sense world in clarity and to think individually and consciously. This limitation is therefore the greatest blessing if we can experience it in this manner. However, we can get to know this only if we can overcome the double 'ego temptation' in the right way. The first temptation is the common, materialistic and egotistic impulse, that becomes ever more intense in modern times. It leads increasingly to the war of all against all, in which hardening and isolated egos fight with each other for supremacy and power. The other tempts us to escape our ego altogether and with it our bodily, soul and spiritual limitations. But then we lose the pearl of greatest price and our true cosmic vocation. What we do when we become true scientists of the spirit is that we learn how to master and spiritualize every aspect of the process of individuation. This is what is meant by spiritual science when it speaks about 'the Christ impulse': finding *in* the earthly ego the true Self, and if we accomplish this, the more we truly transform our egoism, the more we value its coming into existence in the first place, because we know that we must thank our egoism for our ability to find freedom and that without the school of self-love we would never find the way to develop true love. Becoming an individual means to take full cognitive and moral hold on the forces that make egoism itself possible at all, which is the exact opposite of the rejection of egoism. We cannot transform what we reject. Our purpose can only be to learn how to lift up the very same forces that separated us from the spiritual worlds, because we now want to carry our self-consciousness and our free individuality beyond the limits of brain and body, birth and death. In other words, this means that we can learn how to make the unconscious individuation by means of the metabolic-emotive-cognitive mechanism (MECM) a conscious spiritual cognitive capacity. We can work with it consciously to spiritualize the incarnation and excarnation processes alike. Then we practically grasp, nay, we actually become the real solution to this major contradiction and existential problem of individuation.

In the spiritual worlds there are no suitable conditions to develop spiritual individuation and free, self-conscious cognition, knowledge and original human creation. We must bring these capacities with us from this world and learn how to work with them in the spiritual world. What makes us free and creative in the physical world can be lifted in this way to the spiritual worlds, and then, the fruits of free and creative human life in the spiritual worlds can be brought down to the earth, to transform and spiritualize all aspects of our physical and social life.

In the spiritual world individuation itself must be actualized in a purely spiritual way. Becoming a self-conscious self is not naturally given in the spiritual world like it is in the physical world—it must be first consciously created. Plunging into spiritual reality without it means falling asleep, becoming mentally unbalanced, or losing your mind. Indeed if we manage, in one way or another, to experience ourselves outside the physical body, our will to come back to the body and the earth will become ever weaker without creating a new self-consciousness. This is because the intensive life in the spiritual world will erase our individuality and will eventually tempt us to forget our individual life and creative social responsibilities on the earth altogether. We will become increasingly confused, morally and mentally unbalanced and unproductive.

That is, simply destroying the process of representation which is the carrier of the ego consciousness in the physical world, by breaking the MECM, doesn't automatically lead to higher cognition and spiritual scientific knowledge. At the most it leads to ecstatic, mystical or fantastic psychedelic experiences, but certainly not to a new spiritual science in a creative and healthy earthly life. Therefore, our goal is not simply to break free from the limitations of physical life and mental representation, but to take with us its etherized intensive essence as a spiritual extract. This extract of ego-formative forces can only be produced in our human cognition on the earth. It can only be individualized and harvested here, in the body, and not outside it. For this reason it is the pearl of greatest price, the most precious gift of earthly evolution not only to humanity, but also to our universe as a whole. To forsake it amounts to forsaking the meaning of our own becoming and the mission and the meaning of all life and beings on the earth.

This is a centrally important insight gained from the cognitive yoga work: in the spiritual world of real life and spiritual beings and forces, there is far *too much* reality, life, meaning, openness and expansion than we can handle in our present stage of evolution. What follows is that if anything is to be known consciously, and not ecstatically or mystically, outside the body, we must be able to consciously and independently recreate a suitable etheric fabric, skeleton or body, to support our spiritual self-consciousness (as we will describe in detail in Chapters 5 and 8). This etheric body can only be a creation of our freely individualized capacities, and we must learn to create and operate it without the instinctive support of the psychosomatic, metabolic-cognitive physical bodily foundation. The etherized cognitive faculties of individuation can be extracted only from our ordinary egocentric consciousness. But in doing so, we reverse individuation and carry its intensive fruits and seeds from the earth to the spiritual universe. Out of the whole world becoming we have been separated and individuated and now we can use our freedom to carry the fruits of this individuation process back to the spiritual world. We add to the universe new creative contributions that without us, as embodied, individuated and free beings, would have never become part of the evolution of the universe.

Let us again emphasize that we electrolyze water to get pure gases, not because we don't appreciate the role of water in the household of nature and prefer gases, but because we want to understand the mysteries of nature. And this also applies to the spiritualization of human cognition. Understanding how the transition between liquid and gases takes place and vice versa, can help us to become better partners in regulating the cyclic breathing of life between earth and heaven. In the same attitude we approach the spiritualization of individuation. We experience it as sober learning experience, not a frenzied escape from personal limitation or a romantic longing for infinite freedom and bliss. And this objective attitude pays off when we experience the freed life outside its bodily limits and we discover that now this life itself will tell us the reason for its limitation and embodiment. It turns out that from seemingly opposite directions, from both the forces of incarnation and excarnation, we get the same message. The two cease to be experienced as real opposites, because we learn that they are related to each other as the two poles of one life giving rhythm. The forces of incarnation and excarnation alike explain the reason for individuation. They are the only reliable sources of information about the riddle of life and death, not only of physical life but also of the life of cognition, because they administer the processes of individuation from the eternal spirit that governs the two poles of birth and death at the same time. And the more we learn to live consciously outside the body, in the etheric world, we experience also the forces that bring about incarnation and birth, and we can work with them consciously, all the way down to their actualized closed form in the body. We learn to actualize the whole life cycle of birth and death and rebirth, through the most elementary processes of cognition.

From this point of view we can now experience the solution to this immensely significant modern problem. We understand that just as it is true that nothing real can be known of the riddles of the world and human existence and their connections as long as we remain within the limits of ordinary cognition, on the other hand, this is also the only place where self-consciousness can be spiritualized in our universe. Furthermore, once self-consciousness has been spiritualized in embodied physical life and cognition, it must not die here in its cocoon. It can be resurrected from its bodily-cognitive cocoon in a markedly metamorphosed form. And we will carry this essential power of metamorphosis with us, as an individualized capacity of our spiritualized self, in our supersensible life in the spiritual world.

In this manner individuation creates a feedback loop between the spiritual world and the physical world, establishing a conscious life-giving breathing between them. And by means of this, the new life cycle, humanity and the earth become co-creative partners of the beings of the spiritual worlds. We, as self-conscious humans, join our elder spiritual brothers and sisters in this awesome, infinitely creative cosmic journey.

4. Etherization of Sight

It must become a certainty for us that with every ray of light, with every tone, with every sensation of heat and its dying down we enter into a soul-intercourse with the world, and this soul-intercourse must become significant for us.... If we learn, in nature, to receive the soul element together with sense perception, then we shall have the Christ relationship to outer nature. This Christ relationship to outer nature will be something like a kind of spiritual breathing process.

(GA 194, 30 November 1919)

When a light ray streams into your eye, the spirit of the Sun is the substance of this delicate breathing. We breathe in the manifold ingredients of the Sun spirit with our sense impressions.

(Pastoral-medical course, GA 318, 15 September 1924)

With the Christ in ourselves in the right way, we enliven all light on the Earth around us, carry life into the dead light and have ourselves an enlivening effect on the light.

(GA 218, 23 October 1922)

Within the limits of this book it is not possible to enter into the electrolysis of each of the senses and to uncover all of their modalities and operations, as this is a vast field consisting of the concrete applications of cognitive yoga research. Here I will have to limit myself to only a few examples directly related to the main cognitive yoga practice.

Let us first briefly summarize what we have achieved so far, outline the etherization process of perception as a whole, and then describe each stage of the cognitive yoga practice in concrete detail.

So far, we have learned how to stop the inner construction and composition of our mental world, have decomposed the mental picture, and have experienced the two poles in their initial pure states. Mental pictures and representations are decomposed to their two main elements: freed sense perception and freed thinking. That is, their components are electrolyzed, separated and polarized: we get freed sense perceptions attracted to one pole ('the etheric anode', so to speak, where the real etheric equivalent of $+O_2$ is gathered) and freed thinking to the other (the 'etheric cathode', to which the forces of freed thinking – the real etheric equivalent of $-H_2$ are attracted).

The 'electric current' that motivates and fires the mental electrolysis proceeds from our will and devotion to the task at hand. This liberating spark, however, must also be freed from the whole metabolic-emotive-cognitive mechanism and complex. It is also entangled and held back by these forces of hindrance. The stronger our will and devotion become, the more we must come to terms also with the hindering forces working in the unconscious depths of will, desire and feeling. The more we untangle and liberate the inner forces of the MECM and transform them into higher motivating forces, the freer become our perceptions and thinking. This means that a part of the physical, etheric and astral bodies, responsible for this mental composition, is purified and released from its unconscious fetters and becomes free and available to serve a new task. We can individuate these freed bodily forces, make them our own, and use them now to purify, free, intensify and spiritualize sense perception. Without the powerful support of the liberated unconscious MECM forces, that are mainly the forces of will and feeling, we will not have the energy needed to carry the etherization process of perception far enough. This is the place in which the etherisation of sense perception and thinking starts.

The first stage in the etherization of perception beings when we learn how to separate the pure 'sense qualities' from the objects to which they are attached. These can be colours, smells, tastes, sounds, sensations of touch, as well as heat and coldness. Then we purify them further, penetrating beyond the pure quality into the next, higher, force that works through them. The pure qualities of sense perceptions become transparent to the real formative forces of the world that work through them into our body, and mould, shape and nourish our body mainly until puberty. And then we let them stream inwardly as pure formative etheric forces, passing untouched and untagged by the MECM into the innermost recesses of the body. When we have achieved this transformation, we experience how the body's potential etheric forces are stimulated by the instreaming flow of etheric formative forces from the world, and how they respond to their impact. The more the purified formative forces of the etheric world impact the etheric formative forces of the body, the more a gradual liberation of the etheric body from the head downward takes place. By means of the liberation of the etheric body and its free interaction with the etheric world, those forces are also liberated that otherwise are strongly protected from human consciousness. These etheric forces are preserved in each person's unconscious bodily depth, as the purest etheric forces of humanity's earliest childhood. Into these forces the luciferic-ahrimanic beings and influences cannot penetrate.*

That is, during the more advanced stages of cognitive yoga, the purified and etherized world forces, extracted from perception, working in unison with the human etheric body, seek and find their complementary resonances among these purest etheric bodily forces. They awaken, stimulate and activate them, and they, in response, become creative, unite with the in-streaming world forces, and constitute a new etheric stream. We experience how a new etheric stream is conceived when the etheric world and the liberated human etheric body mutually impregnate each other. This new, united world-human stream, becomes a third and distinctly new etheric stream. It is creative, harbouring a newly conceived seed for new bodily-cosmic life. And it is this newly conceived etheric seed that then becomes available as a highly creative potential to be used in the etheric tasks of creating and embodying an independent, spiritual individuality in the etheric world.

In what follows we will demonstrate this process by means of concrete examples of spiritual scientific research taken from the laboratory of cognitive yoga.

---

*These forces are composed, according to spiritual science, of two, deeply connected elements: 1) the pure etheric forces protected from the Luciferic intervention in the end of Lemuria, as described by Rudolf Steiner in his lectures on The Gospel of St. Luke (GA 114). 2) The resurrected *spiritual* formative forces of the *physical* body, or the 'phantom', that can germinate in each person as a seed since the forces of death — the luciferic-ahrimanic forces — have been overcome through Christ's resurrection, described by Rudolf Steiner in his lecture cycle From Jesus to Christ (GA 131).

Colour Breathing

The breathing in of colours and light is the least difficult among the various sense inhalation processes undertaken in the course of cognitive yoga practice and research. The reason for this is that the sense of sight is in the middle between the mostly unconscious bodily senses and the super-conscious senses that perceive the other person.* Furthermore, it is also more conscious in comparison to sensations of cold and warmth, sounds, and especially smelling, tasting and touching.

With hearing, warmth, smelling, tasting, and even more so with the inner bodily and proprioceptive sense experiences (the senses that let us perceive our own bodily movement, balance and life processes), we must invest a greater effort in order to lift them up to full consciousness. These sense perceptions and experiences are therefore deeply affected by the unconscious bodily-soul forces of the MECM and are far more difficult to separate and purify from their capture in representation, emotion, habits and instincts. Their release and the transformation of their intensive emotional impact and deep habitual and instinctual imprint will have to be relegated to the advanced stages of the cognitive yoga practice. This is different in the case of the experiences of light and colours, where the influence on the body and emotions is weak and transient in comparison. Light and colour impressions continuously affect our whole being all day long and yet we move around in the light-filled, clear and transparent space of daily life, which makes our ordinary experience of freedom possible. But it is precisely this aspect which allows us to intensify colour experience volitionally. We can start from a relative minimum of feeling and emotional intensity and grasp it with greater cognitive precision. Vivid colours are the best starting point, because the 'white' hue of pure light is somewhat too

---

*The work in the field of the perception of the other person's 'I', thinking and speaking, is part of the social application of cognitive yoga, called 'social yoga'. I have published the results of this important social application of cognitive yoga in my books and lectures, and have also developed this practice myself in my ever renewed efforts to build spiritual communities, as well as in the school of spiritual science and the Global Event College.

diffuse, scattered, and weak to condense, capture, and assimilate. Because our reactions of desire, emotion, and feeling toward colour are weaker (than the lower soul and bodily senses) the cognitive representations of colour imprinted in body and soul are relatively shallow. On the other hand, the stronger soul and bodily imprints and reactions associated with hearing, smells, tastes and touch sensations are less conscious, because we are protected from them by means of the effective inhibition of the MECM. They are so powerful that they would overwhelm and dampen our waking consciousness, suppressing it to a stage of dreamlike or even dreamless sleep, if we experienced their fully real impact.

When I hear a sound, for example, I immediately lose my (relative) freedom. It takes hold of me more completely than the impressions of sight. I cannot even physically shut my ears like I can shut my eyes. This difference is of course only relative, but is nevertheless helpful in choosing our starting point. Not only is my conscious attention immediately captivated by music, but also — and this is a far greater obstacle to the sensory purification process — sound is instinctively imprinted and captured by the MECM and creates an unconscious nucleolus in and around which my whole embodied constitution of body, soul and mind, is assembled and condensed. What is more, this unconscious involvement with my inner reactions distracts my attention from the fact that at the same time a strong representation is also being formed. It is only because all of our common ideas are based on the predominant sense of sight, that we are not aware that we are also constantly forming representations of sounds and noises. And we are even less conscious of our mental representations of smells, tastes, touches and heat sensations, as well as many inward bodily sensations like balance, movement, fatigue, hunger, disease, and pain. All sensations produce either a semi-conscious or a fully unconscious representation, and therefore cannot be suitable as a starting point for the fully conscious cognitive yoga practice.

Of course for most people today, in the case of colour breathing, the first reaction is 'I don't feel anything when I see blue or red', but this relative neutrality of affect and effect is an advantage. Colour influences and purification processes stand somewhat in between the unconscious bodily senses which are altogether too intense on the one hand, and pure light, which is too ethereal, on the other. Also, the still higher, human-spiritual senses: the perception of the 'I', and the perception of the thoughts and words of the other person, are as difficult to bring *down* to ordinary cognition as it is difficult to bring the lower body and soul sensations *up* to consciousness. Therefore, among the senses sight will be chosen as the most suitable candidate for demonstrating the process of sense purification, etherization and inhalation.

First stage: detaching the quality 'red' from its object

The first step in the decomposition and deconstruction of the 'cognitive composition' in seeing is to concentrate our attention on the colour alone, and disregard the object to which it is attached. As was pointed out above, in the formation of the representation of any object, manifold sense impressions and bodily sensations are amalgamated and synthesized together with many and various concepts, representations, memories and associations. Untangling this complex knot of the representation of the whole object to which a colour is attached is therefore the first step in the purification process. (In the case of pure light, with which we are not primarily concerned here, this would mean, for example, unknotting the representation 'a ray of light' with all its invested concepts and focusing solely on the non-objectified light impression.)

The separation of the pure sense quality from the object to which it is attached is an active cognitive process. We aim to both separate the quality from its object as well as focus our attention on the freed quality 'red', while fully erasing from consciousness the complex body of representations associated with this object or the form or surface to which the colour is attached. This seems to be a daunting task, and as any real empirical scientific research, it requires meticulous experimentation, variation, and verification over many years. Naturally, only an abbreviated report of this can be given here.

The first major obstacle is that it proves difficult to hold the separated sense quality in our consciousness in this object-free state for a long time. It easily dissipates while our attention is immediately pulled back to the manifold representations associated with the object 'red cinnabar' or 'red patch'. Furthermore, being pulled back to the representation of the red cinnabar, reactivates the whole instinctive set of representations connected to it. In no time at all, we find that we have rekindled and relinked diverse chains of representations that we have formed in our life about red things in general, and so on. And then we have to start all over again.

Therefore, when we deconstruct the object, separate the chosen quality and focus our attention solely on its perception, we cannot simply remain passive, because the quality diffuses and slips away from our consciousness immediately. Provided that the work on the purification of thinking is constantly practised, using *The Philosophy of Freedom*, the next step will be possible. After trying many alternatives to hold and prolong the pure quality, I came to the practical conclusion that I have to export and attach a quantity of life force to it from my own resources to keep it alive and growing in its separate, pure state. This force proves necessary for prolonged spiritual experience and research. This solution, however, immediately brought the next problem. (This is how it happens in real research — any solution is but an invitation for new problems.) Now the crucial problem with this move is: if we want to be absolutely certain that we are investigating the red in itself and not our subjective, personal reactions to its influences on body and soul, we must take special care that the energy *we* donate to the red impression flows solely from the red and not from anything else, inner or outer, otherwise attached to this experience. But this still seems to beg the main question. And the cognitive yoga work takes this paradox and contradiction fully into account: if I have to donate the life force, how can it be red's pure force? This force must possess a miraculous power, to give back to the chosen being the essential being of this other being! And so it does, in fact.

Therefore, we have to search for deeper human forces, through which we hope to find what is less personal in our experience of red. And this leads us to the soul and life forces through which we experience the red as a freely given gift. After all, red gives everything it has, it gives itself. In ordinary life we naturally consume and use its gift to serve our personal, sensual, cognitive and practical daily purposes. We aren't interested in the red for itself, but only in how we can use it to fulfil our own needs and interests. But the more we experience the objective gift of pure red, the more we feel an inner need and impulse to give back to the red what we have received from it during our life. This impulse can only come about by itself, from real soul experience and should not come about through autosuggestion or command. We feel the colour red as an inspiration that has constantly blessed us since the moment of our birth and that it continues to give its gift of life in this very moment. When we become conscious of this persistent blessing and grace, it fires our soul and we *feel* the following intensely: we want to give back something of the abundant gifts that we have received from red all our life. This is what establishes the first cognitive-moral bond, an essential subjective-objective, reciprocal determination and exchange of forces between the red and us. And a kind of 'mutual trust' is established as well, without which no further 'cooperation' is to be expected with the forces of the real spiritual world working through red. In a sense, we have to prove to the real spiritual world our loving and grateful acknowledgement of the fact that this red is part of life as a whole, and that through red it is the whole universe that brings us into being and supports us. Only this repeatedly activated selflessness, our ability to experience the pure quality as a world gift apart from our special interests, gradually allows us to return the gift, intensified by our own forces, as a free and loving donation. This 'mutual gifting' makes the purified red quality more intense, vibrant and saturated, not only in comparison to the shadowy 'red' experienced in the perception of 'red cinnabar', but also in comparison to the soul experience of the pure quality experienced thus far. Our donation becomes vibrant when it is reciprocally acknowledged; we experience how it is received by the deeper being of red, and how it calls forth a further, reciprocal inflow of red's deeper life forces that, at least for us, flow more freely and abundantly through the quality red. This mutual interplay becomes increasingly more alive and intense until a mutual exchange of intensities comes about, that is self-intensifying and self-supporting. And now comes a moment, perhaps only after many efforts, in which the experience of the pure quality of red becomes so intense, vibrant, saturated and alive, that we begin to forget ourselves for more than a fleeting second and we experience that our conscious awareness is maintained and carried without our self-conscious reflection. And the remarkable scientific discovery now is that while we forget ourselves the greatly enhanced forces of red take over and support our self-consciousness when we cannot support it ourselves. When this happens we know that we are beginning to find the firm ground for our cognitive yoga research in the field of perception. We note in our lab. diaries this great moment, this event: we have found a path; we know we are on the right track.

Already at the very first stage of the cognitive yoga work we realize, empirically, what the fundamental condition for doing real spiritual science is, namely, how the moral element is truly inseparable from the cognitive and scientific research. One understands now the necessity of developing devotion and love for the truth and essence of all things as Rudolf Steiner emphasized at the beginning of his book, *Knowledge of Higher Worlds*.

Second step: 'falling in red'

The claim that it is possible to forget our daily self-consciousness and yet experience — and retain — an enhanced, higher state of consciousness, must be regarded as an absurd Munchausen trick by most of our present-day science, psychology and philosophy. (Let us be reminded here, however, of the work that is constantly carried on in the second division of our cognitive yoga lab., in the field of pure thinking, where we utilize *The Philosophy of Freedom* to etherize thinking and gradually experience it as a self-sustaining and self-actualizing spiritual being. This activity runs separately yet parallel with the etherization of perception. It helps us not only to keep ordinary thinking and representing out of the way of the etherization of perception, but also provides an *indirect* source of impersonal, spiritual sustaining power in the moment we begin to experience pure perception.) After all, we naturally forget ourselves during dreamless sleep each night. At that time, we lose not only the ability to represent to ourselves our external and internal environments, but we lose also our clear and solid self-consciousness. Maintaining that one can be sustained in an altered state of consciousness that is not less, but more lucid and precise than the clearest state of daily consciousness, is like saying that one can be awake *while* one is asleep. This of course would be a nonsensical contradiction, if one were referring to the *same* state of consciousness. If this statement has a sense at all, it could only mean that one can wake up and become conscious in another, *higher*, state of consciousness while the ordinary state goes to sleep. In addition, any appeal to lower states of consciousness, existing below the level of our normal wide awake consciousness, like mediumistic states, semi-conscious trance, channeling, or ecstatic and psychedelic visions are useless for spiritual science as sources of reliable knowledge. This is because spiritual science takes its point of departure from the clearest modern thinking and solid self-consciousness, which already exist above them, and goes with it upward to fuller and more conscious states of cognition, not downward, to less conscious levels of the soul. Therefore, in the cognitive yoga practice everything takes place in the fullest and clearest consciousness and cognition.

So we want to give up that part of our self-consciousness that depends entirely on our embodied, brain-bound cognition, specifically in this case, on the representations of ourselves and of the red, in order to be awakened to a wholly new red-self-consciousness. This awakening takes place in a new state of conscious cognitive experience. But this means that the stronger power required to become conscious of our different higher 'self' must be given by the 'red'. In other words, our self must become the real world-red, and experience itself through its higher forces. It's a matter, therefore, of real becoming and metamorphosis, not representation or ideation. Instead of self-consciousness, we experience the gift of the consciousness of becoming red. Now what is the real, essential, difference between 'becoming conscious of becoming red' and 'having a representation of red'?

An analogy from daily life can be helpful here, however, we must not forget that this is only a comparison to help us understand better the new state of consciousness. The analogy is one of 'falling in love' or really of any other intense soul experience such as intense fear, angst, beauty, wonder, or becoming one with the world. We all have experienced those intense moments in which consciousness is not lost, but where self-consciousness becomes weak, or even disappears entirely. What disappears in such moments is the reflective reference to ourselves as subjects of our identity and objects of our own attention which is always part of our ordinary self-conscious experience. I can be so wholly filled or overwhelmed by the feeling of love for another being, or feel such awe and wonder in the face of sublime beauty, or be stricken with such unspeakable horror and pain, that perhaps for a second or two, I can really be outside my (embodied, brain-bound, represented) self. Yet I am still conscious and sometimes even superconscious, but the intensity, depth, and breadth of the awareness is not just 'my own' mental image of myself or even of my beloved. Furthermore, this new state of cognition is not a hypothetical combination of the two, which would be something like falling in love and 'at the same time' remaining self-conscious, because it is precisely not 'the same time' in which the two experiences are happening. The new cognition is taking place in a wholly different place and time. Now, bearing this analogy in mind, let us return to the cognitive yoga experience, and observe the essential difference between falling in love in ordinary life and 'falling in red', or becoming red, through this practice.

How can we create a concept of this difference? First, let us emphasize that becoming red through the cognitive yoga practice described here at the pole of sense perception is a result of our own spiritual activity. We experiment and make variations as much as we need in order to arrive at testable, repeatable, results. But this is only the external side of this difference. The essential difference lies in this, that the inner forces that we extract from our own being to kindle and fire this voluntary donation process, offer to red something that it gave us in the first place. It is our purest love and devotion to its gift that allows us to offer red an individualized, free gift of our own forces; and now red, having assimilated and potentized our gift, bestows itself once more. The point is to experience the enhancement of this spiralling rhythm, the intensification of the mutual exchange between the objective red given by the world, our objective devotion to the gift of the world, and our potentiation of this gift through our love of what we received from it through our entire life. Continuing our offering of this gratefulness in this very moment, we follow its reception and further enhancement by the world; here we find red as a real being of the real world. Once more red reveals its being to us, as a gift, but 'we' are now united with this cycle of mutual exchange, we have become one with red's forces and our experience of red.

While we are in this ever less-personal, self-enhancing, self-supporting mutual process of increasingly becoming red, we are metamorphosed, forgetting our ordinary selves. This is an important spiritual scientific distinction: in the cognitive yoga practice, as opposed to the ordinary experience of falling in love, we carry over with us into this impersonal or super personal experience of becoming red, a surplus of energy created by our own volition *before* our ordinary self-consciousness is obliterated. We come to the wedding feast, in other words, well prepared with substantial gifts and offerings. We are not only passive recipients of the gifts of love from our bridegroom, we are active givers as well, and of course, the blessed nuptial will be entirely different! In the event itself, when we go out of ourselves, this surplus is delivered to the red and becomes part of the red that we now become. Becoming red has become, in this way, a mutual exchange of intensities between 'me' and 'red'. I am donating a quantum of my love and forces of devotion to the red. This quantum consists of a freely intensified and grateful giving back of the original gift (or the spiritual-moral capital) that I received from the being of red now and through all my life, which I have made my own (with the added supply of actively produced and accumulated 'interest'). Both of us enter into a reciprocal cycle of mutual enhancement and metamorphosis; both of us are changed through this mutual intensification. This transpires while I am forgetting myself as I am becoming red, while the red in turn is becoming more than the initial red, and, in its turn, has now also a surplus of force to offer back to me. This mutual exchange of surpluses or reserves, as a mutual breathing, plays an essential role in bringing about the next step, in which self-consciousness, after it has been lost in the first experiences of purified red, is coming back from the other side, in-versed as it were, sustained and empowered through the transformed being of red itself. I am becoming red-self-consciousness, that is, I experience consciously the world through the fact that I share now the being and becoming of red in the universe.

Third step: quality becomes intensity

Indeed, in each event in which I enter volitionally into the state of self-forgetfulness, there is always a moment in which I must take a 'leap of faith' and 'fall in love' with, and fall into, the being of red. But again, this leap must be clearly distinguished from similar experiences in daily life. In the cognitive yoga practice, this leap is based on regular and repeated practice. It is a faith in the verified, repeatedly actualized reserves of creative, potentised forces, and I know that, to the extent that I have prepared and stored enough potential forces of devotion and love during the process of the electrolysis and purification of the red quality, these forces will be released to bridge the abyss at the time I take the leap. I am the abyss, the leap, and the bridge, all at once — through the forces flowing through me from both sides. They meet in the middle when the reserved potentials that I bring with me from this side are released when I leap over the abyss, and the answering gesture of red, its acceptance of my offering, flows gracefully to meet me from the other side. The bridge is completed when there is only 'red', purified, enhanced, from both sides of the divide that separates human becoming from world becoming. When we diversify the colour etherization process and repeat it with all the colours, this gradually becomes a bridge woven from all the colours that we become. Indeed, one constructs an individualized rainbow bridge, the Bifrost bridge of Norse mythology, precisely there at the crossing and middle point of the human being and the world.

In the fundamental lecture from November 30, 1919 about the

mission and culture of Michael and the new will of yoga, quoted in the introduction, Rudolf Steiner described this process in this way:

> When our sense processes will become *ensouled* again, we shall have established a *crossing point*, and in this crossing point we shall take hold of the human will that streams up ... Then we shall, at the same time, have the subjective-objective element for which Goethe was longing so very much. We shall have the possibility of grasping, in a sensitive way, the peculiar nature of the sense process of man in its relation to the outer world.... In reality, there takes place a soul process from the outside toward the inside, which is taken hold of by the deeply subconscious, inner soul process, so that the two processes overlap. From outside, cosmic thoughts work into us, from inside, humanity's will works outward. Humanity's will and cosmic thought cross in this crossing point, just as the objective and the subjective element once crossed in the breath. We must learn to feel how our will works through our eyes and how the activity of the senses delicately mingles with it, bringing about the crossing of cosmic thoughts and humanity's will. We must develop this *new Yoga will*.... This must be the endeavour of the fifth post-Atlantean period; namely, the endeavour to find something in the human inner life in which an outer process takes place at the same time.

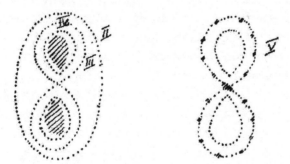

'The Ancient Yoga Culture and the New Yoga Will. The Michael Culture of the Future', lecture from 30 November, 1919, GA 194)

We cross the bridge when the leap of trust and courage becomes the bridge because it opens the deep soul reservoir and releases the reserved potent force that was already created and accumulated through the previous cognitive work. True, it is not a measurable quantitative reservoir. As any self-aware athlete or extreme sport lover can tell you, you cannot quantify in advance how much potential you have actually created and stored in our body and soul. You will only know when it is actualized in the real time of the actual leap, in a moment of danger perhaps, or in the highest, concentrated moment of attention, and sometimes in a rather peaceful occasion of lucid perception and compassionate embrace. But this faith is nevertheless based on realities, on self-actualizing forces that have become part of us through meticulous training. Furthermore, it is also a faith based on knowing the loyalty and benevolence of the colour red, that is, its objective readiness for giving itself. After all, it does make a difference if one can trust the world into which one enters, a trust based on knowledge, grounded in repeated experience that, when one jumps, the world is going to receive, sustain and carry one in the body- and groundless etheric heights. Only by means of generating and actualizing this selfless motivating force, and surrendering all that we have to the becoming red process (including the reservoir of accumulated potential forces), can we let red substitute itself fully for our own ordinary self. World red becomes one's self and guides one as an alter self. It is a fully voluntary step to begin with, which halfway becomes a most intimate metamorphosis, a welcome takeover; an energetic and well-prepared surrender to the absolute world reality of the hosting spiritual being of colour. And when this welcoming embrace is complete, we realize that the whole experience of colour is totally transformed as well.

Precisely at that moment when we have become wholly red, the former experience of the quality of red, which we abstracted from the physical object, disappears. From this moment on we must say that we have not only lost any ability to represent the external colour but that we also lost its qualitative soul experience. The soul experiences of the quality red (expansive, active, warming, attractive, aggressive, etc.) disappear as the representation of red previously disappeared into the soul experience of the pure quality. The qualitative experience of red, that was still our inner soul experience, becomes colourless 'colour' and this colourless colour becomes pure intensity, which feels, wills and thinks itself through us. In this moment, a stream of intensities gushes through what we experienced previously as the quality 'red' and wholly suffuses us. There is absolutely no remnant or reminiscence of the qualities of redness, nor any personal or inner emotional and affective (psychological) experience of the pure quality of red. When we become red there is nothing really 'red' anymore in this becoming, such as we know it and experience it in the ordinary representation of red, as well as in the soul experiences of the purified quality of red described above. The 'colour' of red becomes the colourless colour of pure world power, intensity, becoming.

Fourth step: intensity becomes a revelation of the etheric world

The soul experience of the pure quality 'red' lies between the subjective representation of red, and its real objective intensity as a spiritual world force. As was mentioned above, Goethe pioneered the transformation from the first to the second stage in his study of the moral effects of colours. After we recapitulate and individualize his soul experiments, we continue to the next step, the real spiritual scientific one, which Goethe did not pursue. This is done by following Rudolf Steiner's recommendations in the lecture cycle The Boundaries of Natural Science. What is the exact nature of transition from Goethe's qualitative-phenomenological soul experience of colour to Rudolf Steiner's experience of the purely supersensible spiritual being of colour? The transition occurs when the qualitative soul experience of colours become external to our inner soul life — but we must imagine this externality as much deeper inner world at the same time — and when we exchange our identities with the colours, and become colour while the colour becomes us. We don't take the qualitative colour and experience its affects inside our soul, but rather, our soul goes out and unites itself with the objective spiritual being of colour. The soul does not breathe the colour into its inner life, and experiences it with its ordinary human soul forces, but the colour breathes the soul out and into its external world stream of becoming. We are no longer the hosts but the hosted, not the private possessors of the experience but have become participants in its universal spiritual life. It is the beginning of a truly supersensible experience and cognition, because now we experience how the colour is experiencing itself through us, not the other way around. And the further discovery that we make at this stage, is that the colourless intensity of this stream becomes transparent to something else that works through it. As previously the representation became transparent for the colour's quality and the quality became transparent to its colourless intensity, so now the forces of the spiritual world itself begin to speak through the colourless intensity.

Through pure intensity we are becoming aware of a world force working, weaving, and creating outside in the etheric world and into our bodily being. It is the real etheric world that weaves, operates, and works through the intensive forces of what we used to represent and experience as 'red'. As represented red became pure quality, and the experience of quality became the experience of streams and currents of pure intensity, so now pure intensity opens a gate through which real formative world forces are flowing into our whole being. But having become pure intensity ourselves, we now experience the etheric world as the real being of 'red' experiences it. We experience ourselves spread out in the external etheric world and from there 'we' are streaming through the eyes (and skin) into the whole human being, all the way down and into the body, whose contours and boundaries are becoming at the same time diffuse and indistinct. (Only the outlines of the head remain somewhat similar, but only as a shadowy silhouette of the original form and size of the physical head that we perceive in ordinary cognition.) It is more spiritual and at the same time more bodily, because the external etheric world forces are also the forces that shape and build our body. True, at this stage the external-etheric world experience is still largely formless and the experiences we undergo there will need time to ripen and mature, before they crystallize to become clearly distinct experiences that can be translated and described in ordinary language. But nevertheless, in itself it is a fully concrete, supersensible etheric experience, of being poured out and spread into the vast living world that penetrates and suffuses our physical body also. This world is experienced as intensely alive and vital, crisscrossed by currents and streams flowing from all directions of the cosmic circumference. And because we started this specific research with sense perception and left our physical body through the gates of the eyes, via the gradual purifications and intensifications of red as described above, we know that we are experiencing the etheric world from this perspective. This fact continuously directs our attention back to the body, now from outside, and we begin to experience the relations between the etheric world forces and our own etheric and physical bodies. Such relations will also become the first concrete supersensible experiences we make at this stage that can be described in some spiritual-scientific detail. And indeed we can make some significant spiritual-scientific discoveries through this process that shed light on the whole constitution of the human being in regard to perception, body, consciousness, and cognition. Before we continue to describe the further stages of the etherization and inhalation of perception, we will make a short excursion and describe a few research details pertaining to this field, to the extent that these discoveries are related to that aspect of the cognitive yoga practice described here.

Some spiritual-scientific observations

When we observe the hard skull that encloses the brain as the centre of the nerve and sense system (the senses in so far as they are centred in the brain via the sensory nerves), we realize that it is above all a grave, so to speak, as far as the real etheric formative forces of light and colours are concerned. For the cosmically living etheric forces of light and colour, the sense and nerve centres in the brain are a place they stream into in order to partially die (other parts of them stream through this grave as through an empty space, in and out, circulating in it and around it, with no felt resistance or change). Strikingly, this is the opposite of our daily experience of our head as the centre of command, through which our conscious 'I' is vigorously perceiving, reflecting and directing its acts and deeds. In daily cognition and conduct, our head is our centre that radiates from within outward, but in etheric experience from the outside, the physical head and brain is experienced as a 'death machine' into which a multiplicity of etheric world forces pour from expanded cosmic spaces to be annihilated and transformed into forces of wide-awake ordinary human consciousness. These are the same forces that organize and form the infinitely complex structures of the brain during pregnancy and early childhood, and mostly perish and exhaust themselves in this building. The more the brain cells die and cannot multiply or regenerate, the more the formative forces that build them are free to serve the growing wakeful self-consciousness. Everywhere that sense and nerve tissue is present—which is, after all, the greatest mass of the brain—these dead etheric forces become the forces of wide-awake consciousness. And the forces that we breathe in through the senses interact with these empty and dead forces, in order to make the senses and the physical brain an instrument of self-conscious, clear, earthly cognition.

On closer inspection, in reality the concrete picture is of course infinitely more differentiated. The brain grave is also differentiated in various parts so that we could have drawn a detailed map by means of an 'etheric fMRI'* showing the differentiated etheric processes along the pathways of the different sensory nerves and their various centres in the brain. Indeed, in the dead and dying nerve tissue in the brain, light and colours constantly die and are transformed into the mental forces by means of which we think and perceive and form mental pictures in our ordinary consciousness (the arteries and other regenerative tissues and processes in the brain are an exception). This is a complete reversal of our beliefs about what the head is. This shocking transformation has deep moral and cognitive significance for the cognitive yoga practice as a whole, as will be shown below.

An exact spiritual-scientific observation of the whole human perceptual experience distinguishes three simultaneous etheric streams and their effects and operations, differentiated according to the cognitive level of our perception. The first is the purely spiritual, cosmic etheric stream which is unconscious, or rather super-

---

*Functional Magnetic Resonance Imaging produces detailed neuroimaging based on the increased activity of blood flow to various parts of the brain.

conscious and operates wholly outside and through our body and
ordinary cognition. In ordinary consciousness we have no experience of this stream. The second and polar opposite stream is the
dead, exhausted, etheric stream, released from the physical brain
with the death of each brain cell and nerve tissue, to become the
stuff of our ordinary sensory and mental representations. The third
stream contains the etheric formative forces responsible for the
perpetual regeneration of the sense-nerve system working mainly
through the blood (to the extent that this regeneration process takes
place). Here we confront the greatest riddles of the contemporary
human sciences, concerning the interrelationships between body,
soul and spirit, brain and thinking, and physiology and consciousness.*

We can experience and study the relations and interactions
between the three parallel etheric activities only after we bring the
first, purely superconscious etheric forces into full etheric, or
imaginative, consciousness. Only then do we begin to understand
the true role of the physical sense and nerve system in the human
experience of perception and thinking as a whole. Therefore, we
would never say, as neurophysiology, psychology and the cognitive
sciences do, that the physical, chemical, and electric processes
taking place in the senses, nerves and brain actually cause or produce what we see in the ordinary perception of light and colour
(and all of the other sense perceptions as well). Viewed from the
higher etheric level of cognition, from outside the physical body and
brain, we see that the real function of the physical sense and nerve
process, is actually the very opposite from what neuroscience cur-
rently believes. Not only does it not produce the contents of the
sense perceptions that we experience in our conscious experience,
but on the contrary, it actually devitalizes and kills their intense
cosmic vitality, and only the killed part comes to conscious
experience.† More exactly we should say: the killed part doesn't

---

* Rudolf Steiner described it for the first time in this form in his epoch-making
book, *Riddles of the Soul* from 1917 and later in dozens of lectures.
† In *Riddles of the Soul*, Steiner creates the new term '*herablähmt*' (diminished to
the point of paralysis or 'lamed down') for this process of devitalization.

simply 'come' to be represented in an already existing daily consciousness but this consciousness as a whole (with all its perceptions and experiences) comes into being as a product of this killing process as a whole, part of which is actualized in each momentary perceptual and thinking experience. The real, living, world of light, colour, and other sensations is far too intense and would have totally overwhelmed us and put us to sleep. If we were exposed to the light's full objective world power while still in a physical body, each ray of light would strike us like lightning: we would be burned to ashes in a twinkling of an eye or luckily lose our consciousness and faint. This part of the etheric force is really killed, devitalized, slowed down and disintegrates when it impinges on the rod or cone cells in the eye's retina, causing in them a destructive chemical process and is transformed into an electrical current that flows via the optic nerve and is conducted to the sight centres in the brain. After passing from the eyes to the optic nerves and being processed in the back of the brain, what is left of the original and intense etheric-formative world power is what actually arises in our consciousness as a mere mental image. It is so weakened and devitalized by the destructive forces of the physical brain, that what comes through to full consciousness, when I say, 'this is red', is but a shadowy corpse of the red's objective world creating and shaping force. The same could be said of all of the senses. The brain, in reality, functions as a devitalizing, weakening, mirror that brings the corpse of the real living and intense cosmic being of colour, in its represented form discussed above, to our daily wakeful cognition.

As we pointed out, however, only one part of the etheric forces of light and colour that stream into our brain interacts with the physical bodily process in the eyes and nerves. This part becomes a mirror that brings the ordinary experience of the senses and thinking to consciousness in its dead reflection. Now the same can be said about the relation between ordinary cognition and etheric cognition: as the physical brain functions as a mirror that reflects and brings our ordinary perceptions to full consciousness, so our ordinary cognition turns into a mirror for etheric cognition when it is transformed through the cognitive yoga process described above. Our normal cognition really functions as a mirror through which etheric cognition becomes etherically and cosmically conscious, because we use it as an etheric mirror surface. This mirror does not represent the external world through the senses as does the physical brain. Instead it reflects the real living etheric experiences that come from above, and it brings them to our awakened etheric cognition. This is the foundation of imaginative cognition in the precise spiritual scientific sense.

Now above we referred to the third etheric stream, which is responsible for the metabolic regeneration of the physical brain. This stream is made of the spiritual forces that work through the blood that enlivens itself with fresh oxygen and etheric forces in the lungs and then flows into the brain. This stream also carries, in its warmth forces, the intensive forces of will and feeling that we use to fire the electrolysis of the mental picture. We previously pointed out that we donate these actively created and reserved potential forces to the etherized colour when we unite ourselves with it outside the physical body. Now we are becoming aware that there is also an etheric aspect that underlies this process. When we investigate this blood process further, we become aware that, as the dying physical brain contributes to killing that part of the senses' input that comes to ordinary consciousness, this life force has the opposite effect. On the purely physical level, it regenerates the brain processes and keeps the brain cells alive. But what we discover is that part of its etheric forces emancipate themselves from the purely physical processes of regeneration and serves the etherization processes of perception, described above. However, we need a prolonged period of repeated spiritual-scientific research in this area before we can fully comprehend how it operates.

Our imaginative research finds a firm foundation in this field, when we realize that into this brain grave, living etheric forces also flow in from the whole body. When the blood brings the forces of nourishment and regeneration, enriched with nutrients and fresh oxygen from the lungs, and flows upward to the brain, it is con-stantly giving off etheric substance that flows to the brain as well. If we follow these blood streams inwardly, we discover that what we experience inwardly in our souls as fiery devotion and love to truth, has a delicate physical-etheric correlate. It liberates and spiritualizes the potential and actual etheric forces in the blood. The instreaming etheric world forces, which work through light and colours, unite — through our active cognition and devotion to them — with these etheric forces that stream up to the brain from the heart. This is the physiological-etheric aspect of the etherized bridge-building process described above from the purely supersensible side. In this process, the activities of body, life, soul and Ego intermingle in the most intimate way. This process is called in spiritual science 'the etherization of the blood'. And this etherized stream of blood forces flows from the heart to the brain, where it unites with the purified, etherized, perceptions and supplies our new etheric cognition with a surplus of active and creative forces. We can say that it 'warms and lights up' the otherwise still somewhat shadowy etherized sense perceptions that we extract and purify from our senses. This will be described in greater detail next.

Fifth step: human-world essence exchange

In letting go of self-consciousness, in becoming red and entirely forgetting ourselves, we donated a surplus of self-consciousness to the red; and the red, now as pure world force, becomes self-conscious in and through our etherized perception. In this mutual exchange of self-consciousness, we begin to experience something about the relationships between human evolution and the world as a whole. Our practice starts in the head, but the etherization of seeing (to which we add the same work with hearing and warmth) is not isolated from the whole human being. Specifically through the etherization of the blood, we experience how the whole human being and the whole etheric body are already active in the head. And this will become a foundation for further, more advanced, fields of cognitive yoga research.

One detail from this field of research will be mentioned now because, while it completes the present stage in the etherization of sight, it will also become an essential foundation for the creation of a new etheric body and the embodiment of the etheric individuality (see Chapters 7 and 8 below). As we pointed out above, we discover that when we let the intensive force of light and colour flow through the head, the etheric blood streams to the brain are stimulated and respond in a unique manner. When we observe from outside the body how the etheric forces extracted from the perception of light and colours, strike the etherized blood that flows from the body into the brain, we see that this stimulates and awakens still a higher latent or potential power in the etherized blood. This spiritual potential force always exists in the blood and part of it is actualized to nourish and regenerate the biological life processes in the body. But it has other functions beside the etheric-regenerative bodily processes. In the blood flow are also our soul and spiritual forces. In ordinary consciousness this aspect of the blood remains unconscious and in the etheric cognitive yoga processes, it lights up consciously. When the etherized stream of the light and colour, as world force, strikes the spiritual potential of the blood—which is partly etherized already in the heart—it causes changes in the blood's inner spiritual constitution. It releases and spiritualizes not only potential etheric forces but also soul and spiritual forces. When the two etheric streams merge through the brain, enhanced etheric cognition lights up and when we study this lightening process more closely, we can see how through the etherization process, also a higher spiritual process is taking place. It is really awakened through the meeting and exchange between the forces coming from the body below and the forces streaming from the cosmos above.

What we discover is that this lighting up or awakening of etheric-imaginative cognition is an awakening of the unconscious spiritual forces that create self-consciousness. The reason for this is that the blood stream flowing from the heart to the brain, is fired by the blood's warmth processes, through which the human Ego is living in the physical body. It belongs indeed to the most wonderful experiences that one undergoes in the course of cognitive yoga practice: to participate in this remarkable transformation process of the warmth element, the carrier of the Ego forces, that the instreaming world forces unite with, when they flow through our etherized senses, nerves and brain (and also through the whole skin). We see how, through the fire kindled inside the body by means of the etherization of the blood from the heart to the brain, an intensive 'I' spark is carried to the brain, where it ignites and lights up the etheric world forces, and in this lighting up, the etheric world itself experiences its own 'self' in a new way. What takes place is a remarkable mutual breathing in and out, a reciprocal spiritual essence exchange, which is in reality an Ego exchange, between the human 'I' and the world's 'I'. The human donates an 'ego surplus' released from the blood, and thereby becomes more self-less, and in the place left free, it receives a seed potential of a new-world-Self; and the world in turn becomes self-conscious through the etherized human Ego forces that flow from the heart to the head and through the senses to the world. On the one hand, the whole human being donates a surplus of its spiritualized self-consciousness to the world; and the world, experiencing itself through the human senses and head, embodies and envelops itself in the etherized stream of the blood's etherized Ego-carrying fire, and uses it to become self-conscious.

While we have developed, through cognitive yoga, a fully conscious etheric cognition in becoming one with the etherized stream of light and colours, in which we are now weaving, moving, and living, we have opened up our etheric body—first of all in the head—and made it hospitable and receptive for the real etheric world to use it for itself. This can be actually experienced in imaginative consciousness while we are swimming and flowing outside, expanding to the forces of the world's cosmic circumference. We are looking from the world's circumference back to the body, while streaming, weaving, etherically feeling, sensing and seeing, and experience with the forces of the world how the etheric world is using the streams of our freed Ego forces, spiritualized in the blood, that flow from the whole body to the heart and then to the brain, in order to embody and thereby awaken itself as a self-conscious world Self. This is an event of illumination that far overextends and outshines the boundaries of the physical head. For the whole cognitive yoga practice this event marks a certain culmination in this respect: the etherization of sense perception joins the etherization of the blood and its spiritualized fiery Ego forces, and the mutual spiritual essence exchange, that began with the exchange between the human etheric body and the etheric forces of the colour red, is now intensified, enhanced and raised to the Ego level. It becomes in this way a true spiritual, that is, a fully super-sensible experience, illuminating and actualizing a new, fused human-world Self-consciousness, with the help of which more advanced stages of spiritual scientific research can be accomplished.*

Sixth step: An unsurpassable body threshold

However, this process undergoes a significant modification and metamorphosis when we wish to use the new capacity of etheric cognition to penetrate into the body below the head. When we try to stream with, or inhale the etherized world forces of light and colours, sounds and warmth, from the head into the rest of the body we are slowed down and eventually blocked the deeper we descend into the body. From the point of view of the etherized cognition of sight, it can be said that in a more subtle way this already begins below the eyebrow and becomes increasingly stronger and notice-

---

* Rudolf Steiner describes the etherization of the blood as the process that brings about a union between the human being and the spiritual world: 'A union of these two streams [the macrocosmic stream from the spiritual world and the microcosmic stream from the etherization of human blood] can come about, however, only if man is able to unfold true understanding of what is contained in the Christ impulse. Otherwise, there can be no union; the two streams then mutually repel each other, thrust each other away ... spiritual science must be received and gradually be able so to fire the streams flowing from heart to brain. ... If this comes to pass, individuals will be able to comprehend the event that has its beginning in the twentieth century: the appearance of the etheric Christ.' (GA 130, 1.10, 1911) It is also, at the same time, a fully individualized 'Pentecostal illumination' event, the conscious flaming up of individual spiritual consciousness, which is caused by means of uniting the inner Christ forces that we take into ourselves, with the 'holy spirit' that flows from the spiritual worlds into our etherized senses and thinking. When the two spiritual streams unite, we experience the lighting up of our Spirit Self as World Self, and the spiritual world experiences its own Christ-Self shining back to it from below, from the earth and humanity. (I have described these processes in greater detail in my book, *The New Experience of the Supersensible*.)

able from the mouth region and below the larynx. And most of its intensity is filtered out when we reach the lung and heart region. We discover that the body taken as a whole becomes nontransparent and then even 'hostile' to our etherized cognition and the colour and light forces that stream from the etheric world into the head. As a matter of fact, the body begins to reject and repel it back. We can also experience how each colour is rejected and repelled by different organs. For example, our etheric consciousness that streams into the body with the etheric world forces of etherized green is finally blocked in the vicinity of the lungs. While the world forces of red, though they penetrate a little deeper, are then nevertheless repelled in the stomach region. Here we confront a limit and a border, a real threshold, which repeatedly repels our efforts to inhale the sense stream deeper into the body.*

We realize, therefore, that there are certain lower forces working in the body that cause it to become nontransparent, even resistant, to the instreaming of the conscious, etherized, world forces. Some organs have a strong psychosomatic 'antipathy' to these instreaming world forces and develop an inner resistance that blocks them in specific locations. We realize after further research that this resistance is a kind of astral-etheric autoimmune reaction, coming from

---

* This process of rejection takes place for each sensory-etheric extract in specific and localizable bodily organs. For example, muscles and limb bones repel certain sounds and harmonies. We discover an interesting polarity between sounds and colours. Sounds become audible in ordinary hearing because the speech, jaw muscles and bones reject them. When sounds are etherized and inhaled into the body, these muscles and bones become empty spaces like the nerves in the brain become for the light. When this rejection is overcome and we become one with the sound, its melody, harmony, rhythm and beat disappear as well, because they exist only through the resistance of the muscles and skeleton, and we enter into the experience of soundless music, which flows deeper into the body than the etheric forces of light and colour. In the more advanced stages, after overcoming further bodily-soul and inner organ inhibitions, we learn how it flows out again through the body, reversed, through hands and feet, and connects us with the 'music of the spheres' via the resonance created by the body of the earth and its cosmic movements around its axis; the sensitive, fluctuating, moon's waves and cycles, and the planets' complex dances with the sun in outward cosmic space.

the inhibitive autonomic nervous system, which supplies the MECM foundation in the body. This reaction pushes the instreaming forces of the world away, again and again, in order to protect our daily consciousness. Its function is to protect our delicate self-consciousness and inner soul life and to not let us be overwhelmed by the powerful forces and streams that connect our bodies with the physical, etheric and astral forces of the earth and cosmos. This resistance, as we pointed out above, is what makes individuation possible, because through this opacity and density of body and soul, we feel enclosed in the limit of our skins. This self-conscious feeling of inward solidity is the basis for our modern consciousness, without which we would remain ethereal, flowing beings with no cognitive or moral backbone. Our endeavour is to undo and de-actualize, that is, to etherize the very forces that individuated us by separating us from the world. We achieved it to certain extent with the higher senses in the sphere of the head, particularly in the higher, pre-frontal brain regions, and we strive now to deepen it to include the whole body. Though much has being achieved above in the etherization process of the sense and nerve system, insofar as it is localized in the higher brain centres and functions, it is the middle and especially the lower body that must be confronted now. It is the body (to be specific, certain lower astral forces and influences anchored in its deeper and lower layers) that is responsible for our individuation. As was emphasized above, the aim of cognitive yoga is to individuate and then to etherize individuation itself, the very core of the Ego's formative forces, not to destroy or escape from them. And this goal can only be realized if we succeed in *consciously* uniting the world's etheric forces, streaming in through each sense perception, with the body's own pure etheric forces, whose existence and operation is constantly inhibited, individuated and suppressed by the dominantly astral forces of individuation. Below the border, under this threshold, we must search for bodily forces of a very exalted spiritual origin, that were never used and co-opted by the astral forces of individuation, and have retreated in early infancy into a protected chamber in the deepest recesses of our unconsciousness. But first of all, at this point we come to a certain crisis in our work with the purification of the sense perceptions of sight (and this applies also to hearing and warmth sensations). We experience that we will not be able to break the powerful MECM barrier that separates the conscious mind from the unconscious, unified human-world being. In order to continue to be able to flow together in wide-awake etheric cognition with the forces of the etheric world from outside in, and reach the deeper unconscious virgin-like forces of the body, we must first find a way to penetrate through dense layers and stratifications that appear formidable and tenacious.

When we look for the more concrete causes of this hindrance among the senses, we find them in the inner psychosomatic regions in which especially the senses of touch, smell and taste gather and sediment their astral strata. We realize that the already purified forces of the higher sense perceptions, the etheric forces streaming through etherized colours and light, sounds and warmth forces, are too weak to penetrate this threshold and connect with the pure life forces below it in the lower body. In a very impersonal and yet intimate manner, we must come to terms with and struggle with the senses of smell, taste, touch, and a whole host of related sensations, desires, drives and instincts, bundled together in the core of the whole MECM complex. Furthermore, we find that scents, tastes, internal and external tactile and proprioceptive impressions and pain, pleasure, hunger and similar bodily and emotional sensations, have densely compact and intensive connections to the psychosomatic-biographical unconscious strata of the MECM. In other words, they are like psychosomatic or astral, 'magnets' that gather and glue together all our more or less hidden affections, desires, needs, longings, hungers, and drives mixed in the most complicated ways with our bodily and soul pains, wounds and traumas. They are inscribed, or better *infleshed*, in us since our childhood and are engraved so tightly in our deepest unconscious individuations processes, losses and separations from those we love and from living nature and the cosmos. We find here all our losses, pains, deprivations and wounds that we experienced and accumulated in each step of becoming more separated and individualized in the course of our whole life. They are all hardened, trapped and preserved, like the skeletons of primordial fauna and flora in the geological layers of the earth, mixed and tightly sedimented. For example, we discover that each of our smell, taste, and touch sensations has its own tagged compact strata of 'infleshed' sympathies and antipathies, priorities and favourites, which condense around an intense astral-biographical nucleus of radiating, or better sucking, intensity that has immense power of attraction. Such nuclei tightly magnetize and galvanize the whole spectrum of engraved unconscious psychosomatic strata and sedimentations around them, on one hand, and the diverse cognitive processes attached and affiliated with them, on the other. From there they influence and actually dominate the higher cognitive faculties and sense perceptions, our meetings with other persons and with the natural world, in a subtle, half conscious way, because we don't clearly register their influence as it happens. They are also powerfully connected to our semi-conscious psychic and emotional affects and sensibilities, and from this deeper unconscious stronghold, they attach themselves 'from below' as it were, and 'suck in', contract and harden our cognitive, representational processes. That is, here we learn to know exactly how, from the early childhood, our experiences of smells, tastes, and touches, are connected unconsciously in the most manifolds ways with our conscious cognitive life, emotional and behavioural patterns, our motivating desires, instincts and biographically hardened inclinations, habits, reflexes and traumas. This gives them an unconscious dominance, not only over all instinctive behaviour, but also over our so-called 'higher' cognitive, emotive, and willed soul life.

It must be further noted that in our time it is especially difficult to penetrate through the astral forces attached to our sexual complexes, strata and sedimentations because childhood is increasingly shortened as puberty's threshold is crossed ever earlier. While the astral forces that bring about healthy sexual maturity did not enter the human body before age 12 a century ago, they increasingly do so earlier today. In this way they become parasites, preying on the pure, immaculate forces of childhood, which, had they remained pure, would have made the perception of the innermost processes of the body much more conscious and transparent. They create dense, mixed bodily-soul strata (in the physical, etheric, and astral bodies), composed of desire zones of cold and dead layers, intermixed with layers of burning desires. All this we find in ourselves as a formidable resistance and obstacle, when we try to delve through this threshold, following the etherized in-streaming world forces of light, colour, sound and warmth, and meet the hard core of the astral resistance of the MECM attached to smells, tastes, and touches.

These senses create the impenetrable zone by a double pincer sucking action: from above they suck in and swallow each sense perception and each cognitive process and formation of a conscious mental picture, and from below they suck upward the otherwise pure and transparent bodily impressions coming from the bodily senses of life, movement and balance. They glue them together as it were, making what the outer senses perceive to appear as a physical world populated with external physical objects, and make the inner body unconscious, dense and impenetrable. This causes us to represent the external sense world as made up of material, separated objects, and also to experience our own body as dense, heavy and impenetrable. This also causes the subtle and pure activities of balance, life and movement of the inner bodily senses to remain mostly unconscious. In this manner the senses of smell, taste and touch cause each conscious cognitive process to remain tagged and labelled, glued and meshed together with it, all the way down to the remotest and deepest recesses of unconscious body memory. These deeply engraved unconscious strata, which are bodily, emotive, affective, and also strongly genital, are coagulated together and become dense psychosomatic sediments. This creates the general experience of 'existential density' mentioned above. I feel like I am an 'I' enclosed in the limits of my skin, which I represent to myself as absolute limits, separating 'me in here' from the rest of the world 'out there'.

The most existentially foundational structure of the MECM is rooted in these amalgamations of smells-touches-tastes, and therefore is impenetrable to the etheric cognitive work in the field of the higher senses and cognition. We must seek a passage or a password, to be able to cross this much denser bodily-soul threshold, and we must therefore turn our etherization efforts to the field of the lower middle senses. We realize that if a safe and conscious pathway is to be opened at all, if we are to penetrate consciously below this threshold, the gateway cannot be opened by the forces extracted and inhaled from the higher senses alone, but only from the senses of smell, taste and touch, that are directly and intimately connected with the MECM in the physical, etheric and astral bodies.

Let us also be reminded that parallel with the etherization of the higher senses, we continue with the etherization of thinking. This work continues separately in the etheric world of pure thinking activity. Before we describe how we extend the etherization of perception to the lower senses, to gather the forces needed in order to delve deeper into the lower body, let us describe this thinking work as well. In a roundabout manner, pure thinking, though it operates 'above' and outside the body, nevertheless extracts formative forces, that have shaped and condensed our physical body in the earliest years of childhood. These formative forces of the body find their expression in the mostly unconscious experiences connected to the bodily senses of life, movement and balance. And the etherization of thinking is also etherizing these forces and bringing them to higher consciousness.

Therefore, while ascending out to the wide etheric cosmos, etherized thinking also brings these subtle bodily forces and perceptions to full consciousness. It makes some of the deepest and densest regions of the body more transparent. These purer forces will help us, working from above and from below, to penetrate through and cross over the unsurpassable lower threshold.

5. Etherization of Thinking

For when one exercises consciously the faculty that otherwise 'mathematicizes' within us during the first seven years up to the change of teeth ... one enters into this 'living mathematics,' into this 'living mechanics,' ... what otherwise lives within as sensations of balance, movement, and life.... One unites with this weaving in a toneless music in a way similar to that by which one makes the physical body one's own through the activity of the ego in childhood. This weaving in a toneless music provides the other, rigorously demonstrable awareness that one is now outside the body with one's soul-spirit.

(1 October 1920, GA 322)

Thinking must pass over into the rhythm pervading the external world. The moment thinking really becomes free of the bodily functions, the moment it has torn itself away from breathing and gradually united with the external rhythm, it dives down not into the physical qualities of things but into the spiritual within individual objects.... This thinking yearns to vibrate with the plant as it grows and unfolds its blossoms. This thinking follows how in a rose, for example, green passes over into red. Thinking vibrates within the spiritual, which lies at the foundation of each single object in the external world.

(27 May 1922, GA 212)

Thoughts, then, that are truly experienced, are experienced with the bony system ... [man] must unburden himself of his flesh and blood, he must become a skeleton, he must become of the earth. The thoughts must become earthy in the true sense.

(8 January 1924, GA 316)

Above we described the electrolysis of the mental picture, the separation of thinking from sense perceptions, and the first stages of the purification and etherization of the sense of sight. Then we showed what happens when we go out of the body to merge with the etheric forces of colour and 'inhale' them directly into the body, without taking the detour of thinking about them. We demonstrated how we become conscious of the stream of formative life forces that flow from the external etheric world directly into and through the head, bypassing all of the processes of thinking, representing, reflecting, analyzing, combining, interpreting and naming. The result of the inhalation of their intensive world forces directly into the body was, to begin with, demonstrated in the gradual etherization of the cognitive processes attached to the sense and nerve system, centralized in the brain. This etherization achieved a great deal in the transformation of our ordinary head and brain processes, and kindled the first fully spiritual-scientific experiences of the cosmic, etheric world, through imaginative cognition. But it became increasingly difficult as we wished to descend deeper into the middle and lower parts of the body, and was halted altogether when we tried to cross the barrier of the diaphragmatic threshold. And while the threshold consists of the dense amalgamations of conscious and unconscious soul and bodily experiences, below this threshold also exist those regions of the body and soul which are kept altogether outside any conscious experience. Therefore, in those bodily depths we would also expect to discover the purest, pristine life forces, preserved in wholly unconscious regions, untouched by any personal experiences, desires and interests and memories. We can feel and sense, as it were, through the barrier, that if we would continue to purify our conscious cognition, through further intensive etherization, we would be worthy to meet and awaken this 'sleeping beauty' in us, and stimulate its productive potential. However, this sleep is deep and as the legends tell us, it is also induced — and protected — by powerful spells. Therefore, in order to accomplish this at the present stage of the cognitive yoga work, as we said above, we will need help from two sources: first, from an intensification of the etherization process of thinking, and second, from the etherization of the lower-middle senses, smell, taste, and touch, that are co-responsible for the creation of the lower bodily barrier. Therefore, we will begin by describing how thinking is etherized when released from the sense- and brain-bound mental picture and then we will continue to deepen the etherization of perception. This rhythmic interplay between the etherization processes of perception and thinking is the powerful motor of 'polarization and enhancement' that constantly renews and invigorates the field of polarized forces, through the tension of which our consciousness is spiritualized. While both movements take place separately and parallel, they also continuously enhance one another, and the mutual exchange of their ever more spiritualized forces unfolds naturally, while we focus our conscious attention alternately on sense inhalation and thinking exhalation.

In ordinary cognition we use thinking to interpret our experiences and form concepts, judgements, and conclusions about them. Thinking gives us the knowledge that makes us feel secure and grounded in the physical world, and therefore it enables our personal, scientific and cultural progress in this world. But this knowledge is based on our pre-established memories, interests, sympathies, norms and habits. It is rightly 'conservative' by nature. We want and indeed must know what is useful for us, and could not care less about the true or deeper essence of what exists out there in the world. However, our truest humanity, our being of soul and spirit, cannot be grounded as long as we strive to fulfil only our own physical and natural, social and cultural, utilitarian interests, desires and needs. Also the sources of our best creative achievements in the sciences, arts and moral life cannot be found there. But we can dedicate a few moments each day to intensify the pure activity of thinking as outlined in *The Philosophy of Freedom*. Of course this devotion should never interfere with our physical and social duties in daily life nor estrange us from other people. This activity will allow us to gradually free thinking from the fetters of body and soul and we will begin to experience its inborn and pure etheric forces. Then the representations and mental pictures of 'that tree out there' and of 'I am me inside myself in here' vanish and thinking's liberated and living essence lights up in our consciousness. It becomes what it really is in its spiritual essence, usually hidden because it is so selflessly giving itself to the service of physical life.

That is, through 'electrolyzing' and purifying the 'hydrogen' (thinking) component of the mental picture, around the 'anode' pole of our 'polarization and enhancement' process, we begin to experience and observe the etheric becoming of thinking. We experience what becomes of the potential forces that underlie and motivate thinking, when thinking is no longer used in order to synthesize, reflect, represent, name or define an object or process, externally or internally. What becomes of thinking when we stop ordinary thinking altogether and yet remain conscious (that is, not fall asleep)? Our representations and experiences centred around the 'I think therefore I am' unfreeze, melt, evaporate and thinking becomes 'gaseous'. We learn how to follow thinking's emerging stream of becoming as it develops into the etheric 'exhalation' process of cognitive yoga. We share her bliss of cosmic flight, as she takes us with her to join the joyful expansion of our whole being through her liberated new life, emerging out of the narrow confines of the brain-bound intellect.

Now, this bliss will be morally justified, as long as IT (the etherized, liberated thinking) take us with her as a gift of grace. Pressing for more bliss just because we desire this enjoyment and want to continue to intensify it for its own sake, will not bring us more real knowledge of ourselves and of the world. Sooner or later it will begin to cloud our etheric cognition and imaginative consciousness. Therefore, if we do not surrender at this stage to the one-sided temptation to fly away and escape the body and the earth through the enjoyments of etherized thinking, we will be able, when IT releases us from its graceful cosmic flow, to stand still, as it were, and balance our soul between the powerful upward pull of Luciferic etheric levity and the downgrading force of Ahrimanic gravity. It is far easier to surrender, either to the tempting bliss of etheric flight, or to being pulled back to the physical body, than it is to find the free *moral* etheric balance in the middle between them. But once this balanced position is achieved (it is intensively dynamic inwardly and must be repeatedly established, using all the etheric cognitive forces created thus far) we are able to 'look back' at the physical body. Instead of falling back to the body, or flying away from it, we balance ourselves on the etheric edge in between levity and gravity, grounding our middle position in that part of the etheric body which we have already individualized and spiritualized. This perspective reveals to us other aspects of the formative forces that shape and condense our physical and etheric bodies. If we consciously confront the temptation to immediately seek the source of cosmic life far out there in the tempting cosmic light forces, we will be able to approach, in ever new ways, the riddles and problems of becoming truly human in the universe. And this means, again, to bring to fuller and fuller consciousness the spiritual meaning of incarnation and individuation.*

Paradoxical as it may be for ordinary thinking, which always desires to march on and on, straight ahead to ever new and exciting territories, in spiritual-scientific research the new is discovered in the opposite manner. True spiritual progress or metamorphosis, is a process of 'difference and repetition' or in other words, repetition that creates novelty through essential variations and transformations.† Spiritual cognition is one with the force of life, and *rhythm*, such as that found in circulation and breathing, is the most fundamental force of life. Our research must therefore repeatedly spiral back to the beginning and spring forth renewed and invigorated with new life forces, transforming 'the same' to 'the new' through real metamorphosis. This repetition transforms 'the same' to the essentially different, surprising, and innovative. In returning again and again to the beginning of the investigation, we spiral up to a higher level, since the spiritual path is not linear. As we must repeatedly breathe and nourish ourselves to enliven our body, so we must repeat the most basic spiritual practices to enliven our soul and spirit. Therefore, we are not 'done' with the problems of individuation, birth, embodiment, and death 'once and for all', even if we have experienced them many times. It is precisely in this constant process of renewal that we find the source of our strongest life, because there and only there do the forces of the new 'die and become' of the etheric Christ work.

---

* In Chapter 3 of my book, *The Event in Science, History, Philosophy & Art*, called 'The Event in Philosophy', this process is described at length from a different point of view. The reader of the present book will find it enriching to work with both versions demonstrating the etherization of thinking and its reactualization.

† Gilles Deleuze researched this process from another angle in his major philosophical work, *Difference and Repetition*, (1968).

The spiritual lessons of Death

In those short moments, in which we fire and energize our pure thinking, we cancel the common thinking about our perceptions, bodily sensations and soul experiences. We are then looking back from the perspective of a new state of consciousness, upon our daily consciousness and thinking from the outside. We are looking back and down on our daily consciousness as in daily life we look at a memory picture. Now the first discovery we make is that, without the constant supply of external and internal stimuli, it becomes empty of all force and substance. We discover to what extent our daily ordinary thinking depends on the sensory stimulation from outside or on our desires, will impulses, feelings and memories from inside and how feeble it becomes when required to activate itself without external or internal motivations, substance and stimuli. When it is separated from the whole personal soul life thinking becomes absolutely passive and lethargic, even paralyzed, and it is constantly on the verge of falling asleep. Indeed it is really asleep all the time, but this sleep appears full of vitality and interest as long as it is receiving this constant stimulation and input from the senses and body. But the physical world can fill thinking with force and substance only because thinking first becomes empty of its living cosmic forces. It is more than an analogy to say that, just as in the case of pure sense perceptions, living pre-personal thinking is also 'killed' in each forming of a brainy representation. This is a real paradox: the same external stimuli that awakens thinking to external life, kills its cosmic life. As was the case during the purification of sense perception, we painfully experience the fact that each formed representation is like a real grave and tomb for a previously living, creative, and truly energetic cosmic thinking, and that this death process brings our earthly consciousness to life.

And only then does the question arise in our soul, a question born out of true self-knowledge, out of the experience that we are the grave of cosmic, living thinking: where and how do we find, or produce, the vitality and strength needed to bring thinking back from the dead and awaken it to new cosmic life? What can enable us to resurrect it from the tomb of our soul and the corpses of our representations? And as a matter of factual experience, it must be admitted that we feel as if we stand there quite alone and helpless, and to begin with it seems that we do not have at our disposal forces strong enough to raise the dead.

But all this is still expressed rather abstractly, in comparison to the real soul experiences that we undergo in this process. In order to give an experimental example, let us turn our attention again to the external sense perception of a red patch. We focus our attention on this patch and experience the immediate reaction of thinking that grasps the experience of the red patch and recognizes it as such, namely as 'this is a red patch'. Now we stop the next act of thinking, not allowing it to continue its interactions, interpretations and explanations. Then we also stop focusing our attention on the representation of the red patch and we let it flow through us and disappear. Of course it will come back immediately as a memory picture, that will become a new recognized object, which we must let go of again and again. The duration that we can spend outside ordinary time, between erasing the just formed mental picture of the red patch and the next memory picture (or any other more or less associated image) will grow with practice. Once we succeed in holding the ordinary flow of time at bay, stopping at the same time the flow of future time and past time, enlarge the gap between them, hindering their instant synthesis, we can release duration out of time (as described above in Chapter 2). Then we enter more and more fully into the depth of a decisive moment because, as described above, immediately the forces of elevation and levitation would want to take hold of us and carry us far and away. We must be able to accept the lift but only for a fraction of a second, an inkling of an etheric eye, and stay awake and poise and preserve our presence of mind in this physically empty and etherically full situation. Let us imagine this process once more. While we activate thinking to such an extent, that it becomes free from the senses and brain, we have stopped the mental world from streaming and filling our consciousness from both sides. From the sensory side, we stop the production of new representation of the red patch, and from within we stop the return of a related memory picture. With the one hand of the inner activity of our free thinking we hold at bay the next emerging external representation of the red patch, and with the other hand we prevent a memory picture from taking its place from within. (These 'two hands' are really the soul hands of the two-petalled lotus flower or chakra, located in the astral body between the eyes, formed by the activity of pure thinking, and the process described here allows us to imprint in on the etheric body.) Once we delay and, later, entirely stop the creation of new mental pictures and the encroaching of memories and associations, we ourselves actually start to become this place in between the mental pictures. In this empty space of ordinary cognition, usually entirely filled by the incessant noise and mental products of our brainy intellect, we enter fully into the presence of pure nothing, 'where the human being is zero'.[*] This experience of empty consciousness and nothingness is of greatest importance to the more advanced states of the etherization of thinking and cognition as a whole through cognitive yoga. It is experienced in such a way that we say to ourselves: when we delve into this empty space from above, from the etheric world, we delve into the same place that is usually filled up by the reactions of thinking to the constant daily inputs from the senses. This is where, in ordinary cognition, thinking first creates and then remains bound to the mental pictures it formed of objects and processes. In creating each and every mental picture, another portion of thinking exhausts itself, and really dies, and each mental picture is therefore a singular grave of a certain force of thinking invested in its creation. When we first create a mental picture of a red patch, then cancel its further consolidation and memorizing, what is left, to begin with, is the grave of *this specific mental picture* and in this grave lie its concrete, individualized, corpse. Coming from above, with the etheric forces of etherized thinking, this allows us to locate exactly the place, time and process in which living thinking dies. This cognitive place turns out to be the only cognitive place through which thinking's death can be brought to full supersensible consciousness. If we cannot precisely find this location and this process of death, we will not be able to find the place of its resurrection, nor generate the forces

---

[*]Schiller made this fine observation in his *Letters on the Aesthetic Education of Man*.

needed to actualize this resurrection. In this case the whole process of the etherization of thinking will go amiss from its very beginning. That is, the lack of real self-knowledge may lead us to believe that our thinking is 'living', but because this life does not arise from the confrontation with and overcoming of real death, this livingness will have a luciferic twist from the start. If this false vividness is not recognized and corrected, it can lead to many errors and illusions concerning so-called 'living thinking'. To avoid this error, we have to be able to enter peacefully into this mental grave and befriend its death forces. We must be able to remain clear-headed, composed and objective, which are the qualities our practice with *The Philosophy of Freedom*, if properly done, has given us. That is, to be poised inside the 'place of the skull', without wishing, because of angst and suffocation, that it will be filled with new life right there and then for our own sake. The life that is to be born there, must come solely from the new life that we would create. When we do so, we are confronted by a real presence, who comes to meet us from within this grave, a presence that embodies, clothes and individuates itself in the mental remains of thinking. In this manner, we actually force it to make itself imaginatively visible and uncover its otherwise well-hidden and guarded true being. (One cannot but recount these events as they truly occur, no matter how strange and paradoxical they must appear to our ordinary understanding.)

In this grave of thinking we undergo a significant experience, which wholly transforms our etherized thinking and cognition. When we stop the habitual activity of the brain-bound intellect, the forces that are used to produce mental pictures by reducing and devitalizing cosmic thinking, cannot roll on to do their accustomed job. They are forced to abstain from this work. They are released but they still remain eager to re-engage with each new sensory or mental stimulus. They are no longer mobilized and invested in the production, formation, and consolidation of representations. In ordinary cognition these formative forces of the intellect (originally robbed from living cosmic thinking) don't come to the light of consciousness, because their operation is constantly hidden and suppressed in and behind its mental products and because our consciousness is intensely focused, engaged and interested in these mental results.

They are hidden behind our desire to know and explain everything in its materialistic sense. In our daily consciousness we are aware of the mental picture only in so far as we desire its object, we need it, and we are invested in and concerned only about its usefulness. The forces that brought it about remain hidden behind the finished picture that direct our desire and will to the object we need and use. These formative forces sustain and shape our ordinary cognition and consciousness but they don't show up in the same cognition. They are also invested, and therefore become invisible, in the mental fabric and constitution of the mental picture. Now, in the darkness of the grave of consciousness, when we abstain from the creation of a new mental picture and refuse the return of a past memory picture, they emerge, because they are always on the alert ready to attack and possess any new experience as usual. However, we have deliberately stopped their activity in the very act, and now, because they find no prey, no new sensation and impression to capture, devour and digest, they remain, so to speak, hanging loose in the dark, empty, and somewhat mouldy mental air in the skull's cave. There we can catch them in the moment of their mental emergence into and through the physical-etheric brain, becoming externalized and visible for a second, but before they take hold of a new external or internal sensory or mental being or substance. They are ready for the kill, burning with astral-mental desire, but we prevent it from happening, and therefore we can experience them in their full, dark nakedness, as pure brainy death forces. Now their texture, threads and filaments become iridescent and visible and appear like an imaginative 'thought skeleton', which as a matter of fact expresses very exactly their essential nature as forces of death. In the above described process, they are unearthed and brought to a clearance of visibility in the darkly luminous light that fills the mental grave in the cave of the skull, which is, in each person, the always present and individualized hill of Golgotha.

In this dusk between the worlds, in between the dying out of the light of ordinary cognition, based on clear-cut and dead representations, and the stream of living cognition, still in a state of potential, the forces of death become alive and animated. It is a very special kind of life, this life of death in which we participate now, as these forces are the forces of our own (dying) being. But our active participation infuses it with new life, and makes it increasingly concrete and substantial. The important point is to realize that it is *we* that become the *whole* process and event. We enliven this death and we become this resurrection as an individualized spiritual self-conscious activity. This becomes our innermost spiritualized 'I' activity, experience and substance for all time to come. Here — and only here — can we ground our self-conscious, spiritualized self, whose activity alone can carry us through all the worlds, to the highest and back to the physical, with full self-consciousness. We will remember, spiritually speaking, this self, in each new world and will therefore always be able to incarnate with it back on the earth and bring the rich fruits of our experiences safely back home.

And this becomes the fundamental imaginative event at this stage of the cognitive yoga practice: this newly experienced and individualized dead etheric thought skeleton will fulfil the same role in etheric cognition that nerves and bones fulfil in physical life and physical cognition. Indeed, bone and nerve tissue share the same embryonic origin, and in the bones' formative processes, the death process of the nerves continues further until final ossification and death, which is held back one step in the nerves themselves. The nerve is like a bone which has not become fully hardened. Therefore, in the flat bones, to which the skull bones belong, bodily life and substance are solidified and killed to the outmost possible extent. This etheric skeleton functions as a cognitive basis and foundation for imaginative cognition, being the deadest etheric substance in the human constitution. The conscious experience of this etherized bone and nerve skeleton not only frees one from the unconscious fetters of death, but enables a transformation of death into a living, vital force. Forcing death to embody itself in the spiritualized activity of cognition described here, means to bring it into the living and warmly human light of etheric self-consciousness which it most anxiously avoids. It means to make it alive as well. This is one and the same process, because we are essentially dealing here with the death forces that innervate all human constitution and consciousness and also all natural kingdoms.

The being of death now becomes visible and alive as an independent being. Living death has many gifts. It becomes our etheric bone-nerve skeleton and fabric, which steels and supports our etheric body and etheric cognition and gives them the tough yet flexible, etheric elasticity, resilience and endurance, which is indispensable for real etheric creation and life out in the wide open etheric world. Using this etheric body and cognition, we may venture — later on — into the World Wide Web of cosmic life and ground ourselves out there in firm etheric embodiment and spiritual cognition. And as we shall see, because we freed and redeemed these forces from the clutches of death in its individualized form, it will serve us well to transform the cosmically tempting forces of Lucifer for the good. (The spiritual father source of our personalized being of death, or 'death Angel', is Ahriman himself, macrocosmically speaking.) This is the reason why the lessons of death are indispensable spiritual lessons, a foundation stone for both the advanced stages of the etherization of thinking as well as for the building of the etheric individuality itself.

Strange as it may sound, the being of death, once spiritualized and resurrected in this way, becomes both a friend on our path, as well as an essential spiritual guide and teacher. We meet death in its pristine form, befriend it and learn a lesson from it that no other being in the universe can teach us. It teaches us this indispensable spiritual lesson, the lesson of death, called also 'the lesson of individuation', without which the liberation of thinking from the fetters of brainbound representation will either shatter and end in resignation (succumbing to Ahriman's temptation), or become ecstatic, mystical or psychedelic (succumbing to Lucifer's temptation). It demonstrates the contradictory and enigmatic meaning of death as something that enhances life and consciousness (and this also allows us to better understand Goethe's wisdom-filled statement: 'nature invented death in order to create abundant life'). Death teaches us not in words and concepts, but in living and moving, worldwide pictures, which can only be translated into rather abstract concepts and prosaic words. The basic message is that what we know as 'humanity' and 'the human being' during physical-organic embodiment, though it appears to be only a tiny and insignificant part of the universe, in reality is a most vital stage in its whole spiritual evolution. Death shows us by demonstrating 'in front' of our spiritual eyes, that the divine spiritual worlds secrete and actualize bodily individuation through conception, birth, and growth until death, like a caterpillar spins its own cocoon, in order to go through a remarkably creative process of metamorphosis. And what emerges out of this divine cocoon—so our new spirit companion tells us, is our resurrected and Christ permeated 'I'. This is the true whole human being, the firstborn that will redeem and return the earth and all her beings to the spiritual worlds from which they descended. Death shows us how it is his mission to help us find the way in and out of bodily incarnation in an organic body. He operates on both sides, guiding birth and death alike, and guards the limits in space and time that constitute this miraculous divine cocoon, without the limitation of which the whole spiritual cosmos would have never achieved individuality and self-consciousness. In reality birth isn't there in order to annihilate cosmic life, and death isn't there in order to annihilate earthly life, but both are the in-breathing and out-breathing of becoming. The narrowing and expanding of life and consciousness are like the two poles in between which individuation, human freedom and human love become possible. Death's task is precisely to make cosmic becoming far more consistent, independent and therefore also stronger than it could have been without it. Indeed, human freedom and love can become strong enough to be individualized *and* cosmic at the same time only thanks to the being of death. By means of the grace of the gifts of death (that is, incarnation and excarnation or birth and death taken together), after going through an evolutionary phase of individuation and separation, humanity will add a fresh and wholly unique individualized stream of becoming to the spiritual worlds. In this way, death becomes a teacher of the meaning of individuation in the universe and shows its true nature as a faithful guardian of the fountain of eternal, creative and living becoming.

The event of cosmic thinking

The fundamental truth that we understood and actually *became* as we received the schooling and the lessons of death, is that this individualized event of Golgotha, the death and resurrection of human cognition, can alone give us the etheric firmness we must have in order to remember our self when we excarnate with etherized thinking into cosmic life in the light-filled etheric worlds. It allows us to continuously free our dead thinking, raise it from the grave of representation, and follow its resurrection into the cosmic worlds, while taking with us an unforgettable lesson concerning the true cosmic meaning of our 'I' and our individuation.

At that moment we experience a significant spiritual event: the event of thinking's cosmic rebirth, its release and metamorphosis, its becoming world, its cosmization. Now we can modestly let ourselves fly with thinking's released life stream into the cosmos, and celebrate 'the event of cosmic thinking' without forgetting the creative cosmic significance of human life and becoming on the earth. This flight takes us in two different directions at once: higher in the direction of the existing cosmic etheric sun, and deeper into the new 'sun in the earth'. If we avoid putting these orientations into spatial representations, we can feel that their spiritual essences are one and the same. We experience only one sun-line, arch, and circumference through midday and midnight, sunrise and sunset, spread out there through the whole radiant etheric universe and 'down there' in and through our physical body that has become transparent. This also lets us see through the transparent etheric depth of the earth that lights up and reveals the indwelling, earthly sun life of the etheric Christ.

If we truly go through and assimilate death's lessons described above, the etherization of thinking and our ascent to the sunlit cosmic world will be experienced as carrying in its wings an etherized extract of the powers that materialize our body and individuate our pre-individual, cosmic, consciousness. We carry with us into the cosmos, on the wings of the cosmic rebirth of thinking, an intensive extract of the cosmic formative forces that cause human individuation, embodiment, birth, death, and materialization in the first place. Now this extract can consciously unite with the cosmic sun forces that guide both the life before and after death, through our incarnation and individuation. These forces surround and penetrate the body from all sides. This experience of etheric cosmic thinking, will be (again paradoxically from an ordinary point of view) a fully conscious supersensible experience of the process by means of which the human body is actualized, and becomes filled in with what we usually designate by the abstract concepts of 'substance' and 'matter'.

The threefold metamorphosis of cosmic thinking

This is a fact of experience that can be observed in all clarity and exactness: the thinking spiritualized by means of *The Philosophy of Freedom*, released from its brain-bound attachments to the body, takes a spiritualized extract of the bodily formative and constitutive forces out with it into its cosmic flight. These are the forces that have shaped our body from its conception until approximately the cutting of the second teeth. When we look back at the body from the etheric world, where we are united with the forces that constituted the body, we discover that the forces that contract, condense, harden and shape the body's connective tissues, cartilages, bones, the skeleton, teeth and the nerves and brain mass, are highly spiritual forces. Furthermore, these are the same forces in which we are totally and unconsciously immersed in the first years of our lives, while our baby consciousness is busy learning how to master the sensory-motor dynamics of our quickly developing baby body and mind. These bodily contracting, condensing, building and shaping forces are experienced in their pristine, spiritual state, as etheric, creative, cosmic forces which at the same time are the forces of cosmic thinking. We experience what Rudolf Steiner continually described, from the most varied points of view — that only later in life, after the hardest parts of the physical body have been sufficiently formed (bones and second teeth), do these forces become free from their bodily work and available to power the first developmental stages of logical and mathematical thinking. In other words, when they complete some of their primary organic and physical tasks, they are free from their previous, highly spiritual, bodily work and become the formal and abstract concepts of conscious thinking and cognition. They become increasingly available as the child's elementary cognitive forces and continue their emancipation from the body and bodies through childhood and puberty. The force that becomes conscious as thinking is a cosmic, living, body-building force that has completed its organic bodily tasks. Each concept and representation that the child learns to form uses an emancipated and abstracted residue of the bodily constitutive and formative forces. As long as they were mostly building the body, they were real spiritual cosmic forces, and because they were real they were also unconscious. This is the law of human embodiment: the forces that build, shape and enliven the body are real cosmic forces, that is, spiritual forces. All bodily and materially productive and formative forces are spiritual and therefore work only unconsciously in the present stage of individuation. And what gradually emerges as conscious thinking (and also the conscious experience of feeling and will), is what has completed its unconscious, spiritual, bodily work and become free for conscious mental and soul life. Only after the forces of the spiritual world have completed their real task in the constitution and formation of the body, an empty and lifeless shadow of them, a dead corpse, is freed from the spiritual bodily tasks and becomes available as a force of our modern and awake self-consciousness. They become conscious precisely because they are now devoid of the absolutely powerful creative spiritual forces, which are capable of shaping and condensing real matter and real bodies. We as self-conscious humans can only make reflected, abstract ideas about bodies, when the bodies are already created by the cosmos. But we make those abstract ideas — and this is the essential point here — by means of the spiritual leftover of the cosmic forces that created the bodies in the first place. Real creative life, that produces substance, consigns it and shapes reality, has become mental-image, the conscious ability to form concepts and mental pictures about those finished cosmic material creations. This transition, transformation and translation of the unconsciously working, high spiritual forces that cause the body's substantiation, consolidation and formation, into forces of clear and conscious thinking, is one of the greatest riddles of all human becoming.

In ordinary thinking we don't know that our clear-cut and

abstract logic, mathematical and geometrical thinking (as all other conscious mental and soul forces) originates in the cosmic spiritual forces. These are the forces by means of which the child's incarnation is spiritually shaped through the infinite spiritual wisdom of 'measure, weight, and length', that is, through the still purely spiritual and dynamic relationships, ratios and harmonies. These forces work from the whole cosmos into the developing child. Spiritually speaking, these forces of the highest 'musical' wisdom are fully alive as they work, shaping and building the body of the child in the first seven year period and especially in the first three remarkable years. Thus he finds his first bearings in time and space while he learns to stand up and walk, speak and think, and he does so by the still unconscious perceptions of the bodily senses of balance, movement and life.

This is how humans can think and grasp the world by means of the laws of abstract and formal logic, mathematics and geometry, and use them to understand and implement the laws of mechanics and engineering, to build machines and transform the external physical world. But what we think and use in a material and mechanical way is a shadow image of the sublimely creative and artistic forces of cosmic mathematics, geometry and harmony, which form the human body and indeed all material and organic bodies in the universe. As Rudolf Steiner points out in his lecture about the new yoga, quoted above,

> when one exercises consciously the faculty that otherwise 'mathematicizes' within us during the first seven years up to the change of teeth ... one enters into this 'living mathematics,' into this 'living mechanics,' ... that otherwise lives within as sensations of balance, movement, and life.... One unites with this weaving in a toneless music in a way similar to that by which one makes the physical body one's own through the activity of the ego in childhood.

Only thanks to death's teaching and lessons are we in a position to inwardly connect, in our own conscious spiritual activity, these three realms of reality, which are considered to be totally different and disconnected from each other in daily cognition: the realm of objective, spiritual-material unconscious body formation, the realm

of self-conscious but lifeless human thinking, representations, concepts and ideas, and the realm of consciously etherized and spiritualized thinking. Through cognitive yoga, we realize that, when
ordinary thinking becomes cosmic thinking, it completes a full circle
in the spiral of becoming, because it becomes one with the same
cosmic thinking that has created our bodies unconsciously since
conception and birth. What now lives and weaves consciously in
our etheric cosmic thinking and cognition are the same spiritual
formative forces that build our body, and all material bodies in
nature and the cosmos in the first place. The realization that these
are three stages in a process of metamorphosis of one and the same
spiritual (and at its lowest spiritual level, etheric) world force, is a
discovery that is only possible through modern spiritual-scientific
research. Through the etherization of thinking by means of the
cognitive yoga practice, we experience, therefore, the following
remarkable threefold metamorphosis of thinking:

First, before our ordinary thinking becomes ordinary and think-
able in conscious, personal, human self-consciousness, it works as
an unconscious cosmic and spiritual bodily building force, that has
factually transformed *itself* into real working, living, formative
substantial and material processes and bodies.

Second, as a part of this creative spiritual force completes its
body-building work, it emancipates itself from the substantiation
and formation of the bodily-organic functions, and becomes available as free and dead mental forces. This is the reason for the human
capacity to develop conscious thinking (while the other part continues to unconsciously nourish and regenerate the body, in a
gradually weakening capacity, until death).

The third stage in the metamorphosis of thinking is when it again
becomes etheric and cosmic as demonstrated here. But now for the
first time it is a fully self-conscious spiritualized thinking that unites
with the otherwise deeply unconscious spiritual body-building
forces. We, as self-conscious beings, can experience, through our
individual 'I', the same high cosmic forces that created our bodies,
in which we have unconsciously incarnated since conception and
birth.

We realize, therefore, that our ordinary and self-conscious mental forces are the middle stage in the metamorphosis of one and the same spiritual stream of creative cosmic forces. On the one hand, it builds and forms our bodies unconsciously in early childhood and the other hand, we can develop it ourselves in full self-consciousness outside the body. In the middle stage, between the two poles of the unconscious and the superconscious creative cosmic thinking, ordinary human thinking develops. This thinking is also in the middle potential between the formative spiritual forces of the past and of the future. It is a metamorphosed residue of the highest spiritual forces of birth that gradually exhaust themselves in bodily growth and formation, and at the same time the seed potential of future spiritualized, transformed, self-conscious cosmic cognition. This is again the pearl of great price! If we only look at the content of our conscious minds, we may experience it as only a reflection and representation, a filtered out corpse, in comparison with both the unconscious formative forces that build our bodies and the fully conscious cosmic thinking experienced outside the body. But it gave us self-consciousness, clarity, exactness, logic ... and all the unique gifts that only earthly thinking and cognition can offer in the universe. This can only be achieved in the middle phase, because without it there is no third phase, no conscious spiritualization of self-conscious thinking at all. But this is what spiritual science is all about: the newest spiritual stream of modern humanity. And then, if we walk faithfully in the pioneering steps of Rudolf Steiner, and separate thinking from sense perception, decompose the mental picture, experience and resurrect the death forces of cognition and thinking, we experience how this selfsame, ordinary, abstract, dead, thinking is metamorphosed into the purest, life-giving thinking, that unites wholly with the same original spiritual force and beings that create the physical earth and all its physically incarnated beings as well as all sun and galactic bodies in the starry heavens. And only then can we realize: now *we* experience ourselves, our spiritual selves, to be one inside this stream of cosmic forces, and we experience how it flows through us. We experience how these forces, filled with divine wisdom, beauty and might, originally substantiated, contracted, condensed and shaped our physical body since our

conception. And now we have transformed them, thanks to thinking's clarity, into self-conscious spiritual-scientific cognition.*

The whole process of metamorphosis of thinking, its birth, death
and resurrection, is enacted and repeated consciously by means of
cognitive yoga in the middle phase of this metamorphosis, in each
moment of waking life. Taken in this sense, each moment of cognitive yoga practice accomplishes in a nutshell the whole cosmic
drama of human life on the earth. It is a real seed, which contains in
its stages and events, consciously, the whole movement and
development that humans go through unconsciously through their
whole life by activating and resurrecting, in this very moment, the
potential forces of thinking. It brings to light our pre-birth cosmic
existence, our descent to the earth through bodily incarnation, the
gradual development of our earthly self-consciousness during
childhood and puberty, and the stage of consciously going through
the portals of death through self-conscious spiritual cognition. This
whole process becomes our individualized self-conscious 'I'
activity. That is, first of all, in our daily mental life we recapitulate
the same body-building process in the building of each single
mental picture. As we saw above, each forming of a representation
is a small embodiment and incarnation process, in which free cos-

---

*Precisely when thinking is released from the body, it shows that what we call
'thinking' in ordinary cognition is an abstracted and emancipated corpse of a
force unconsciously active in the inner bodily formative processes and its
adaptations to space and time during embryonic and early childhood development. It is experienced as a kind of bodily formative, indeed, musical logic,
mathematics and geometry, through which the baby learns to master the basic
experiences and learning processes of controlling the bodily senses and faculties connected with the development of balance, movement, and action. It is
also interesting to follow Husserl's genetic phenomenological studies in this
direction, because here he gets as close as he ever did to spiritual science. As
Don Welton finely pointed out in his book, *The Other Husserl* (2002): 'At yet a
deeper and final level of genetic analysis Husserl discovers that space and time
themselves are not just "forms" but are generated, on the one hand, by the
interplay of position, motility, and place, and on the other, by the standing-
streaming flow of the process of self-temporalization itself. Husserl's studies of
the self-generation of space and time are clearly the most difficult of all his
genetic studies.' (p. 254)

mic forces from sense perception and thinking alike, captured by the brain, are contracted, condensed and hardened. The sum total of all our mental pictures constitutes our 'mental body' and 'mental stuff'. And only when the unconscious formation process of the representation is complete, do we wake up to truly full self-consciousness, saying: that is a tree out there in space separated from us. Each sense perception and thinking, naming, cognizing, and forming of a mental picture is a kind of a small, subjective mental birth on one hand, and death of a cosmic stream of life on the other. And each formed representation, as a corpse of cosmic life, functions as a solid 'mental body', a contracted and condensed cognitive ground, on which we can stand up inwardly and become individualized, self-conscious, and independent in our ordinary life of cognition. This is how representation is conceived, born, grows old and dies a mental death of hardening. In doing so, it organizes and builds the skeletal and therefore self-conscious mental struc- tures, shells and envelopes, described for example in the phenom- enological observations of Husserl and the structural investigations of Piaget. A mental structure crystallizes around its originally living and unconscious stream of growth and becoming in order to actualize and individuate human self-consciousness in the physical world. But what structuralism cannot comprehend is that deep inside this corpse, in the grave of the skull, a seed of its original cosmic life is preserved, under the hardest mental covering, and it lies dormant, asleep, as a divine potential, awaiting the awakening impulse of self-conscious humans. As we could point out above (in Chapter 4) the exact place and process by means of which Goethe's phenomenology becomes spiritual science in the field of perception: here we can exactly delimit the place in which structuralism and Phenomenology become spiritual science in the field of thinking. When this impulse is flowing in and through this grave, it awakens the potential cosmic seed of life and spiritualizes its cosmic forces. And our human, individual, cognition, becomes the place through which we go now, in each moment, wide-awake, through the gates of death into eternal life, that we experience while living in the body. On all levels of our human existence and becoming, we actualize the cycles of individuation, birth, death and the resurrection of spiritualized cognition. And thus we become on the earth, co-creative participants and partners with the Gods.

Back to our senses

The more we develop and strengthen our cosmic thinking, the more we draw nearer to the mystery of its living source. Everything is experienced as an etheric, cosmic-earthly rhythmic heartbeat, pulsation, and breathing. More concretely, it is experienced as a universal source of warmth, light and life, indeed an etheric sun-like source, embracing all matter and life. It nourishes humans and the kingdoms of nature, as well as the higher beings on earth and in our cosmos, and it brings the earthly and the cosmic into mutual relations of harmony. We feel attracted to this source with our whole freed etheric being and with our emerging spiritual individuality. This becomes, therefore, our real future goal in the etheric world. We want to prepare ourselves for this meeting. In order to make this possible, we know that we will have to gain forces strong enough to actualize two real creative tasks in the etheric world. First, to consolidate our independent and creative spiritual individuality, and second, to build a fitting individualized etheric body to embody this individuality in the etheric world. We will need these two achievements in order to facilitate the meeting with the source of universal life.

And yet, the more we strive in this direction, the more we realize that we lack the necessary moral-cognitive forces. And we feel that, if we want to draw nearer to it in fuller imaginative consciousness, we will have to first make ourselves worthy of such a meeting. Again and again, when we venture forth into the wide open etheric world, we will either soon lose our etheric cognition and plunge back into ordinary consciousness, or, conversely, lose our focus, sobriety, and self-consciousness, and fly around aimlessly, not able to coordinate and navigate our journey. Without the moral-spiritual conscience, which alone is our compass in this new world, our etheric GPS loses its bearings, and we soon realize that we are straying away from the cosmic source of life which we aspire to reach.

We realize sooner or later that we have yet to intensify and complete the etherization processes of sense perception, so that it can help us cross the formidable lower threshold to search for the treasure of the purest potential bodily forces that we still need to extract. Without them, we will not be able to fulfil our cosmic mission and our cosmic flights will be continuously aborted. We must find the inner strength to renounce further cosmic flights and concentrate all the forces gained so far in our work with the spiritualization of human consciousness and cognition through the bodily senses and the *whole* body. We know that the pearl of greatest price is still to be discovered and actualized in the strongly guarded depth of the body.

Let us, therefore, direct our spiritual forces back to the physical world, the physical body, and the etherization of perception. And as we demonstrated above in detail during the etherization of sight, we must now concentrate all our cognitive efforts on the etherization of the lower-middle senses (smell, taste and touch). For reasons to be explained below, the sense of smell has been chosen as an example for our present demonstration. It will lead us safely into and through the labyrinth of our lower nature.

6. Etherization of Smell

The experiences of the senses of smell, taste and touch are sedimented as it were on top of what we would have experienced through the senses of balance, movement and life ... through the fact that they are imposed on one another, there arises a solid self-consciousness in man; thereby he feels himself as a real self.... The one striving for Imagination wends his way through the sensations of smell, taste, and touch, penetrating into the inner realm so that, by one's remaining undisturbed by sensations of smell, taste, and touch, the experiences stemming from balance, movement, and life come forth to meet one. It is a great moment when one has penetrated through what I have described as the sense-triad of taste, smell, and touch, and one confronts the naked essence of movement, balance, and life ... one has reached something that one experiences initially as the true inner being of man because of its transparency.... What one finds is a true organology, and above all one finds within oneself the essence of that which is within equilibrium, of that which is in movement, of that which is suffused with life ... we experience what on the one hand, what we have obtained as Inspiration from pure thinking – the life that at a lower level is thinking, and then becomes a thinking raised to Inspiration – and on the other hand what we experience as conditions of equilibrium, movement, and life. Now we can bring these modes of experience together. We can unite the inner with the outer. The fusion of Imagination [created by spiritualized sense perception] and Inspiration [created by spiritualized thinking] brings us in turn to Intuition....

(GA 322, 3 October 1920)

Let's turn now to smell. A scrutiny of the present position of the scientific research concerning the sense of smell or olfaction, will allow us to better understand its central position among the senses, and also within the whole MECM complex. Because it is directly connected to the higher, middle and lower functions of body and mind, it also influences them in the most immediate manner, powerfully controlling our whole human constitution. As in so many fields of knowledge and life, recent natural scientific research has corroborated many of the results of spiritual science in this field too.

Olfaction is considered among the oldest senses in vertebrates and the only one that establishes a direct connection between the brain and its environment. While other senses must pass through different cortical filters, olfaction goes from the environment right into the highest centres of the brain. Furthermore, olfaction never sleeps because we always breathe and perceive smells. It is significant that olfaction coincides with the nerve pathways and centres that also serve memory and emotion in the limbic system, and this explains the enormous memory retention and the vital intensity of events in life that were assimilated and tagged through olfaction. The olfactory sense also uses brain regions directly responsible for the processing of emotion, motivation, fear, memory, pleasure and attraction. Neuroscientists have coined the term 'higher olfactory functions' to describe those brain functions which combine cognition (memory, intuition, perception, judgement) and olfaction.

Bearing this in mind, let us continue our research in the department of cognitive yoga in the lab. of spiritual science. It must be remembered, that the etherized cognitive forces, extracted from sight and from thinking, described above, support our present efforts from the background. Now, when we inhale the sweet scent of a rose, the first thing we have to do is to separate and purify the qualitative element of the scent from the air that carries it. For this purpose, we have to find where the stream of the inhaled scented air bifurcates into a coarser air that flows down through the nasal cavity and the upper and lower respiratory track to the lungs, and a subtler scented stream that flows from the nasal cavity upward into the brain. We find that the bifurcation is located right above the nasal cavity. From this location the air stream flows downward and the pure quality of the scent streams along the olfactory nerve pathways to the olfactory centre between the eyes. When we grasp and hold fast to this bifurcation place, we can also train ourselves to move deeper into it and widen the differentiating fissure in between the two, which usually remains imperceptible and veiled because our attention normally follows the experiences of pleasure or displeasure that we have with the scent. This veil is woven from our emotional investments in all of our sense perceptions and the

various desires, pleasures and displeasures that arise in our perceptions of smell, taste, touch, coupled with their corresponding
unconscious inner bodily sensations. The only way we can progress
in the cognitive yoga's sense breathing process at this stage is to
actively renounce the solid commitments invested in our attachments to smell's emotions, desires and pleasures. When we succeed
in doing this (and in practice this is a difficult task, demanding
robust discipline and patience), we discover at the same location the
source of a third stream that splits off from the other two. A stream
that is subtler than the pure qualitative scent is split off from the
main scent, a stream of pure etheric intensity that is finer than the
scent quality to the same degree as the latter is finer than the air. It is
released from the same place in which the original inhalation stream
was split into the coarser air and the finer scent. However, even after
we succeed in registering its emergence point and releasing its
emanation from the two other streams, we cannot hold it fast for
very long in its pure form. Not only is it extremely fleeting and
evanescent, but also the instinctive emotional attachments to the
experience of the quality of the scent keep intruding back into
consciousness. The problem is made all the more difficult because
the experience of the pure qualitative element of the scent is still too
close and similar to a normal instinctive-emotional smell experience
and hence it repeatedly blunts the subtler etheric perception and
cognition. The pure qualitative experience of the scent appears
coarse in comparison with the pure intensity and it continuously
veils it and wins over our attention. And we realize that we will not
be able to overcome it and take hold of the intensive etheric stream
in its purity unless we develop a method that can transform our
olfactory experience to such an extent that it will agree to free the
third stream and let us grasp it and follow it on its own terms.

1st step: From quality to intensity

After achieving the capacity to focus on the purely qualitative
experience of the scent, which in itself is not an easy requirement
and demands repeated practice over long periods of time, we must

be able to allow it to ebb away again. However, letting an accomplished soul and cognitive achievement go isn't easier either. The
pure sweetness of the rose scent that fills us after its release from the
inhaled air is much more powerful and inwardly persuasive than
our daily experience of the scented air mixture. Paradoxically, our
success in the first separation, purification and extraction of the
pure qualitative scent from the physical air, makes it that much
harder to let it go and progress to the separation and extraction of
the third stream, the pure etheric intensity, out of the qualitative
scent. It clings not only to the inner parts of our brain but to our
inner bodily organs as well. Its sweetness becomes, with all its
subtlety, a source of profound, even if more refined, pleasure. We
must find the strength to give up this body and soul experience of
being saturated with the finest inner sweetness. We must also
confront the fact that when we succeed in letting it vanish, it leaves a
greater sense of lack and emptiness behind and that our emotionally
invested longing will become as intense as its sweet fullness and
saturation was before. The problems will be better understood if we
know that the lower bodily organs and also the inner parts of the
brain have a strong astral, addictive tendency toward sweetness of
all sorts, including many pleasurable but also distasteful scents,
tastes and touches. Therefore, when we actually empty the scent's
fulfilling pleasurable presence we are left with a negative shadow of
the very same aura and intensity. Producing this empty nothing, or
an extract on the negative side (-1) of the scent's quality, is difficult, because the scent haunts our attention and clings to it. For a
long time, we still feel this remnant of the highly diffused scent as a
disturbance at the background of our attention. Slowly and reluctantly it becomes rarified, then eventually unnoticeable, and finally
it is ready to take its leave from our attention. But we will have to
learn at this point to humbly admit that we are attached to the smell
much more than it is attached to us. When we discover the cause of
our difficulty in getting rid of our attachment to the scent, we have
to face this fact. We find out that what actually makes it stick to us so
stubbornly is caused by (beside the more easily recognizable
attachments to the last vestiges of the pleasurable sweet scent itself),
a much deeper unconscious experience. This experience comes to

consciousness only reluctantly and in it we find that the bodily sensual impressions, perceptions and sensations of smell (tastes and touches, and so on) actually ground us in our body, nay, really make the body into *our* individual body. We face the fact that we have a 'sentient or sensation body' that produces and grounds an embodied existential feeling of self. We are constantly capturing the subtlest cosmic radiations and sensations and condensing them into an individualized sensation body, and embodying our self in its 'astral flesh' of sensations, pleasures and displeasures, desires and affections. We discover our safe, sensual-sentient cave, warmed up by digestion and the blood, inwardly self-loving, embracing and welcoming. We alone possess it as a private hideout (actually 'hide-in') to use and occupy according to our needs and desires. Each morning when we wake up and indeed at every moment of our waking life, we constantly fall in love with and fall into this sentient-soul body. We smell ourselves inwardly all the time, and taste and touch ourselves inwardly, and this constant self-smelling, tasting and touching that never stops in the unconscious depths, grounds us in our sentient soul and body. Thanks to this unconscious astral process of bodily self-perception, sensation and enjoyment, in which the forces of smell play a central role, we have a body that we love in the most egotistical sense of the term, more than any other body among the infinite number of earthly and cosmic bodies. So trying to let go of this self-loving and self-constituting, warm body of smells, tastes and external as well as internal bodily touching and sensations, is like making a volitional choice to die; separating from a beloved and comfortable place of secure and hidden, private, earthly dwelling. Only when we are ready to face this fear and let it go, will the scent aura and substance really be free to leave us. We have also liberated it from its imprisonment in our sentient body- and soul building processes, and it can therefore return to its true cosmic stream of becoming. As an act of thankfulness for this self-less liberation, it may gracefully allow us to participate in its return to its cosmic source and share its true being and becoming as a real objective world force from now on.

What remains when the pure qualitative element disappears entirely is, to begin with, really nothing, but the nothing tips over below its zero point and becomes more empty then nothing. When we stop resisting the disappearance process, and still remain conscious when our supportive body feeling falls away and the experience of bodily dense-fullness becomes truly empty, something in the disappearance process of the pure sense quality will 'invite' us to follow it in the direction of its infinite 'line of flight'. This empty body-shadow of pure physical nothing becomes a vehicle for an embodiment of new etheric existence. We have to learn to feel 'embodied' in this no-body place of empty nothingness, as we naturally feel embodied, secure and fulfilled with solid sentient soul substance in our physical body, and love it with the same intensity of affection. If we succeed in sticking with it and let it carry us, we will find out that we are transformed in two directions at once. On the one hand we are becoming expanded following the line of flight of the infinite, self-diluting experience of scent, while on the other hand, the empty centre from which we expand takes us over to itself; we are becoming infinitely diffused at the periphery and emptier than nothing in the centre of the vanishing quality. We are vanishing at the periphery and centre simultaneously. And then comes a moment in which the escaping movement towards the infinite horizon and the vanishing movement towards the infinitely emptying centre become one movement. But then it is no longer 'movement' in any physical, spatial-dynamic meaning of the term. By now any last residual dose of the original qualitative scented stuff has completely vanished from our being and consciousness and the last attachment to the embodiment in bodily sensations has vanished with it. Everything is inverted in all dimensions: upside becomes downside, inside out becomes outside in and vice versa simultaneously. We now find ourselves fully 're-embodied' in reverse in the substance-less situation of pure negative intensity. It takes us over as we become its 'minus' site, its emptied-out nothingness. And we experience that this emptiness is no longer something we possess, but, conversely, that it begins to possess us. We know that we are fully negatively 'embodied' in this disembodiment when we feel that it swallows us, in a manner of speaking. The possessor of the qualitative scented experience becomes possessed by its opposite, etheric, nothingness, and is pulled with it until the possessor wholly surrenders its possessing power. Therefore, in the depths of the intensive 'negative rose scent', a remarkable inversion and reversal of the 'owners' of the etherization event takes place, in the fullest *Umstülpung*. Once again, this requires from us the great readiness to let go, and the confidence that it will guide us safely and benevolently to visit its innermost being.

2nd step: from intensity to etheric world force

It is important to emphasize, for reasons of scientific exactitude, that the above described process of 'rose takeover' doesn't emerge from the centre or from the periphery of our attention, because when it happens, we no longer 'have' centre and periphery; we neither own nor control them. The situation and event no longer match our ordinary perceptions and concepts of centre, periphery, movements of expansion and contraction, and so on. We have, precisely speaking, become *their* inward intensities of rarefaction, etherization, dispersal and evacuation. As long as the self-emptying hole in the centre and the expanding circles that vanish at the periphery are still our experiences and perceptions, we are essentially still in the centre, that is, we are experiencing the qualitative element as an *inner* process, and we still possess a residue of the common centre/ periphery, inner/outer dualities of ordinary cognition. When this comes to an end, to full inversion, it comes from 'the back' as it were, from 'behind' us, as a stream of etheric, cosmic human becoming that gently embraces and holds us and carries us away altogether on its path.

When we have honestly relinquished our embodiment in the soul and sentient body through the etherization process of the sense of smell, without in the least relinquishing our previously gained, etheric, conscious awareness, we become willingly one with the pure etheric being and becoming of the scent. Obviously, as human beings in our age, there is something unsettling in the idea that one should become another being in order to know it. Modern people want to know everything from a safe external observatory and remain onlookers without essentially changing themselves. This is understandable of course, as we still live in an age in which the impulse of individuation in the physical body is strong, even though this is caused by the inertia of past ages that now can be and must be reversed. Indeed, the timely impulse to create sound ways to transform human consciousness has already begun in the last century and a self-conscious method to open the gates to the etheric and the spiritual cosmos in a new way, exists through spiritual science. As modern people we all experience, in various degrees of intensity, these two opposite drives, and the cognitive yoga practice described here aims to harmonize them in a timely manner, that is, to demonstrate the first, elementary etheric step, as part of the development of a modern spiritual science. In this first step it is therefore absolutely essential that we retain our fullest freedom and human dignity, and live, breathe, and cognize precisely while our whole being is truly metamorphosed into another being. The freedom of following a kind invitation to become another being means *giving up* oneself, not putting oneself down. It is not experienced as annulling one's freedom, but, on the contrary, as an infinite elevation and spiritualization of freedom through the truest devotion and love to the other being that one is invited to become. This experience of metamorphosis, of coming to be hosted by the true being of the other, through love fired by the highest freedom, is going to be the most beautiful experience of a humanity progressing in the right way. Therefore, in the future the following must be increasingly understood: that *any* true knowledge demands becoming one with its subject 'matter', which is not matter at all but real spiritual being, because everything, including what we term inanimate or material, is in reality spiritual being and beings. So, if we want to know the essential innermost nature of any other being, we must become this being and this means that we must be gracefully invited and allowed to do so. We can do whatever it takes to prepare ourselves, but then we must await an invitation and benevolently be given the gift of hospitality by the hosting being's wholly objective stream of world becoming. Only in this manner can we venture to accomplish a conscious spiritual scientific research of the real etheric becoming processes of the world from the point of view of the etheric world itself.

Empirically speaking, it is only at this stage that we can fully corroborate the fact that this intensive, unified rose-world-human stream of becoming that we have changed into, has its origin in the third olfactory stream described above, which was separated from the two other streams of the physical air and the pure scented quality. True, we had already experienced it at the beginning of our work, after the trifurcation of smell was accomplished, but this experience was, to begin with, more external, for we couldn't yet enter into its inner being and becoming. We realized that it is liberating itself and streaming all the time from the trifurcation point, where the physical air, the pure qualitative scent and the pure intensity separate from each other. But now this trifurcation point (which physically speaking, is located in the neighbourhood of the olfactory nerves between the eyes) because we have become this point of emergence ourselves and experience that we ourselves are constantly divided into the three streams with each inhalation and smelling. The extracted third intensive force has nothing more in common with our mental pictures or inner soul experiences of a 'rose flower' or 'rose scent'. But it has all the more to do with subtle formative forces that build the world and the body, which a wholly different being, call it a 'cosmic rose', inspires. (However, this expression is misleading because it uses the representation of the real physical rose, and therefore the reader is advised to bear in mind that during the actual spiritual research on this level, I avoid all representations, comparisons and metaphors linked in whatever way to experiences connected with the physical rose.)

As was demonstrated above in Chapter 4 through the etherization process of sight, this is the exact point in which the subjective is fully transformed into the objective in the course of cognitive yoga research. We are no longer breathing from within outward and back as in ordinary thinking and perceiving, because we are not centred in our body. We are breathed out from the body and into the other being and then we flow from outside into our body and experience what the real forces of the world, working through what used to be the rose scent, experience when they work inside the body, shaping and moulding, nourishing and sustaining it. As the ordinary olfactory representation of the rose scent was purified and its pure quality was extracted from the air, and as the pure scent quality was further purified into pure intensive force, now the intensity is revealed as objective etheric world force that carries us with its flows and streams of becoming. We discover that the stream of pure intensive becoming that took us over to itself is woven out of the world's forces that constitute a subtle or etheric 'spirit' of the rose scent. (Another way to represent this would be to call the air of this specific stream of becoming its 'body', the pure quality its 'soul', and the pure intensity its 'spirit', but such abstract definitions would only mask the reality of the becoming process we describe here.) Furthermore, the subtle and intense power of the world-etheric being flowing through the rose scent isn't similar at all to the representations we make of its sense perceptible as well as its pure qualitative correlates. As was the case with the intensive world forces extracted from the colour red above, this stream of forces of becoming is also an objective etheric world stream that flows into the human physical and subtle bodies from the whole cosmic periphery. And when we flow with this stream from outside into the body, we experience the fact that it has the potential to penetrate much deeper to the lower processes and organs of the body that resisted and pushed away the etheric forces extracted from sight and the other higher senses.

3rd Step: Merging the two etheric streams

What the purified etheric extract of smell offers us, as an objective world and body formative force, is the first clue that we can create the password needed in order to cross the threshold that guards and seals the core of the metabolic-emotive-cognitive-mechanism (MECM). Its penetrative bodily power is considerably stronger than the etheric forces extracted from the world forces that stream into the body from the colours, light, sounds and warmth of the external etheric world. These more powerful forces extracted from smell (to which the forces extracted from the sense of taste and touch are added) establish, to begin with, a certain resonance with the lower subtle forces of the body that lie below the threshold of the diaphragm. This resonance helps us locate and decipher a cognitive path that would lead us safely through the thickets of the MECM into the lower bodily regions, whose unconscious autonomic functions inhibit and repel the cognitive pathways opened by the intensities and forces extracted from the higher senses. The world forces that work through etherized smells into the body come from more compelling and potent cosmic sources and directions, and they have the capacity to negotiate and create subtle links with bodily processes below the diaphragm. We experience now that if we can raise them to a sufficiently vigorous and clear etheric cognition, they can unlock this door and open a narrow path that descends into the deepest subtle bodily processes and functions, which are guarded and well hidden.

Therefore, at this stage of the cognitive yoga practice, we must marshal all the forces we have generated so far, from both etheric streams of perception, seeing and smell, and bring them together in order to enhance and intensify our cognition accordingly. Then, with their united strength, focused and concentrated on one point, we will be able to recapitulate the etherization of perception from the beginning, in order to raise it into an even higher level of etheric cognition and consciousness. Such repetition and recapitulation form a vital part of the cognitive yoga practice and research. One must spiral back again and again to the original practices of each process, in order to move on to a higher level. And in our specific research about the transformation of sense perception, 'higher' means actually 'lower', that is, the higher the cognitive forces we develop, the deeper we can descend into the recesses of the body. By penetrating more deeply into the body with ever greater cognitive capacities, we can sense that we are on the verge of breaking through the strong lower bodily blockades. In our case here, it is the fully conscious crossing of the threshold of the diaphragm that requires repeated and prolonged cognitive efforts that, in reality, take decades of energetic work.

In this united etheric stream, by a mutual exchange and an enhancement of their different formative forces, we weave and interlace a new thread out of the etheric forces that flow into the body through sight and smell from the external etheric world.

Let it be borne in mind that in the present spiritual-scientific lab.

report we are limiting ourselves to describing only two examples of the senses that represent the higher and lower poles among the six senses that make up the group of the middle senses among the 12 senses (sight, hearing, warmth, smell, taste and touch). The middle senses are located between the three higher senses that perceive the 'I', thinking, and speech of another person, and the three lower senses that perceive the life, movement, and balance of our own body. However, in the real and complete cognitive yoga practice at this stage, the third etheric thread that we are unifying is made from the mutual enhancement of the six middle senses as a whole.

Now if we want to achieve the greater potency with this united stream there are two conditions that must be fulfilled. First, we have to start all over again by going back to the brain itself, since it has locations and processes in it that could not be spiritualized by means of the etherization of sight alone (and in fact we bypassed them in our report on the etherization of sight in Chapter 4 above). This means, in other words, that the lower bodily barrier, or dia-phragmatic threshold, sends its inhibitive branches from below and builds its centres also in the brain, and it must be experienced and confronted first of all in there before we will be able to confront its strongest core in the depth of the body. We cannot consciously penetrate into the protected regions and organs of the inner and lower body before we etherize its corresponding extensions and centres in the brain. Therefore, we must first unlock the tightly closed and guarded gates of this threshold in the brain. And second, to fulfil the task ahead, we must gather all the forces that we can from the etheric processes accomplished thus far. We need to gather them in a more external-etheric manner from the dynamic processes of the etheric body as a whole, in so far as we can gather them at the present stage. This will allow us to activate and actualize the united stream of cognitive etheric forces acquired thus far, gather their subtle radiations and potencies from the whole body, in order to focus them in the brain. (Such an 'excursion' may appear to be an arbitrary interjection in the orderly and step by step description of the present cognitive yoga research, but in reality everything com-municated here is loyal to the actual research processes and stages. Such 'excursions' belong to the healthy and invigorating rhythm of empirical spiritual-scientific research, because we create phases of rhythmic expansions and concentrations in order to maximize the strength and quality of the forces needed in each concrete next task in the main line of research.)

4th step: Gathering the needed etheric forces

The following short 'excursive' observation will be limited to a general outline of an infinitely complex and intricate multiplicity of active and creative subtle etheric bodily forces. Our observation finds a clear path in this maze when it follows in the footsteps of the new united stream, composed from the world's creative forces flowing together through the higher and lower middle senses. This stream is experienced in various parts and organs of the body in highly differentiated ways. When it streams in and out of the organs, it stimulates them to become inwardly etherically active; they begin to resonate and radiate, and discharge their subtle activities and streams in a more visible manner. (These concrete research details can be of use in spiritual-scientific medical and curative research and practice. Here I will limit myself only to few research results chosen because they demonstrate aspects of the present cognitive yoga practice.)

Again, let us return to our starting point. We begin at the tri-furcation point above the nasal cavity, but now we have at our disposal the united, twofold stream, composed of the two categories of extracts from the senses. This stream is therefore very potent and intense. Now we are one with the united stream itself.*

---

*In reality, as was mentioned above, we must remember that at this stage we actually have at our disposal the etherized forces of all the six senses working together: etherized forces from hearing are flowing through the largely expanded ears, warmth etheric forces are flowing through the whole circumference of the etheric double of our physical skin, together with the bodily, deeply penetrating etheric- and astral-extractions from the etherized sensations of tastes through the mouth cavity and alimentary canal to the inner metabolic organs; and all of them are enveloped by the etherization streams extracted from the various individual experiences of touch spread through the whole etheric surface of the skin.

First we experience how it radiates as it were from an inner region behind the space between the eyes, lighting up the forehead and brain, and pours down and fills the whole body, and how it begins to circulate inside it. We experience that it has certain affinities with certain organs of the body, into which it either streams faster and/or upon which it has deeper and more long-lasting impact than others. One main branch streams from the nasal cavity and circulates inside and around the middle part of our body (the chest), and from there it branches as it were into three distinct streams that flow to different regions, and come back again to the region of the heart and lungs, to reunite, and branch out again. One of these streams flows down through to the solar plexus and the diaphragm into the metabolic, reproductive and also limb organs and systems. Another branch flows up from the chest to the head and gathers itself, to begin with, inside the frontal lobe of the brain and concentrates its forces especially between and behind the eyes, innervating the pineal gland, while at the same time flowing and circulating along the lines of the olfactory pathways into the deeper brain centres. There it develops strong resonances with certain parts of the middle brain and when it circulates back from the brain to the body and joins the general stream around the chest, it carries those brain forces along with it to the whole body; and a third branch remains in the middle region, and it specifically bathes and innervates the inner dynamics of the heart's systole and diastole and the lungs' rhythmic inhalation and exhalation. Here it develops certain affinities to the oxygen-rich red blood that flows from the lungs to the head and back to the lower body.

Now one important detail can be mentioned here. The organs stimulated in this way, like the liver or heart, for example, begin to become sensitized. They become increasingly 'sense like', on the one hand, and 'gland like' on the other (of course we are referring to subtle, etheric processes). The heart begins to produce and disseminate a certain bodily awareness, an inner sensitivity, we could have almost said (remembering the limitations and misleading nature of common words when used to describe subtle processes) that the heart is beginning to develop a certain elementary 'bodily cognition' all of its own, which in turn, radiates and branches in two main streams. One stream radiates from the heart's region upward to the head and feeds and enhances the etherization process described above while the other radiates downward and informs the lower metabolic parts of the digestive and reproductive systems. We notice that among other subtle effects, the liver is especially becoming strongly stimulated, answering the heart's streams with its own creative responses. Their mutual resonances and oscillations have important medical and cognitive value. (It is interesting to note that the rose scent in particular has a powerful influence on these mutual etheric interactions between heart and liver.) We shall return again to the whole etheric bodily dynamics after we have gathered the stronger forces needed for the deeper and lower bodily tasks.

5th step: Etheric brainwork

We are now in a position to recapitulate and deepen on a higher level, armed with the stronger etheric forces extracted from smell, the brain processes accomplished above through the etherization of sight. Let us be reminded that in processing the etheric forces of the sense of sight (and the other higher senses) we have first of all separated part of the etheric brain from the physical brain and worked with its intensive world forces. Now that we have at our disposal stronger cognitive-etheric forces of the two sense streams combined, enriched by etheric forces gathered from some of the whole bodily etheric streams, we recapitulate the same process in the brain. But now we are starting directly with the etheric brain itself, applying these stronger forces to it. From a vast multiplicity of active and dynamic etheric forces to which the etheric brain is opened and activated in this way, we will single out again only one thread, because it is directly related to our main task: to open a passageway to the strongly guarded threshold that leads to the lower bodily regions. This way must pass through the corresponding regions and functions of the brain. We must therefore revisit those parts of the etheric brain that we couldn't separate previously from the physical brain. At this point, we can now traverse and unlock the inhibitive MECM functions and centres in the brain with the stronger etheric forces extracted from smell and sight combined together. In this more advanced, subtler, and precise etheric brain operation, we are working with the already separated part of our etheric body attached to the higher regions in the pre-frontal cortex. Now we are uniting them with the etheric forces extracted from smell, taste, and touch. Because of this, we can let the intensive, etherically speaking more robust forces of smell energize the higher forces of sight, and also let the higher forces serve as the 'eyes' and guide the whole operation deeper into the middle and back parts of the brain. Next, the freed etheric forces lead us not to the experience of the hollow, empty physical brain (as did the forces extracted from the higher senses of sight, sound and warmth alone), but to what can be called 'the bodily brain'. This is where the sensations of smell, taste and touch are most immediately active in connecting the metabolic-limb system with the emotive and cognitive systems. These are the denser, middle and posterior regions of the brain that regulate the synthesis and amalgamations of our basic cognitive, emotive, rhythmic and instinctual functions. In what is described below we are reporting what happens to these functions when we apply to them—from above as it were, working from the freed etheric body of the higher brain functions down to the physical, bodily brain functions—the full power of the intensified inhaled sense streams as a synergetic unity. This will obviously be a very specific etheric brain operation, selected for the sake of scientific experimentation and clear demonstration, but in reality this united stream works together with all the other subtle fibres and threads woven in an etheric bundle that is infinitely differentiated and complex.

To begin with, we focus our full attention again to the region behind the eyes and the olfactory process. We find out that the force we extracted from the etheric dynamic of the whole etheric body indicated above, can be directed in such a way to stream up from the whole body and collect and concentrate itself in this location. When it is gathered there, it shows distinct affiliations to cognitive etheric processes connected with the etherized blood radiations that we worked with in connection with the etheric inhalation of light and colours. What was lightening up in the empty physical brain, by means of the etherization of the blood, as 'world self-consciousness' (see Chapter 4 above) used that part of the etheric brain separated from the higher brain to become conscious of itself, while, at the same time, gifting us with the cognitive power to gain and sustain etheric world-consciousness. But armed with the newly etherized sense of smell combined with etherized sight we are led not to the higher brain, but on the contrary, we are lead to the locations in which the etheric brain is powerfully united with the physical brain. This unification is the foundation of the whole MECM in the brain. What becomes markedly conscious here is precisely how the cosmos creates an inhibitive body of individuation to serve our evolutionary needs to become separate and free egos. The discovery made at this stage is that there are forces active in the etheric and astral worlds which interact with the human brain and body in such a way to create the MECM all the way from the brain down through the pathways of the autonomic (sympathetic and parasympathetic) nervous system to the solar plexus and the ganglia of the lower, metabolic-reproductive regions of the body. This bodily, etheric and astral system suppresses and removes from our consciousness the influences and beings acting through the infinitely intensive and rich planetary and cosmic etheric and astral worlds. It works by inhibition and blockade. In this way the individuation and separation of a self-conscious ego is protected from the whole living cosmos and made possible. The cognitive yoga research reveals to what extent the sense of smell and the related senses are part of a whole planetary-cosmic complex of forces that bring about, in the course of human evolution, the inhibition of the real spiritual forces of the external astral and etheric worlds. This inhibition, in the last resort, is caused by the luciferic-ahrimanic forces active in the entire human constitution. This process, centralized in the MECM in the brain, is most intimately linked to the senses of smell, taste and touch. However, after its etherization, it causes the very opposite effect: it gives a powerful impulse to the separation process of the middle and lower etheric brain from the physical brain. This happens especially in some of the most emotive-libidinal-erotogenic and therefore densely autonomic, instinctive (and powerfully inhibited) psychosomatic centres and functions.

Now we enter these locations from the other, free cosmic side. We have become inwardly one with this etheric stream, and by consciously flowing with it to the core centres of inhibition, individuation and separation, we experience that the same forces, now purified, reverse the inhibitive functions to their exact opposites. In other words, the liberation of the inhaled stream of sense perception from our personal attachments and its purification from all subjective human needs and desires, make it into the best tool to accomplish the reversing process of bodily-soul individuation. It becomes such a powerful liberating power, precisely because of its strong affinity with the instinctual bodily activity of the MECM in the first place. Here it provides the best key to deconstruct it and open its gates to allow the full 'unzipping' and separation of the etheric body from the physical body, all the way from the head to the feet. This separation process of the etheric body from the physical body starts in the higher brain, moves to its centre, and culminates in the lower brain functions and spinal cord, and then proceeds through the larynx to the heart, to flow into the depth of the lower body in order to eventually reverse and turn the whole tightly inhibited and closed, body-world connection inside out.

This can be more completely understood if we remember the result of the previously described process of sense perception's purification, intensification and inhalation. We have condensed an intensive force extracted from the purified rose scent and have let it impact our body directly, without intervening mental processes. Then we returned to the brain with intensified forces stimulated and harvested from the processes, organs and functions in our whole subtle body. From these various intensive bodily reactions and radiations, the stream of smell selects, gathers and condenses an intensive cognitive potency. Uniting with the etheric streams flowing through eyes, ears and the whole etheric warmth inhalations and regulations through the etheric skin, it gathers them together, concentrates their potencies, focuses their most intensive, synergistically working forces behind the eyes and directs it to stream deeper into and through the brain. We become aware that it creates its main stronghold in the two-petalled lotus flower, or chakra, behind our eyes, as a centre of intensification and radiation, through which the whole world-body's sensory-etheric stream becomes especially productive and cognitive. This happens in and around the region in which, physically speaking, the pineal gland is located. (This gland appears to be a kind of a tiny localized physical condensation, crystallization and expression of this intensive productive world-human etheric stream, and not its cause.) From the pineal region, these etheric radiations and streams split into many threads, the central ones of which irradiate and innervate the whole inner and posterior brain, sending rays that link with and intensely inform the currents playing around the pituitary gland (hypophysis), the amygdala and hypothalamus regions, and through them flow to the mid-brain and brainstem.

Expressing ourselves through the common anatomical terminology (we shall describe presently the same process from an etheric point of view), this united etherized sensory world stream, has mutual affinities with the radiations of the regions associated with the subtle activities of the hippocampus and amygdala. These activities are responsible, through their diverse connections and affiliations with the hypothalamus, for the activation of the autonomic nervous system, which in turn, is responsible for the suppression and inhibition of the always present connections of the body with its planetary and cosmic environments. This amygdalahypothalamus synthesis is the major centre of bodily individuation, responsible for the fundamental, existential or ontological inhibition and hence for the separation of our being from the whole living universe. This separation already begins in our early infancy, and reaches a certain bodily culmination with sexual maturity. In this brain region the suppressive influence of the MECM is strong and its etherization and reversal process that causes a separation of the etheric body from the physical body is therefore more difficult. This separation is therefore also the key and pass to the lower regions of the body, giving us the cognitive forces needed in order to cross the solar plexus and diaphragmatic threshold.

In the more advanced stages of the work, this stream will prove to be especially fruitful, when it offers an essential contribution to building the etheric tool used in the substantiation of a new etheric body and an independent etheric individuality in the real etheric world outside the physical body.

Let us now describe the whole etherization process of the brain in some concrete, more imaginative detail.

6th step: Imagination of the etheric brainwork

If we want to give an exact imaginative description of the brain process as a whole, we must ask the reader to cooperate with us as we go along. This description requires, like the other concrete etheric research details, an intensified inner cognitive activity and participation from the reader as well. As described above, this work starts in the 'trifurcation point' between and behind the eyes. In this place we now gather and concentrate the greatest intensity of extracted world forces and the added etheric forces from the whole body. There it exerts the greatest etheric pressure. It presses inward; it seeks to open a path between the eyes and through the whole brain from the anterior to the posterior lobe.

We experience now on a higher, etheric level, what we experienced above through the hollowing out of the physical brain, when we first separated the brain's physical and etheric bodies in the higher, frontal, functional regions of the brain. But now the whole process starts in the purely etheric brain and proceeds from there. The etherized, inhaled, sensory world forces radiating and streaming from the front to the back of the etheric brain, actually hollows out a tunnel-like formation through the whole middle etheric brain. And the more the etheric tunnel deepens and elongates, it is also enlarged, until we experience that not only the etheric brain but that the etheric head as a whole is opening up. There's no other way to describe it, than saying that we feel as if our etheric skull cracks open, the brain's etheric equivalents of the hemispheres are disconnected, separated from each other, turn inside out, and are etherically flattened, spread out and expand like the petals of a flower, or two wings of etheric flight. An *Umstülpung* inside out and outside in, that is, a full inversion of the etheric brain and the etheric head takes place the deeper and longer the etheric 'tunneling' proceeds. At the same time, while this opening process is taking place, the tunnel (which is already an open tunnel, unfolding and expanding upward while it bores deeper in) has reached the base of the etheric brain, the etheric cerebellum and etheric brainstem, and it pours its intensive forces directly into the etheric spinal column. That is, while the tunnel expands and eventually cracks the etheric brain open, the stream of world formative forces from the centre between the eyes continues to bore its way inwardly, rippling, expanding-contracting, pulsating, through wave-like etheric cascades, pouring itself and descending downward along the etheric spinal cord and reaching its lowest etheric base. Reaching the etheric base, in provokes a release of potential life forces yoked and suppressed there, as if coiled in and upon itself in an etheric, intensive shell, seed or cocoon. Now it is liberated and shoots back, very much like the fastest lightning movement of a snake uncoiling its tightly held looped rings as it strikes; and it fires up backwards through the etheric spinal cord into the etheric brainstem, flowing through the opening middle etheric brain all the way to the etheric starting point between the etheric eyes, through which it continues to flow and illuminate the surrounding external etheric world, until it loses itself in far etheric expanses. This process actualizes and consolidates a repeated, rhythmic, spiralling current, reciprocally streaming between the external etheric world, etheric brain and spinal cord, and the lower etheric body and back to the etheric world. It flows with immense speeds like an electric current in a circuit that energizes itself from the etheric world through the etherized sense perceptions of the higher and lower senses, to the etheric brain and etheric spinal cord and back again, increasingly flowing in both directions simultaneously. We feel as if not only our head and brain, but our whole back is opened up from behind to etherically perceive and cognize the surrounding cosmic etheric worlds.

When this etheric current flows to and fro through the point of outmost intensity between the eyes, it activates a clear multi-levelled kaleidoscopic imaginative vision, enlarging it gradually as the circulating current is intensified. The same process is often referred to in various esoteric traditions as the opening of the 'third eye' (in spiritual science the chakra between the eyes is referred to as the two-petalled lotus flower). However, the representation of an eye, taken from the physical body, really misrepresents the functions of this wonderful astral organ and its etheric counterpart. Therefore, an exact scientific distinction must be made between the two. It must be emphasized that true imaginative 'seeing' is different from physical seeing in all respects. For example, unlike our physical eyes that can only observe in one direction from within outward and have only a limited forward view of the world, the 'third eye' has a simultaneous panoramic etheric vision, and it can view the whole etheric brain process, as well as its connections to the surrounding etheric environment and cosmos, from all directions at once.

Furthermore, all other functions of the physical eye that enable ordinary sight but remain mostly instinctive and unconscious are fully conscious in etheric seeing. This applies above all to the motor aspects in the eye's muscle movements and focusing processes. In physical seeing they are partly unconscious, reflexive and automatic. Indeed, our voluntary eye movements, which we *can* consciously regulate, function unconsciously most of the time. In etheric-imaginative perception, all movements must be consciously activated and regulated and the navigation in the etheric space is wholly dependent on conscious human-world operations, which cannot be described in detail here.

There is another major difference between physical and imaginative seeing. The physical eye grasps what exists as light, colours and shapes in the real world, and because the contents are already given in the external physical world, it grasps them as such in a passive way ('passive' refers here only to the *content*s of ordinary perception, and not to the activity of perception itself). The reverse holds true in imaginative seeing. Imaginative seeing is a productive, creative operation. The third eye must first actively produce the substances and formative forces it needs for its vision out of the real world-human, human-world process described above. Then it must actively draw and paint what it will 'see' in the universe and the human body through multiple real movements, radiations and extensions. It can only perceive if it first creates the drawings and mouldings of what it is going to see, by means of an actual etheric-imaginative painting; however, its 'paints' are taken not from any subjective psychic source, but rather from the consciously etherized and cognitively transformed perceptions of the etheric world and etheric human body. For this reason, its extraordinarily rich and manifold artistic creations and productions are, strictly speaking, objective. It imaginatively paints, sculpts and cognizes the world that it sees, using the actively purified and etherized colours, lights, sounds and warmth forces, energized by the extracted and intensified etheric forces of smell, taste and touch. These provide the etheric sweetness and aroma that it has extracted from the real etheric world through the cognitive yoga process of inhalation described above.

The opening and activation of the third eye, or two-petalled lotus flower, is part of the transformation process of the etheric brain as a whole. When it is used to co-produce and study the process that shaped and activated it, it paints and perceives a remarkable picture of the transformation process of the etheric brain. This picture must be understood as an objective etheric or imaginative, perception; it is actively produced as an etheric, living, extract of the whole process and illuminated by exact imaginative cognition. First, it portrays the result of the release of the etheric forces from the strongest attachments to the MECM centres in the physical brain, second, its opening up to the whole etheric cosmos, and third, the merging and integration of the etheric forces of the individual etheric body with the forces of the etheric world.

This is one real Imagination of the flowering process of the brain: it becomes an unfolding chalice of radiating inner light, opening, awakening, and growing towards and together with the light of the cosmos as a flower unfolds its enclosed petals towards the light of the sun. Its wonderfully flashing and shining radiations reach to the farthest cosmic spaces above, merging with spiritual radiations emanating from the sun, moon, planets and stars, and communicate far and wide with the etheric formative forces of all natural and earthly beings. It is a magnificently dynamic, ever awake and active organ of light, like a flowering, adorned crown, with the third eye as its stirring wheel, by means of which the united human-world's living forces are regulating, harmonizing, and directing the circulating ebbs, flows and currents of etheric perception and cognition. This flower that is formed and matured through the cognitive yoga practice becomes the main organ of etheric world-human, human-world cognition and consciousness. The etherized and released etheric brain becomes a rhythmic, breathing, organ, a flowering chalice that produces, gathers, and cognizes detailed supersensible knowledge, grasped through clear imaginative perception and consciousness. The etheric brain becomes a cognitive, breathing, rhythmic organ and function that monitors and co-produces the living reciprocal breathing and exchange of etheric becoming between the human and the cosmos.

It is the first independently built supersensible, etheric organ, used by spiritual science, as an individual achievement of modern spiritual scientific research.

In the above described process, we have in fact also transformed our etheric brain into a livingly cognitive, conscious, breathing rhythmic system. It has become not only a new etheric brain and etheric sense and nerve system, but at the same time a dynamic rhythmic system of etheric cognitive breathing open to and synchronized with the world. From the external etheric world, it takes in living formative forces through the etherized senses, inhaling them directly into the etheric brain and body, and exhales the etherized forces of the body in turn out to the external etheric world. The etheric brain becomes a centre of rhythmic etheric breathing, and can henceforth be used to regulate and cognize the processes by means of which our etheric senses breathe in and out with the etheric world. Thus the inhaled world forces and the exhaled body forces meet, interact, and mutually exchange their potencies and influences. We learn in this way to observe and study the exact interrelationships between the macrocosmic and microcosmos etheric streams: how the macrocosmic stream forms and nourishes the human body and how the microcosmic human body answers this stream etherically. Since this is an etherized cognitive breathing process, everything takes place in full imaginative consciousness. Through the etheric rhythmization of the brain, the two streams of becoming unite synergistically: the becoming self-conscious of the etheric world and the becoming world-conscious of the human being merge and reciprocally, mutually, interlace and produce one world-human creative and breathing cognitive stream. Through the etheric brain, which is etherically cognizing and breathing, this united world-human stream becomes, in its fullness, illuminated and self-conscious, bringing to full consciousness the great future event through which, in the next centuries and millennia an increasingly spiritualized humanity and earth will merge with the spiritual worlds and the spiritual worlds become increasingly human. Also the meaning and significance of the coming spiritual event of the twenty-first century, which I have described in my recent lectures, begins to be visible in its first spiritual outlines.*

The same purification, etherization, and extraction process is accomplished with each sense perception, quality and intensity, and is varied, adapted and applied to specific subtle bodily parts, organs, processes and functions. Then the whole united and complex world-human etheric web circulates and streams from the etheric brain to the etheric world and back, and increasingly also through the etheric body as a whole. And this circulation naturally expands, via the larynx, to liberate and activate the etheric forces in and around the physical heart and lungs, while it seeks to unite with the purest potential etheric forces sensed and felt below the strongly guarded threshold of the lower body.

7th step: Etheric heart work

As described above, it is first through the liberation of the etheric brain from the physical brain that world consciousness and human self-consciousness light up in an intensive etheric essence exchange. The two-petalled lotus flower with its etheric extensions becomes the centre of the new etheric human-world brain, through which the united human-world 'I' lights up in the most lucid world-self-consciousness. Through this etheric essence exchange, the world

*See my book, *Spiritual Science in the 21st Century*, 2013.

becomes self-conscious through the human and the human becomes world conscious through the world. The repeated rhythmization of this essence exchange makes the etheric brain into an organ of etheric rhythmic cognitive breathing: the knowledge-creating organ of the new yoga. When this organ matures and becomes fully operative, with the third eye as its cognitive centre, it interacts and converses with the radiations streaming upward from the whole body on the one hand, and with the etheric world on the other. It answers the bodily radiations by connecting them with the macrocosmic etheric stream and lets the macrocosmic stream descend deeper towards them, and in this descent, it meets them halfway and focuses its activity in the etheric heart region. There, in and around the physical heart and lungs and the chest as a whole, a new rhythmic function is established in the etheric body. This organ connects and regulates the inhalation and exhalation of the world-human life streams through it rhythmical movements, streams, and radiations. It becomes a conscious rhythmic system of forces, responsible for the vibrantly living and mutually enhancing breathing relationships between the etheric world and the human etheric body. (This occurs via the astral centre and etheric forces of the larynx, which have an important formative function, that help consolidate and form the etheric currents that flow from the head to the heart and back, about which more will be reported later.)

The more the rhythmic etheric cognitive activity is expanded and transferred from the head to the heart, the more we can use the heart as an organ of imaginative cognition as well. Then in certain graceful moments we can actually experience, through the etheric heart, how the etheric world's pulse and breathing becomes human. This is one of the most beautiful and rewarding experiences in modern spiritual research. In one and the same moment of life, we experience how the human breathing, pulsing and circulating rhythmic system (that includes all the rhythmic processes and functions of the whole body), synchronizes in real time with the etheric world's heart pulse and breathing. (We can only experience it consciously for single moments; otherwise we would be totally overwhelmed, set ablaze and consumed by these divine fires. But physical minutes are eternities for real etheric experience and cognition.) We can also say: the etheric world of living and formative cosmic forces in-breathes us and takes us out and over into itself, while it out-breathes its etheric heart pulse and breathing rhythm and embodies them in our subtle bodies. In our own subtle bodies, we experience how the etheric world expresses its heart pulse and breathing rhythm when it builds, shapes and organizes the human body from conception, pregnancy and birth (and especially in the 2nd seven-year period, between the ages of 7 and 14), from the whole living, ensouled and spiritual cosmic circumference. And becoming part of the etheric world's heart pulse and breathing rhythm, outside the physical body, we experience how the human heartbeat and human breathing, to the extent that it has been liberated from the luciferic-ahrimanic influences, synchronizes and harmonizes with the etheric heartbeat and breathing of the cosmos, and we feel that we are drawing closer to the spiritual heart source (the etheric Christ) of universal life. When we look back at our body from outside, we realize that this body — in its true, always pulsating, vibrating, breathing, etheric life and form — is an individualized embodiment and formation of the world's etheric heart pulse and breathing. Its forms and functions are embodiments of the all-embracing, pulsing, surging and weaving cosmic life, that remains unconscious in daily life and cognition, and come to consciousness through cognitive yoga's etherized sense- and thinking breathing. Furthermore, we experience that now, breathing in and out the real living world forces, being breathed ourselves in and out of our body through the world's etheric heart pulse and breathing rhythm, our whole being becomes a singular heart and pulse beat in the circulation and pulsation of the cosmic heart, and we begin to individuate it closer to their source. And while an actual merging with the cosmic source of life must remain at this stage a future goal, a devoted feeling of loving trust imbues us, carried by the pulsating forces of the life source itself, that such merging is essentially attainable by the human being in our time.

At the same time, when we experience this nearness to the cosmic source, we also feel the awakening of the same forces of life, healing and resurrection in the depth of our own body. We feel that, working from the centre of our etheric being, and intensifying the mutual breathing with the etheric world, will make it possible to merge the cosmic Christ forces from the whole cosmic circumference with the pristine forces of life and resurrection active in the deeper unconscious regions of our soul and body. Now, since the etheric body is liberated and integrated with the etheric world from the head to the heart, it gives us the needed etheric forces to cross this lower bodily threshold in a fully conscious way and fully unite the etheric Christ forces that work in the universe with those in the depth of the human etheric and physical bodies.

7. Birth of a new etheric body

In the solid organism there is produced what we call a seed of life.... This etheric seed which lies in the deepest levels of subconsciousness is ... entirely hidden from ordinary consciousness ... if today we allow ourselves to be inspired by moral ideals, these will carry forth life, tone and light into the universe and will become world-creative ... if there were only a dozen people filled with moral enthusiasm, the earth would still ray out a spiritual, sun-like force!.

(18 December 1920, GA 202)

The fact of supreme importance is that man can now take his treasures with him from the physical plane into the spiritual world.... Before the eyes of the Spirit a world arises in the future, a world which has its roots in the physical as our world once had its roots in the spiritual. Just as men are the sons of the Gods, so out of what men in the physical world experience by rising to an understanding of the Event of Golgotha, the body will be formed for those new Gods of the future, of whom Christ is the Leader.

(22 December, 1908, GA 108)

Just as from the body of Adam the bodies of earth-men are descended, in so far as these men have the body that crumbles away, even so are the spiritual bodies, the Phantoms for all men, descended from that which rose out of the grave ... we must think of the Phantom as multiplying itself, as does the cell which gives rise to the physical body. So, in the evolution which follows the Event of Golgotha, every man can inwardly acquire something which is spiritually descended from the Phantom which rose from the grave ...

(11 October 1911, GA 131)

A further intensification of the cognitive breathing from the head to the heart, empowered by the heart forces of the etheric world as described above, enables us finally to overcome the hardest MECM barriers and cross the threshold of the diaphragm. There, in the metabolic and reproductive processes and organs we consolidate the third functional centre of cognitive breathing.

Through the etheric work accomplished in the etheric head and heart, and the mutual essence exchange with the corresponding forces of the etheric world, a conscious and expanding rhythmic system was created. This functional and free cognitive and creative system is the result of the merging between the macrocosmic and microcosmic life streams. It is a united world-human etheric stream of becoming, enhanced by means of repeated cognitive etheric inhalations and exhalations. It was established first in the etheric head and brain. This is a necessary starting point, that guarantees that all further, advanced etheric work, will be actualized in the most concise and lucid state of cognition, which greatly enhances the best modern clarity experienced in ordinary pure thinking and sense perception. There, through the head, it first became an individualized organ of etheric world-human breathing self-consciousness, a conscious organ of clear imaginative cognition. Then it was shaped through the larynx and poured into the heart and lungs and all other rhythmic processes. It became an independent etheric rhythmic system of pure formative forces that lifts to consciousness what always transpires unconsciously in the organic bodily rhythmic system that regulates all the physical rhythmical and circadian processes. Using the etherized forces of the rhythmic systems of the heart and lungs, separated from its bodily-organic foundations, the cognitive yoga practice became a movable and flexible 'middle' organ or system of etheric rhythmic forces that can be moved freely through all parts of the etheric body. We can volitionally and consciously transfer, relocate and operate its functions in any part of the body in which we wish to regulate, harmonize and perceive the interactive etheric respiration and inspiration between the world and human forces. We learn to breathe with the whole etheric body, which, as a whole is a cosmic-human living rhythmic system. And we learn to cognitively actualize the mutual exchange of the instreaming etheric world forces and the inner etheric-bodily forces. We can regulate, navigate, and cognize how they interact with each other in any specific organ or function inside and outside the etheric and physical bodies. And when we concentrate this etheric cognitive activity in the lower body, we experience new aspects of the etheric mutual exchanges between the world and the human body.

Crossing the lower threshold

When the above described work on the etheric brain and etheric heart has progressed thus far, we experience that we are getting help from an unexpected direction. The source of this help lies in the streaming together of the whole cognitive yoga work presented above. This work has three main components. First, the purification and etherization of the higher middle senses of sight, hearing, and warmth. Second, the purification and etherisation of the senses of smell, taste and touch. It must be remembered that these are objective world streams, pouring into the body from the whole formative forces of the etheric cosmos. At the same time, on another level, thinking was gradually etherized as well, which had a powerful influence on the whole etherization processes of the hardening, death-bringing forces in the body. Then we united the two streams of the etheric forces of the six senses. This synergetic unity produced forces to transform the etheric body, first of the whole brain and then from the head to the heart. While this work with the inhalation of the etherized sense forces was going on, the etherization of thinking was overcoming the forces of death in the body and activating the forces of the bodily senses of balance, life and movement (as described in Chapter 5 above). Apart from the three higher senses, that grasp the 'I', thoughts and words of the other person (which are transformed in the social department of cognitive yoga), an etherization of all nine senses began to work in unison (though to begin with, this took place unconsciously, as we eventually discover) while the above described conscious transformations were accomplished. Now, through the transfer of the cognitive-rhythmic centre from the head to the heart, it is emerging into full etheric cognition. When the etheric body that controls the inhibition and individuating centres in the brain has been liberated from the physical brain, the pristine and pure lower bodily forces begin to resonate and vibrate in harmony with them, but this was still taking place from afar, unconsciously. But now they respond actively to the inhaled etheric world forces that flow through the purified senses and through the etherized brain and heart, and begin to 'converse' with them. Furthermore, the subtle, physical and etheric organs and processes of the lower body are as if awakened from a sleep of long ages and are stimulated to become productive. This productivity 'answers' in the affirmative in such a manner that the instreaming world forces can now begin to flow uninhibited, down into the lower body. A mutual interaction ensues, in which each stream stimulates the other and reciprocally enhances the etheric and physical productivity of the other. The bodily forces interact with the world forces by producing their own subtle forces, streams and radiations and this, in turn, allows the world forces to flow into the lower body ever more freely. This 'conversation' however, must mature in order to become a full 'agreement' between them, and this alone can create the functional 'bridge' across the lower threshold. This results from the further intensification of the inner, moral activity and substance of the continuous cognitive yoga practice. It brings about the bridge-building process that finally allows us to cross over the solar plexus threshold. It also has a moral-spiritual aspect that must be mentioned at this stage.

If we put it in more pictorial language, we can say that the guardian of the lower world (the ever-awake dragon the keeps vigil over the dormant eternal, youthful fountain of life) demands a key or password from the whole upper etherization process streaming down from the head and heart. It demands this key to safeguard us and the treasure alike from a premature crossing of the threshold and a misuse of the most precious forces of humanity and the cosmos. Not only are the highest and purest forces protected from our misuse there, but we are also protected from our wildest desires and evil inclinations that lurk in the same depths and from which our daily consciousness is protected. When the dragon is pacified it can for the first time go to sleep, having fulfilled its mission, while the sleeping beauty (the virgin, paradisal, life forces) and the fountain of eternal youth (the forces of resurrection), can wake up to new and conscious etheric life.

The result is a harmonized, regulated 'mutual agreement' between the real etheric world forces flowing into the body through the etherization of the sense-breathing and inhalation, and the pure forces of the lower bodies. This agreement works through and beyond the bodily threshold of egotistic individuation. Once this mutual exchange of etheric forces and mutual etheric conversation is established, the previously purified and extracted world forces flowing through the higher middle senses of sight, hearing and warmth and the lower middle senses of smell, touch and taste, find their counterparts in the pristine bodily organs and processes. The merging together of all the forces extracted from the purification of the higher and lower sense perceptions, with the etheric support of the etherized thinking, now resonate with these pristine bodily forces, increasing the world-human power to achieve maximal bodily impact. Due to the moral purification we have undergone, the danger of their egotistic misuses has been sufficiently overcome. Thus this 'mutual agreement' means that the inhibiting barrier can be lifted, the luciferic-ahrimanic MECM can become transparent, and the pure forces coming up from the lower body can meet and merge with their cosmic equivalent from the world, through the transformed senses, brain and heart.

Let us be reminded that from the very beginning, it was the soul and spirit forces working in the heart that brought about the etherization of the blood motivating the whole spiritual scientific work. These forces of love and devotion to truth constantly fire and nourish the etherization processes in the head, of perception and thinking alike. When the etherization process of the brain descended into the heart region, as discussed above, it meant also that the forces of etherized blood, that were, to begin with, used for the etherization of perception and thinking in the head, can be used now in their fullness to etherize the lower body as well. This gives the liberated, etheric, rhythmic system the added forces necessary to cross the threshold and build a conscious, cognitive, 'etheric bridge' over its abyss. The lower body receives the united function of the etherized head and heart operating together as one functional etheric system. In this system, which is really the liberated etheric body itself as a whole, both become one: etheric cognition, created first in the etherized brain, and the etheric rhythmic system, the beginning of which was also created in the rhythmic etheric cognition in the etheric brain and further developed in the heart. Now the lower body has added the third functional system to the forces of head and heart that are already united. It adds the productive-creative potentials of purest etheric and physical forces, that is, of pristine life and resurrection, the source of higher production of life and substance. And these forces, awakened, stimulated, are nourished by the purest extracts from the etherized forces of sense perception and thinking, which means the finest brain extracts and substances, warmed us and enlivened in the etheric heart process. It takes in the cognitive head forces and the rhythmic heart forces and gives back to them its creative and productive forces. The etheric body becomes a whole first in the lower body when the third, metabolic etheric function is added to the other two. It is becoming a combined 'productive-rhythmic-cognitive etheric system'. It functions as an active and creative cognitively breathing and pulsating function that operates inside the lower body in unison with the etheric chest and head processes, united with the macrocosmic etheric forces.

Now the creative becoming processes of the etheric world, flowing into the body and inhaled through the etherized streams of the senses, unite with the pure creative forces of the body's own becoming. Both streams, the macrocosmic and microcosmic etheric streams, mutually intensify and enhance each other consciously. In this way a lower bodily correlate is constituted for the mutual becoming of the world and the human through each other in the head and in the heart, described above. And when we study the whole threefold etheric human-world body, we experience the following.

As we saw above, to begin with, in the head region, through the etherization and inhalation of lights, colours, sounds and impressions of warmth, a first individualized mutual exchange of self-consciousness took place between the human and the world. The world became self-conscious through the human and the human became world-conscious through the world. Second, with the help of the forces extracted from the etherization of smell, taste and touch, this functional rhythmic centre was extended downwards and founded in the heart (with the support of the etherization processed along the spine behind and larynx in front). The etheric world heart pulse and rhythmic breathing becomes human, and the human heart pulse and breathing becomes part of the cosmic pulse and breathing. Third, in the lower body, through the further intensification of the merger between all the senses' inhalation and the backup of etherized thinking, the lower body is also stimulated and becomes creative, merging its creativity with the instreaming productive and formative world forces. This merging leads to the production of new etheric and subtle spiritual-physical substances, forces and organs.

In this way cognitive yoga becomes a source of a life-giving breath of becoming. It becomes a movable, dynamic, middle rhythmic system, encompassing the whole body, working in and between the head, heart and abdomen, using the etheric heart as its operative rhythmic function. This function harmonizes and regulates the whole etheric body. In the head it becomes individualized as a cognitive rhythmic, breathing, etheric organ of world-human knowledge. In the heart it becomes an individualized pulsating and breathing organ of cosmic etheric life, monitoring and regulating the breath of becoming between the streams of mutual exchange of world-human, human-world life. In the lower body it becomes an individualized, rhythmic, life and substance giving and creating source, through which etheric world-human, human-world pro-duction of new living forces, substances and matter, is actualized. Through cognitive yoga, a holistic unity of the three etheric func-tions is accomplished: an etheric synergy which is cognitive, rhythmic, and bodily productive is created, through which, in each of the three functions, all are operating. A mutually interconnected and interrelated etheric ninefoldness is created in this manner. In the etheric head, cognition is made rhythmic by the cosmic-human heart and substantiated by the productive lower bodily forces. In the heart, the etheric human-world heart pulse and breathing becomes cognitive and productive, and in the abdomen, bodily-etheric productivity becomes rhythmic and cognitive. This three times three etheric essence exchange, between the human being and the cosmos, becomes cognitively conscious, active, and productive.

Mutual fructification between etheric body and etheric world

Let us focus our attention again on what is taking place in the lower body. We must imagine that now the whole etheric body participates in a threefold mutual essence exchange, conversation and agreement, between the etheric body as a whole and the etheric world as a whole. This threefold essence exchange forms something entirely new with the purest etheric forces awakened in the lower body from a millennia-long slumber. An entirely new element is created thereby, that was not there before, neither in the external etheric world apart from the human physical and etheric bodies, nor in the human bodies apart from the etheric world.

When the cognitive rhythmic breathing process is carried through the threshold of the diaphragm into the lower body, we experience two major events. The first is the establishment of the functional cognitive-rhythmic-productive activity in the lower body mentioned above, which also releases the etheric body as a whole from its last major bondage to the physical body. This adds a third and new experience of the relationships of the etheric body and the etheric world. Second, we discover that the lower body, through its etheric cognitive-breathing interactions with the productive forces of the world, becomes itself productive. A third venue of mutual essence exchange between the etheric world and human body begins, of world-human productivity, which culminates in an 'etheric birth event'. It can also be said, not metaphorically, that through this mutual exchange of productive forces, the etheric world becomes a fertilizing father source and the etheric body becomes a productive mother source, and together they conceive the becoming of a new embryonic etheric body that will become a source of a new emerging etheric world. Let us study these processes in greater detail.

When the rhythmically productive etheric abdomen is firmly established in our etheric body and cognition, we feel the need to learn to breathe anew and more deeply with the etheric world. We let the threefold breathing and pulsating activity of the etheric body as a whole flow from below upward, in reversed direction to the etherization process we accomplished from above downward through the senses. We let it flow from below through the now etherized pathways of the autonomic nerve system (which after being purified functions as the main channel of the cognitive bodily etheric streams), into the heart, larynx, and brain. On this pathway between heart and brain our forces gather themselves in a new way around the larynx. This location was already stimulated during the upper etherization processes described in Chapters 4 and 6 above. But its more concrete buildup remained somewhat veiled in the background. For example, when the etheric brain-spinal cord process was established from the etheric brain down the etheric spine and upward again, we focused our attention on the etherization processes along the spinal cord. At the same time, however, another, but purely etheric frontal 'spinal cord' is finely formed, through the activated astral chakras, as the work progress from head to heart and abdomen. There, between head and heart, we could indeed register that the larynx organ was activated as well and we were conscious that its formative activity informs the etheric streams in their transition from the etheric brain to the etheric heart. But its formative activity comes to full consciousness only after the etheric body in the lower body has been activated and brought to full etheric consciousness as described above. Then, on the way upward, which now takes place along the etheric front of the body and not through the backbone, we build a new etheric 'spinal cord' with its 'etheric nerve system', that is, a firm and consciously built etheric scaffolding for the newly created, future orientated, etheric cognitive frontal function. And through the forces of the lower body, the purest metabolic, productive and reproductive etheric forces, now released from their physical commitments, the etheric body around the larynx centre is formed and activated, and we learn to use it also to 'speak out' our etheric life and breathing into the wide open etheric world. It shapes our reproductive, heart and head radiations with what can be called, 'the creative human-world-word', by means of which our interaction with the etheric world becomes spelled out and articulated, formed, into etheric vowels, consonants, syllables, syntax and vocabulary. (Essentially, everything we accomplish in the etheric world, as will be described in detail below in Chapters 8–10, is actualized through this spiritual speaking and articulation process.)

Now via the larynx we gather the whole etheric body, energized and formed through the whole metabolic-reproductive, heart and larynx assembly of etheric forces, and let it stream in and through the free etheric brain, to achieve a certain needed intensity of outward radiation. Then through the etheric brain and etheric senses (indeed through the whole etheric skin) we let it speak, radiate and flow, as it is articulated and formed, far into the surrounding world, using the two-petalled lotus flower between the eyes as the organ of radiation, perception and navigation. Now this organ is further enhanced because first, it receives, via the larynx, a formative and articulated stream of etheric forces from the etherized metabolic and reproductive processes of the lower body; second, this stream is thoroughly potentized and rhythmicised via the heart centre. These articulated, rhythmic and substantial etheric forces radiate outward through the etheric brain, senses and skin and extend far beyond the limits of the physical body. There, outside, they substantiate, articulate, illuminate and resonate with far and wide planetary and cosmic etheric beings, substances, streams and forces. This etheric activity is made possible because the etheric metabolic-reproductive forces joined the heart and brain via the larynx and its forces are streaming now in synergetic unison through the creative activity that emanates from all the etheric and physical organs and processes *as a whole*. And the etheric world responds and answers these spoken, articulated etheric radiations of the body by enhancing the flow of its world forces into the body.

It is as if, pictorially speaking, the fully mature etheric body, resurrected from its physical sheaths, forms itself into a human-cosmic message, that it sends far and wide into the spiritual worlds. It has something essential to communicate to them about the present and future accomplishments, potentials and duties of humanity in the universe. And what is registered is a distinctively positive, affirmative, cosmic answer, that empowers us to continue in our work, and indicates the next future tasks ahead.

When we experience this enhanced mutual exchange of etheric forces between the whole etheric body and the etheric world, we learn that we must entirely change all our physical concepts about space (and even more of time, but this cannot be described in the limits of the present study).

The etheric human-world body

The above described threefold etheric activity stimulates and awakens the etheric body as a whole and streams with it into the general etheric world. We experience in this way the essential openness between the human etheric body and the cosmic etheric world. While in our physical consciousness we experience our physical body as distinctly separated from the surrounding physical world, the very opposite is the case with the etheric body. On the one side, it is bound to the physical body that it must constantly nourish and shape, and thereby it assumes also a similar structure and boundaries. On the other side, it is open to the whole etheric, astral, and spiritual worlds, from which it constantly receives vital life forces. But it also gives forces back to the universe, and these are the forces that are engraved in it by our soul-spiritual activity during the course of our earthly life. It becomes a fact of direct experience when the etheric body and its interactions with the etheric world are brought to full consciousness as described above. Not only do we realize the deep scientific truth expressed in Valéry's poetic insight that 'the skin is deepest', but we realize that the whole 'inner' bodily space, in which the inner organs, tissues and functional systems are embodied, is in spiritual reality not at all located 'inside' the space enclosed by the skin limits of the physical body. Already the etheric-functional space isn't at all located inside the body but in the external etheric world. Etherically speaking, we must learn to map a radically new etheric spatiality and topographic topology of the relations between 'body', 'organs', and 'world'. In this new topography, the body's inner space is but the world's infolded external space, and conversely, the external world is a body turned inside out and infinitely multiplied. It is therefore really misleading to say that the etheric body and its forces and organs radiate out far and wide because this is still described as a force working from a centre to the periphery, and this way of thinking is still part the ordinary, physical and linear 'Euclidean' mapping.

In the new etheric map of the body/world continuum, first of all, the etheric body and all its forces and organs are parts of infinitely vast, planetary and cosmic, assemblages and networks of functions and interconnections that weave outside the inner physical space of the body. Abstractly expressed, the human body appears as an infolded and contracted infinite external etheric cosmos and the cosmos as an inverted, expanded and infinitely multiplied cosmic human body. In concrete reality, the body's inner organs appear as integrated and functional members of the planetary and cosmic etheric and astral bodies, which in itself is composed of a multitude of etheric bodies, streams, swarms of beings and occurrences. What we discover is that all inner organs and processes are neither 'inside' us nor, for that matter, 'outside' us, but that we are outside ourselves: inverted inside out with everything that is inside our spatially experienced body limits and inner contents. But then trees and animals, mountains and seas, clouds, rain and lightning, sun and moon, are in the etheric world-body continuum, our inner forces and organs, while the etheric and astral counterparts of liver, kidneys, lungs, heart, are cosmic bodies and beings. The inner organs and organic processes are spread out as etheric-astral natural, biological, meteorological, atmospheric, planetary and cosmic streams and functions, and participate in infinite flows of universal becomings. And that place we mark as 'our' body is a unique site of micro-macro planetary and cosmic composition, synthesis and individuation. We realize that what our senses perceive and what our thinking represents as an external world, distinct from our inner world, is not simply an arbitrary mistake or illusion, but a profoundly meaningful and exact *reversal* and inversion of the true state of all etheric, astral, and spiritual affairs. The etheric, astral and spiritual worlds are a differentiated human being multiplied to infinity, the cosmic archetypal Anthropos, Adam Kadmon, while 'our' body is a whole cosmos contracted, microscopically synthesized and individuated together.[*]

---

[*] In this manner the modern cognitive practice leads, through fully conscious spiritual-scientific empirical research, to a rediscovery of the truth of ancient mythic conceptions, such as that the human is a microcosm of the macrocosm. This causes us to greatly admire the grand wisdom of such ancient mythological world conceptions, gained in a more instinctive and dreamlike state of consciousness in comparison with our modern scientific approach.

When we turn our attention from the exhalation and merging of our etheric body with the etheric world and observe the inhalation of the etheric world forces into the body, we experience that these forces stream into us from the whole etheric-cosmic circumference of the universe. They constitute and form our body from its conception and birth until death. This etheric cosmos supports our bodily growth, nourishment, metabolism, and reproduction, respiration and circulation, and regulates them through its creative, artistic and living cosmic pulsations and breathing rhythms. As a matter of fact, these cosmic rhythmic processes regulate our metabolism and growth processes through their regulation of all human rhythmic, circadian and circulatory organs and functions, including breathing, blood circulation, heartbeat, as well as the changes of sleep and waking. And we become increasingly aware of the fact that the same living, rhythmic, pulsating, etheric forces that nourish, build and shape our body, also build and sustain all other earthly, natural and cosmic bodies. We experience that our body and the body of the earth and all its kingdoms and creatures, are 'one infinitely multiplied and multiplying world-human etheric body', a shared etheric planetary body, open to, and suffused by subtle cosmic radiations, streaming in from the whole circumference of the cosmic firmament and environment. This also includes the planets, sun and moons of our solar system, as well and the farthest fixed stars of our galaxy. We begin to have a firsthand experience of human and earthly life from the point of view of that exalted cosmic-sun being that united Himself with the human body and the body of the earth, and said: '*This is my body*'.

The above described etheric human-world body becomes perceptible because the mutual exchange of etheric forces between our etheric body and the etheric world, when it is enhanced by the etheric stream located in the lower body, is denser in comparison with the etheric breathing and exchange in the heart and head streams. We can say that through this lower bodily stream the etheric world constantly fructifies and builds up our subtle bodies, not only during conception, pregnancy and early childhood, but as long as we are physically alive. It is substance creating and consolidating, and the birth forces and processes continue to nourish us through our metabolic limb and reproductive systems day and night as long as we continue to nourish ourselves and breathe physically. While this process, strictly speaking, is etheric, that is, purely supersensible, we must point out that its influences nourish, shape and organize all the subtle, microscopic processes of the physical body and earth. And future researches in this field will demonstrate ever more concretely the fundamental truth of spiritual science, namely, that everything physical in our bodies, on earth and the whole universe is a direct manifestation and expression of the spiritual. From this supersensible perspective, all concrete details of subtle chemical, physiological, biological, geological, metallurgic, meteorological and stellar natural and cosmic realities are led back to their real, active, spiritual causes. It will be understood by more and more people, not in theory only, but through their own life and practice, how Rudolf Steiner could research and demonstrate in such concrete detail the myriad ways in which the whole human body and its subtle constitution is embedded in the whole supersensible cosmic and planetary environment and how the human being, down to its most physical organization, reflects the creative work of sublime spiritual beings and processes. Through the cognitive yoga practice described here, we can experience firsthand, in an elementary manner, what spiritual science has described from its beginning, that spiritual, astral and — in our case here — formative etheric forces are working in and through all the subtle forces that underlie objective, natural, physical, biological and planetary-cosmic realities in the real physical world.[*]

Reversal of puberty

As described above, when the pure etheric stream of becoming, flowing from the purified sense perceptions, impacts the body

[*] Let us be reminded again that such general descriptions communicate only the preliminary stages of the real, concrete, cognitive yoga etheric research. Concrete details are researched and discovered in life itself, according to specific questions, problems and requirements, especially in the fields of agriculture and nutrition, medicine, education and social life.

directly, it awakens in the body its dormant and potential reserves of pristine, subtle forces that lie below the solar plexus and diaphragmatic threshold. Through the opened and disinhibited gates of the MECM, distilled and etherized sensory inhalation can flow deeper into the brain and body and cross over the lower threshold into the abdominal regions. There it nourishes, awakens and stimulates the pristine pure vital forces of the body and releases part of the etheric body from the basic physical functions of metabolism, growth and reproduction. These forces join the freed etheric forces of the etheric heart, larynx and head, and as we demonstrated above, interact with the etheric world as a whole.

When we observe how the whole etheric world interacts with the whole etheric body, we notice first of all, a general intensification of the threefold etheric operative systems and functions described above. In the etheric head, we notice how our imaginative world thinking and perception is stimulated; in the heart region, world pulsating and breathing becomes increasingly more individualized; and in the lower body, substance creation is stimulated by etheric growth and nourishment processes fed directly through the general etheric world. When we focus our attention again on the lower parts and processes of the etheric body, and delve deeper into the forces stimulated by the interaction with the etheric world, we experience a powerful awakening of the subtle, pristine forces of the lower body. This is first of all, a more general experience, but the more we are able to practise the whole, threefold, world-human etheric breathing between the lower etheric body and the etheric world, the more we experience how the deeply dormant, spiritually speaking, purest reproductive forces of the body are becoming especially awakened and stimulated. This takes place on a non-physical, purely etheric, subtle level. Then we experience on a higher cognitive level, which can cognize deeper the hidden processes of the body than was possible before, a reunion of the world-human, macro and micro streams of etheric forces. It is as if the world's formative and productive forces merge intensively with the body's life forces. But now this union activates still deeper layers of the body's own original life forces. The two streams merge together again in this place, but now we see how the whole etheric body's mutual exchange of pure etheric forces with the etheric world is concentrated in a still deeper bodily level. The general stream of life forces from the etheric world, which we inhale through our etheric breathing, contains the highest creative and formative, body-shaping forces. This intensified stream permeates and thereby awakens and stimulates the holy treasure, the forces of the pure and long protected reproductive forces. They come from the deepest metabolic-reproductive recesses of the body, even before the red blood is formed (that is, before it takes in the synthesis of hemo-globin and iron), from the purest etheric-paradisal force of the cosmos and humanity. The previous etherization process in the blood flowed from the heart to the brain and then back to the heart as cognitive processes via the larynx. This is an etherization of the red blood, in which iron, the earthly metallic substance, is already incorporated. The deeper and enhanced etherization begins before the intake of iron, where the blood tissue itself originates. Indeed, these forces originate in the metabolic processes where the white lymph is produced, before it joins the red blood, and in the bone marrow, before the red blood cells are formed, activating human-ity's long protected, purest childhood formative forces, showing how deep this etherization penetration goes into the physical body itself. This etherization produces life forces different from the forces produced by the etherization of the already formed blood in the heart that flows to the brain as we demonstrated above. Now we co-create with the whole world, by bringing together the subtle etheric productive world forces and the forces of our threefold etheric body, and focus their synergetic effects in these earliest and purest bodily depths. As a result, we witness how out of their union a new, third, united human-world stream is produced. This mutual exchange and merger is repeated and intensified as etheric breath-ing from the very first beginnings of the cognitive yoga practice, from the head to the larynx and heart and now in the abdomen and limbs. At this stage it reaches a certain culmination. By means of this intensified mutual exchange we experience the fullness of the human-world, world-human, etheric merger with the cosmos, and now we become aware—with holy awe—how it awakens and stimulates the pristine forces of our bodies, and how the whole cosmos most purely unites with them to bring forth a new emergent etheric stream of becoming to expression. Thus a new third stream is conceived through the merger of the world formative forces and the bodily potential life and resurrection forces, and this stream is endowed with unique productive potential. This process also helps us to answer some of the most difficult esoteric riddles related to the reproduction and sexual life of the present human being.

To begin with, we experience this process as what can only be described as a reversal of the bodily processes taking place around the age of puberty (in healthy development it takes place toward the end of the 2nd seven-year period in the life of the child, around the twelfth year. It then continues into the 3rd seven-year period with the earthly birth of the astral body at the age of 14). The above described etherization of the lower body allows us to observe quite objectively the reversal of what takes place unconsciously in puberty. In puberty the unconsciously working forces of the astral body penetrate and transform the forces of the etheric and physical bodies, causing earthly soul development and sexual maturity. These astral forces are in themselves the purest forces of cosmic love, and below all conscious affections and desires, they also unite with the purest etheric-physical forces in the human body. What mostly comes to consciousness today, however, are precisely the individuating, egotistic luciferic-ahrimanic forces that cause a far stronger 'infleshment' and hardening of these pure love forces. This causes the above described impenetrable astral-etheric-physical mixture of the MECM complex and sedimentation between the instreaming productive forces of the world — which are, essentially, an expression of the world's creative love forces — and the luciferically infested and ahrimanically hardened physical organs and forces of reproduction and sexuality. At this stage of the cognitive yoga practice, the forces of reproductive love, bound to the physical body, are purified through the etherization of the blood, perception and thinking, that etherizes and brings to consciousness the reserved purest forces of humanity's pre-luciferic childhood. There, forces protected by the deepest sleep of unconsciousness in the lowest recess of our bodies, are liberated and resurrected. They are lifted out of the hardening physical, etheric and astral bodies and organs, suffused and enlivened by the purest etheric world-human productive forces. Thus the original pure astral and cosmic forces of love can again flow freely and directly into the body and unite there with the purest force of humanity's childhood, untagged by the luciferic and ahrimanic forces. This process is experienced in imaginative cognition as a unique spiritual event, which can be also called a regained and conscious, uncontaminated event of 'pure puberty', leading to new and holy (that is, pure and free from the egotistic influences) 'marriage' between the cosmos and the human being and to an immaculate fertilization and conception of a new life body. And this new pure puberty and marriage between heaven and earth conceives new offspring of wholly new human-cosmic life.[*]

Reversal of the separation of the sexes

In this way, the productive and reproductive etheric-astral process, captured and sedimented in the transition between the 2nd and 3rd seven-year periods of life, is liberated from the capture by the hardening forces of the MECM. To these luciferic forces, joined later by their ahrimanic counterpart, we owe our extreme individuation and the speeded up earthly development of our strong ego-centred

---

[*] In this way the 'sleeping beauty' awakened to new life in the protected depth of the human body, described above, is again a microcosmic expression of a planetary macrocosmic Christ permeated process: 'If you take in your hand a piece of granite containing quartz, you can say: This piece of granite with its quartz will at a future time be alive again. It has lived in former ages and today it is dead. It has formed solid ground upon which we can walk about. When we did not need to walk, the solid ground was not there. But one day it will come to life again. In fact, we can say that the earth sleeps as regards cosmic space — only the sleep is long, 15,000 years at least. When the earth was alive it was awake, it was in connection with the whole universe and the life forces of the universe brought forth upon it the great beasts. Later, as solidity was reached, these forces brought forth the human beings. Human beings nowadays have a pleasant time of it on earth — of course in regard to the universe too — they can go about on solid ground. But this solid ground will wake up again — it is really only asleep — it will wake up again and become active life ... someday it will be alive again, it is between life and life and is really only asleep'. (Rudolf Steiner, GA 349, 17 February 1923)

consciousness and life. The good Gods further also used them to divide the whole purely spiritual, astral and etheric primeval cosmic human being into the two bodily sexes. Before this division, humanity was still wholly embedded in the cosmos, endowed with pre-personal and dreamlike, cosmic spiritual consciousness. The Spirits of Form (the Elohim led by Jehovah), who are the givers of the 'I' to humanity, divided it into two sexes, and enclosed each sex in a polar opposite bodily compartment. This division of the sexes has closed off and sealed each bodily sexual form, and the incarnated human Ego could only experience itself in a half of the whole spiritual human potentiality, which, in turn, has increasingly darkened the spiritual consciousness of the spiritual worlds as the incarnation in the body got ever stronger and denser. Humanity was incarnated into these divided and sexualized human bodies, which function as the main instrument and foundation of individuation and the formation of personality, because the human spirit and soul could never have achieved freedom otherwise. If we forever remained cosmic, asexual, and non-individual beings, we would also never have developed self-consciousness, freedom, and true love based on freedom.

As we saw above, when the new etheric, cognitive-rhythmic system encompasses the threefold etheric body, it also becomes an organ of creative cognition inside the lower part of the body. Then the following process becomes perceptible. The whole interaction or breathing, between the etheric world and the liberated threefold human etheric body, described above, becomes a sacred ritual of fructification and impregnation. As the purest productive etheric world forces, flowing into the body through the purified sense perceptions and thinking, fructify the subtle reproductive parts, organs and processes of the lower body, the body answers this fructification with opening up its innermost and primordial and immaculate forces, kept in a deep secret place of reserve, protected from the influences of divisive sexuation and conscious egotistic desires, fantasy and deeds. Concretely observed, we may say that the whole mutual fertilization between the etheric body and etheric world is concentrated in a finest etheric thread, mentioned above as the fullest etherization of the blood from foot to brain. Activated through the whole cognitive yoga etheric breathing, it flows in the threefold etheric body between body and world and head and limbs. It connects the deepest spiritualized reproductive forces, flowing from below via the etheric heart, and articulates and forms them through the creative formative forces of the larynx. The mutual fertilization comes to full imaginative cognition via the two-petalled chakra and nourishes and activates its etheric-physical expression in the pineal gland. This is the microcosmic expression of the same reproductive cycle in the macrocosmic etheric world through which the Gods constantly create and recreate the worlds. In this way spiritual science becomes the mediator and midwife that bring about the new human-world etheric fertilization and birth. Into these unconscious depths of the body only the purest forces of the etheric world can penetrate, flowing through our senses and purified by our best moral impulses, because in those regions of the body and the earth only Christ's primordial, paradisal forces are working together with his eternal forces of resurrection. As the Logos, the cosmic Word, became flesh as a physical human being, so from now on the flesh is beginning to become Word: it is etherized and spiritualized again. The human being becomes the world resurrecting and enlivening Logos, and this takes place inwardly through the human body and the body of the earth.[*]

There, at the same time, we witness and partake in a sacred 'immaculate conception' event that unfolds in our own living flesh and blood. And this immaculate conception brings something new into the world: it conceives a new human-world etheric being. What is conceived is a new offspring of our human-world, world-human

---

[*] Rudolf Steiner describes the cosmic-planetary foundation of this process here: 'Of what then does the earth consist, since it was penetrated by the Christ-Spirit? To the last atom the Earth consists of Life, since Christ permeated it, and the atom is ... a sheath that encloses a spiritual part; this spiritual element is a part of Christ. Now take anything that is of the Earth; when would you be judging of it correctly? When you said: 'This is a part of the body of Christ!' What else could Christ say to those who desired to know Him? In breaking the bread made of the corn of the Earth, Christ could say to them: 'This is my body!' What could He say in giving them the juice of the vine, which is the juice of a plant? 'This is my blood!' Because He had become the soul of the Earth'. (GA 112, 7 July 1909)

etheric becoming which is, etherically speaking, super-sexual, that is, in which both sexes are merged, transformed into a new creative force. It is a future creative and co-creator child that the earth offers the cosmos through humanity as a stream of new cosmic becoming. The old father macrocosmos, that once gave birth to the natural earth and humanity, and is now dying in our mature individuation as a modern people, is reborn, because we, as free humans, become the future oriented 'young mother source', and because we unite ourselves with the eternally born son, the sublime sun spirit that became the spirit of the earth. Each individual human being harbours a new individualized Christ-given seed of a new cosmos to come. A new cosmic seed-child is conceived that, if rightly fostered, can later be born out into the wide universe, and we are now consciously parenting its becoming.

The body, fructified and impregnated with the purest etheric world forces, becomes self-reproductive, and its productivity merges in turn with the productivity of the world, flowing back into it through the doors of conception and perception. The physical senses that were opened after eating from the fruit of knowledge, as a result of the luciferic intervention in Lemuria, after which humans became conscious of their sexuality, individuality and mortality,* become the pure gateway through which the forces of the Tree of Life are individualized as a new etheric human-world child. The doors of sense inhalation become also the outlets for new life streams of exhalation, formed, articulated, out-spoken via the etherized larynx centre, because the pristine, virgin forces of the body, after becoming fructified by the purest forces of the etheric world, begin to become

---

* 'Then the eyes of both of them were opened, and they realized they were naked; so they sewed fig leaves together and made coverings for themselves. Then the man and his wife heard the sound of the Lord God as he was walking in the garden in the cool of the day, and they hid from the Lord God among the trees of the garden. But the Lord God called to the man, "Where are you?" He answered, "I heard you in the garden, and I was afraid because I was naked; so I hid.... Cursed is the ground because of you; through painful toil you will eat food from it all the days of your life ... until you return to the ground, since from it you were taken; for dust you are and to dust you will return."' (Genesis, 7–10, 17)

world productive. It is now in its turn impregnating the world with its newborn forces. A 'mutual impregnation' between the purest reproductive forces of the world as the 'father' source, working through his 'son', the individualized free love forces in us, and through our body as the 'mother' source, is taking place. And we are the newborn humans, the free co-creative stream of becoming in the cosmos. It is this individualized and spiritualized human self that is the newborn world-human, cosmic baby. The result is that a new life stream is flowing from within the incarnated, physical, human becoming into the spiritual world, and we are in fact co-parenting and co-harbouring a new cosmic child. We are becoming world pregnant, world birthing and world child all at once. And it is this world-self, fructified by the world, that becomes a source of world's productive becoming, harbouring future world forces. It co-creates with the spiritual world, for the world, a new stream of building, enlivening and healing, youthful forces of the future.*

These imaginative pictures give expression to a profound spiritual scientific truth: it is absolutely true and scientific to contend that the human-earthly body becomes a living fountain, and it produces fresh streams of life-giving 'cognitive oxygen' that flow into the world. And as previously the etheric world fructified and impregnated the

---

*The purest nourishment that this human-world spiritual baby must receive comes from the finest etherized sense perceptions and the most purified bodily mineral extracts described above. This is also the Grail's nourishment that flows from the dynamic, circulating source, about which the North spirit advised Rudolf Steiner when he asked her concerning the Grail's whereabouts. It is called 'Ganganda Greida', 'circulating cordial', or 'travelling sacrament' in the northern Grail legends. Rudolf Steiner described the Grail's nourishment as follows: 'The legend of the Holy Grail tells us of that miraculous food which is prepared from *the finest activities of the sense-impressions and the finest activities of the mineral extracts, whose purpose it is to nourish the noblest part of man all through the life he spends on earth*; for it would be killed by anything else. This heavenly food is what is contained in the Holy Grail.' (25 March 1913, GA 145) ... 'Now, to whom is this food to be handed? It is really to be handed — as is revealed to us when from the exoteric story we enter into the esoteric presentation of it in the Mysteries — it is really to be handed to the human being who has obtained the understanding of what makes man mature enough gradually to raise himself consciously to what the Holy Grail is.' (26 March, GA 145, my emphasis)

etheric body with pure formative forces flowing through our sense perceptions, now it is the individualized humanity, and the earth's body, that in turn fructifies the cosmic world with its own youthful fountain of life. This body is not only a new life body, but it is also supported by an etherized, resurrected seed of a new physical body, who's archetypal 'Phantom' has been multiplying itself in us since the Mystery of Golgotha. It is nourished and brought to imaginative cognition by reproductive etheric breathing. It is a firstborn offspring of our joint human-cosmic creation, an independent etheric body that harbours future seed forces of a new universe.

In my book, *The Spiritual Event of the 20th Century* I called the embryonic stream of becoming also 'the earthly-human sun' because what is produced here is the co-production between a resurrected, Christ imbued humanity and earth, and the cosmos. This constitutes a new sun-star centre, a newly conceived seed of a future sun and cosmos which the earth is becoming.

Now, with these seminal forces of the individualized earthly-human sun, we are in a position to turn to our creative etheric tasks in the etheric world itself. But the forces needed for the purely etheric tasks can be created only through the etherization of the modern cognitive and moral forces that originate in the physical body and on the earth.*

---

* We note only in passing that through this modern cognitive yoga practice, we reach in a fully self-conscious way, that is, through pure cognitive activity and without any external manipulation of the physical body and physical breathing, the same goal that the Kundalini masters achieved in the traditional practices of yoga. These practices are no longer adapted to western bodies, mentality and social life. Let us also add in passing that at this stage, we discover that without any manipulation of the physical breath, a subtle modification takes place all the way down to the real bodily and physiological levels. Then, implausible as it may be sound, at this point the metaphor of water's electrolysis gives way to a real process, by means of which real, though quantitatively very subtle, life-giving, etheric, oxygen is produced, when the physiological synthesis of CO_2 through the breathing is subtly, to begin with, homeopathically, reversed. In this way we can also study in detail the spiritual physiological foundations of the regulatory and rhythmic system that controls the centres of breathing, blood circulation and the circadian clocks that regulate sleeping and waking.

8. Birth of an etheric individuality

For each human being who searches for the godly fountainhead, the great World-I, in the realm of the surging, wafting 'I', can perceive it as the archetypal image of the individual 'I'.... Through this also a breath of human freedom is drawn in human development: right at the peak, so to speak, of the continual 'I' the human being is placed and then formed through the divine 'I'.

(14 December 1908, GA 108)

In our unconscious embodiment and individuation in the physical world, we start with a given body that is a sublime fruit of the creative wisdom of billions of years of spiritual evolution. With its help we gradually develop our free personality. Bodily individuation precedes and therefore supports the gradual maturing process of our soul and spiritual human personality in the physical world. When we enter into the etheric world (the first real supersensible world) with our newborn etheric body, we must accomplish in full self-consciousness a similar process of individuation. This means that we have to consciously learn to become independent co-creators of our own spiritual individuality and embody it in a proper etheric body in the etheric world, without the support of the physical body and the soul life supported by the physical body.[*]

When we compare the individuation processes between the physical and the etheric worlds, we can say that in the etheric world the process is reversed. It is our task, which is also a 'test' of our spiritual capacities acquired in our spiritual-scientific work in the physical world, first, to 'read' and 'interpret' our situation in the

---

[*] In the spiritual world, spiritual guidance and instruction fulfils the highest modern ideal, because it *completely* depends on the pupil. That is, free initiative is the rule and what we want to receive we must, paradoxically speaking, first freely conceive and actualize by means of our own individualized spiritual cognition. In the limits of the present study I will describe only the human side of this development and not the nature of the intercourse with the spiritual teachers.

spiritual world, by developing, solely by means of our own cognition, the ability to understand its language. Second, we can decide to take free initiative and actualize our independently chosen task in the spiritual world, solely by means of our own forces. And the first task, the nature of which we must conceive, research, and actualize by means of our own cognitive forces, has three interrelated stages: first, we must conceive and give birth to an independent spiritual individuality in the etheric world. This being is called in spiritual science 'Spirit Self'. Second, we must embody it in a fitting etheric body in the etheric world, and third, in the first 'three years' of its spiritual childhood, we must develop its basic spirit- soul and bodily capacities, and learn to use them as an independent self-conscious spiritual individuality in the etheric world.

In the course of the above described stages of cognitive yoga practice, a real metamorphosis of human cognition, consciousness and being was realized. We have now at our disposal, as operative forces and cognitive faculties, two integrated world-human streams of purified etheric formative forces. The first stream—extracted from the inhalation of sense perceptions—brought about the 'body birth event' described above. This birth was caused by the mutual essence exchange with the forces of the etheric world. A new embryonic etheric body was conceived through the mutual fertilization between the pure life forces of the world and the immaculate, pristine etheric forces of the human being. In this new stream we have the potent source of life forces needed in order to create and embody an independent spiritual individuality in the etheric world. On the other hand, parallel with the etherization of perception, thinking was etherized as well, as we showed above in Chapter 5. There we have created a second stream of etherized life forces, extracted through the release and exhalation of thinking from its physical embodiment. This etherization of thinking has led us to the 'cosmic thinking event'. This event actualized two related faculties: first, by graduating from Ahriman's school of death and extracting its lessons and secrets from him, we developed the faculty needed to perceive, spiritualize and condense the etheric forces that create what is commonly referred to (this is Ahriman's language) as 'physical' or 'inanimate' matter. Second, by entering in the right manner into the etheric world, overcoming the temptation to be carried away from the earth by the seductive forces of the Luciferic etheric levity and blinding, dazzling light, we have developed the ability to humbly approach the proximity of the cosmic source of life. Christ's etheric forces, full of love, wisdom, beauty and creative potentials, which humanity needs so much on the earth today and in the near future, flow through this source. These two related spiritual capacities, derived from the etherization of thinking, join the capacities derived from the etherization of perception, to give us the forces needed for developing and maintaining our etheric individuality in the etheric world.

Now while we were practising the etherization of sense inhalation and thinking exhalation in the above described practice of cognitive yoga, the formative forces that shape self-consciousness itself were also transformed and etherized. While our attention was directed to the purification, intensification and liberation of perception and thinking, the forces of the active self-conscious 'I' went through their own metamorphosis. This resulted in a new stream of becoming, which we also called above an 'individuation of individuation', which means, in other words, the spiritualization of the *core* forces of the Ego itself. This was taking place mostly in the background, while our attention was focused on the etherization of perception and thinking and their applications. But now that we unite their forces, this central spiritualization of the Ego comes to fuller spiritual cognition.[*]

The spiritualization of the formative forces that create all other representations also transformed the forces that shape the repre-

---

[*] According to Rudolf Steiner's indication, quoted above in Chapter 5, the spiritualization of the forces of perception create the supersensible faculty of Imagination, while the faculty of Inspiration is derived from the spiritualization of thinking. Their combination creates the faculty of Intuition, by means of which also the eternal 'I', spiritual Ego or Spirit Self, is created and perceived. Now, while in the present work we limit our research to the etheric world and use primarily the faculty of imagination as our main tool, this faculty is, on the other hand, thoroughly penetrated by the forces of inspiration and intuition. In my book, *The New Experience of the Supersensible*, I described in detail the creation of this faculty, which I called an intuited and inspired imaginative faculty.

sentation of our self. It has been decomposed, and the mental husk, the dead envelope, was transformed into living, conscious etheric formative force, that does not mask but reveals and expresses the deeply unconscious real kernel of the 'I'. This kernel is highly spiritual, which means that, while incarnated in the physical body, it works through the deeply unconscious, creative forces of the real spiritual will (and this includes the forces of instinct and pro-creation), and therefore is bound to and inhibited—for our protec-tion—in the lower bodily organs and functions. The mental picture that we make of this real 'I'—and in ordinary cognition we only have a mental picture of it, not its reality—is metamorphosed gradually during the cognitive yoga breathing into an increasingly conscious spiritual and real capacity. This individuation or actua-lization of the self-conscious, real willed self can be called 'reversed individuation', which means also 'spiritualized individuation'. It is subtly registered while it is taking place constantly in the back-ground of the above described cognitive yoga breathing, between senses' inhalation and thinking's exhalation, allowing time for the naturally slower moral purification, before its powerful real forces will be released from the lower body. Gradually, the rhythmic etheric breathing of perception and thinking, fired by the love forces working through the etherization of the blood, and also extending to the pure metabolic and reproductive forces, is intensified to such an extent, that it begins to become the very substance, form and activity of our real spirit 'I'. In this manner the self-conscious human 'I' learns to individuate the activity of metamorphosis that matures during the *whole* 'polarization and intensification' cyclic breathing process.

What started as a mere ordinary mental picture: 'I am this or that', becomes the extracted, intensified, pure etheric force of metamor-phosis, actualized through the repeated, cyclic, cognitive yoga etheric breathing. But only when the freed etheric body and the corresponding forces of the etheric world have united and created the new human-world third stream, as described above in Chapter 7, is the true 'I' fully released as well, supported by the forces of the newborn etheric body. It can now take charge of the whole etheric process, being its child as well as its parent, so to speak. A self-conscious etheric thinker, perceiver, knower and creative operator, or artist, is actualized, who knows how to incarnate and excarnate consciously and volitionally, to enter organic embodiment and exit it at will and feel at home in the physical world and in the open etheric world. This new 'I', a consciously willed, spirit imbued, spiritual self, was active of course in the *will power* that animated and energized the whole cognitive yoga work from its very first steps. But, to begin with, it stayed more in the background, substantiating and energizing the whole etheric breathing processes but not coming to full consciousness in itself as a *self-conscious spiritual self.* Now it comes to the fore and can be baptized with its true spiritual scientific name: *Spirit Self.* Through the two etheric breathing movements that it created, it has two hands or wings of passage, pictorially expressed, by means of which it learns to recreate itself as a self-consciously, etherically embodied, spiritual individuality in the etheric world. Through the metamorphosis of the process of perception at one pole, it learned to master the forces of birth and incarnation, and through the metamorphosis of the forces of thinking at the other pole, it learned to master the forces of death and excarnation. That is, on the one hand, it masters and consciously actualizes the unconscious processes of bodily embodiment, connected to the processes and forces of birth, and on the other hand, it learns to consciously actualize the forces of disembodiment, that cause physical death and release of the soul and spirit from the physical body. Both become the spiritual 'hands and feet', or more precisely, wings, as an expression of the innermost forces of the spiritual becoming of the Spirit Self in the etheric world.

The making of the Spirit Self

In order to transform and condense self-consciousness into self-producing and self-actualizing spiritual individuality, as a real, spiritual, force being, creative and active in the etheric world, we have to mesh the forces extracted from the two events of transformation described above: the body event which culminated in the birth of a new human-world etheric body, and the thinking event, which culminated in the experience of the vicinity of the cosmic source of life of the earth and humanity. Both events embody the fullness of the released forces of birth and death, of metamorphosis, and only the fullest merging of their extracted spiritual essences can be used to actualize the etheric birth and development of a real spiritual individuality in the etheric world itself.

In physical life our etheric body is engaged in a downhill task of taking care of the organic life processes of metabolism, growth and reproduction, fighting the forces of death as long as it can. In our cognitive yoga practice, we had to wrestle with the forces of organic birth and death alike, in order to spiritualize the growth and death forces of the physical and etheric bodies alike. In the etheric world, on the contrary, we have to embody the forces that served the dis-embodiment process on the earth, or to incarnate the forces of excarnation. This is the fundamental paradox of our human exis-tence, to which we already referred above: in everyday physical life we gain real feeling and experience of a physically real, embodied and substantial personality because the infinitely strong cosmic life is *unconsciously* subdued, suppressed, and depleted in the building and formation of our organic physical body. We experience our-selves as *more* substantial, alive and solid the *less* spiritually real we become, and the less we experience the real spiritual world. This is simply our given human, existential experience; it's our most fun-damental daily physical reality in the present age. The cognitive yoga soul breathing, leading to the etherization of the senses at the pole of sense inhalation and to etherization of thinking at the pole of thinking's exhalation, allows us to transform these birth and death forces into real world forces. When we do this we are not weakening or giving up our self-consciousness, but on the contrary, we are infinitely enhancing it. We carry this spiritual self-consciousness and its intuited, inspired, imaginative cognitive faculties with us into the etheric world. But while sojourning outside the physical body in the etheric world, we are nakedly exposed to immensely powerful cosmic forces. If we are not imbued with the spiritualized 'I' forces, which we actualized through spiritual scientific life and research in the physical world, we will suffer greatly from the impact of this all too powerful cosmic life. As we saw above in Chapter 5, this impact has major consequences. It's powerful anti-gravitational pull and intensity of life is so overwhelming that it subdues all the forces of our soul that still depend on the physical body for their existence. And this means practically all the forces of our self-conscious and personal soul life. Its forces pull us away from the earth and disperse us in the vast, light-filled cosmic periphery. Our soul forces are dispersed as well and any experience of an 'I' centre and identity vanishes entirely. We are gracefully protected from this misery when we fall asleep and lose our self-consciousness every night on leaving our physical and etheric bodies. Today only spiritual scientific development gives us the full forces to sustain awakened self-consciousness and cognition without the natural support of our physical and etheric bodies. This is the reason why modern humans must infinitely strengthen their soul life and cognitive faculties in order to enter the spiritual worlds consciously. They must infinitely enliven and resurrect all their life and soul forces in order to enter the world of pure cosmic-spiritual life forces, breathe the rarified etheric air that the Angels breathe, and remember that they are an 'I' being. However, once we have entered rightly into the spiritual worlds (and let it be emphasized once more that the etheric world is, in this respect, already a fully real supersensible world), the situation is immediately reversed. When we enter the supersensible world, when we are fully immersed with our whole being in its forces, we must learn how to do the very opposite of what we did in order to enter it. Now we must learn to subdue, contract, devitalize, and condense cosmic life in order to be able to originally create a consistent and self-conscious spiritual individuality, which is solid enough and has enough 'etheric consistency, mass and gravity'. Otherwise, we will only be able, perhaps, to 'peep' into the spiritual worlds, and then be immediately pulled back to either our normal daily consciousness or into dreamless sleep. To live, move and actualize our whole being there (as long as the graceful spiritual guidance allows us, because this should never become a matter of wilful personal desire), is possible only to the extent that we are able to use our abundant reserves of enlivened and strengthened soul and life forces, procured on the earth, to counterbalance life's overwhelming etheric abundance. Only the extracted, spiritualized, essence of the forces of death, which we transformed consciously through the above described cognitive yoga work, make this possible. Otherwise we will vanish into thin ethereal air in the vast universe, and will never be able to embody our spiritual individuality in substantial and firm etheric flesh and blood.

But where is the living source of the mutual exchange and transformation between the forces of birth and death to be found? Where does life become living death and death become a fountain of new life? This stream of becoming is called in spiritual science, 'the Christ impulse'. It directs and regulates the planetary and individual processes of sleep and waking, birth and death, incarnation, excarnation and reincarnation. When it is experienced self-consciously in this manner, and individualized through the spiritual scientific activity described here, this impulse reveals itself as the essence of humanity's Higher Self, or, again, in its individualized spirit form, it is called 'Spirit Self'.

Again, let it be emphasized that the power needed for the next steps of the cognitive yoga practice can only emerge from a reserve of forces produced and accumulated in the background while the etherization of perception and thinking was the focus of attention. And this reserve is accumulated always in the crossing point between the inner and outer, in-breathing and out-breathing, in the place in which the two etherized streams of perception and thinking mutually exchange and merge their spiritual essence with each other, forming a united, synergistically potent spiritual power. This crossing and *Umstülpung* activity *is* our true 'I'; there our Ego is spiritualized in its core and becomes Spirit Self. In this place we cannot speak any more about the rhythmic in and out movements of breathing, conceived spatially or even in time, but only about a fully real actualization of the power that is responsible for all rhythms and pulsations in our body and in the universe. This power sends its pulses and rhythms into time and space from an intense 'non-moving' place. It is the unmoved and immobile mover, whose innermost activity is the essence of metamorphosis: purest actualization of actuality, pure spiritual being. This is how Aristotle

experienced it for the first time in the evolution of human consciousness, as the full intensity of self-actualizing potentiality that
harbours the dynamic, energetic, creation of the *Entelechy*.* Today,
through the forces of the Consciousness Soul, the entelechy is
becoming the creative, active, self-intensifying and self-metamorphosing spiritual activity, which becomes in us an eternal Individuality beyond time and space altogether.

When we harvest the intensive forces of the Spirit Self extracted
from the mutually united events of the spiritualization of perception
and thinking, the modern, individualized, non-moving mover 'I' is
also actualized. It is the intense and potent source of the real will
forces that create and substantiate our physical body and bring us
into physical incarnation, and then destroy this body to lead us back
through death into the spiritual worlds. We can say in all truthfulness that this being—the true 'I', the Higher Self—arises out of
Christ's death and resurrection. Now, in the etheric world, we must
become self-conscious builders of our world existence as self-
conscious beings. And as here on the earth we use Christ's life forces
to recapitulate in ourselves the overcoming of death, so in the
etheric world we must learn how to reverse them and use the forces
of resurrection first of all to kill the all too living cosmic forces in
order to give birth to an individualized Spirit Self and embody it as
an independent individuality in the etheric world.

Die and Become

Therefore, strange as it may sound, the truth must still be expressed:
in the physical world, in which death predominates, we must imbue

---

*This spiritualization process of the power of the eternal human entelechy or
Spirit Self is given to humanity in our age through Rudolf Steiner's spiritually
multiplied 'I' accomplishment, supported by the ever-growing forces of his
eternally preserved etheric body. The forces of this etheric body can be individualized since the end of the twentieth century. The original seed of this
divine Self was first planted in the 'I' impulses of Moses and the Prophets,
individualized in Aristotle, and spiritualized for all time through the resurrected 'I' of Jesus Christ.

ourselves with Christ's life forces created out of the overcoming of earthly death, in order to transform our individual death forces into forces of stronger life; in the etheric world, where there is only infinite life and abundant light and beauty (experienced to begin with as belonging to the domain of Lucifer) we must, first of all, transform this infinitely tempting life into fully conscious spiritual death in order to achieve full self-consciousness in the etheric world. In the physical world, when we 'fire the streams flowing from heart to brain' and apply cognitive yoga practice to physical cognitive life, we are able to take in something already dead – the mental picture – and resurrect it to new spiritual life. However, the joy of new and liberated life is already, and rightly so, mingled with pain because we experience consciously that *unconsciously* we (not 'we' as self-conscious subjects but rather as part of an objective world process) have killed living sense perceptions and thinking in order to produce the dead representation that we now resurrected. But the given existence in the etheric world is abundant life, not death as in the physical world. And this means that in the etheric world we have to do this killing process, which on the earth is taking place unconsciously – in full consciousness and voluntarily. In order to produce and maintain strong enough self-consciousness in the etheric world, we must contract and condense cosmic life into consistent and individualized selfhood. If we want to know something in the etheric world – anything, from the tiniest etheric beings and currents to vast cosmic vistas, events and beings – we must contract and condense our perceptions, and make them into self-conscious contents of real imaginative cognition.

In the physical world we are threefold consumers: we eat, breathe and know in the physical world by *unconsciously* killing and assimilating the content of our consumption. First, we must devour natural beings and transform them into dead foodstuffs to build our individual physical body, second, we kill the world's life-giving oxygen into death bringing carbon dioxide, and third, we kill our living sense perceptions and thoughts, and we assimilate them – as dead mental substances – in order to build our personal mental life and identity and individualize our soul. And this unconscious threefold death process makes us physically, organically and psychologically strong, independent and alive. But this is a given, objective, world process that takes place unconsciously in our bodily, soul and mental organizations. We become self-conscious and free, separated from the real spiritual worlds, due to this unconscious threefold killing process. However, now, in the etheric world, everything can only happen in fullest imaginative cognition. Individuation is still the same process here and there, since the killing process must also be accomplished in the etheric world, but now for us it must happen in full consciousness. On the earth we are asleep to the killing process that individuates us, and in the etheric world we must do it ourselves consciously. If we want to develop a full and free, spiritual individuality with clear, lucid, imaginative consciousness, and if we want to develop fully 'embodied' (etherically speaking) individual cosmic life out there, this will be our first chosen task.

Our Spirit Self that we developed on the earth through the overcoming of death must become a fully conscious killer as well as a conscious life-giver. It must subdue and contract any part of cosmic life, which we may encounter at any given moment in our etheric development, in order for us to consciously integrate it into our free etheric being. And then, it will have to breathe new life into it and resurrect it, through its own self-conscious etheric cognition. This is the only way in which we can become—and therefore know—this cosmic life at all. Without this process, our Spirit Self, will remain bodiless and will lack etheric consistency, body, skin, limbs, and individualized spiritual faculties, without which it will have no consciousness of *self* out there. Therefore, first and foremost we have to actualize this process in our own etheric being, in order to create a self-conscious etheric individuality. We have to learn how to produce, from intense, yet very fine and subtle ethereal and light-filled streams of life, a consistently solid and sustainable, self-limiting, etheric embodiment and individualized spiritual faculties, in order to become a real individuality in the etheric world. This is a shocking fact of human existence on all levels of real supersensible life. We must utilize the forces of resurrection that we individualized from Christ's death on the earth, in order to actualize death-like forces and processes. Otherwise we would never become fully free and creative cosmic agents, as we should become in the present age of the Consciousness Soul, and would instead remain dreamy and airy-fairy will-o'-the-wisps, tossed around by each and every etheric and astral current and being, without the ability to direct our supersensible cognition, actions and life in tune and in sync with the cosmic rhythms and events that we want to serve.

But also our feeling life is strongly differentiated in the physical and etheric worlds. This is the reason why the more our self-consciousness increases in the etheric world the more intense both our joy and our pain become. The astral world, the bearer of all feelings in their purest, most intensive nature, is much closer to the etheric world than to the physical. In the physical world we are sheltered from the immense intensity of the feelings, sympathies, antipathies, pain and bliss that, for example, the dis-embodied human souls of the so-called dead, experience after death, when they lay aside their physical and etheric bodies. Though also in the etheric world we are not yet fully immersed in the real astral life, this life powerfully penetrates the etheric world. The ability to balance intense and polar soul experiences is required to a far greater extent than in physical soul life, because without it no 'normal' soul life is possible at all in the etheric world. The Spirit Self is grounded safely only in these purified and spiritualized forces of the astral body. A balance and harmony between the blissful creative joys, which is part of the very existence of the etheric world, on the one hand, and the intensive pains, loneliness and resignations, caused by the self-inflicted death processes necessary for modern individuation out there, on the other, must be first achieved. A solid, self-conscious and self-active, etherically embodied spiritual individuality is constituted on the feeling level, only by means of this hard-won balance. And this soul constitution is the stable ground on which etheric indivi-duation and later embodiment in an appropriate etheric body can be consciously accomplished. Therefore, only the etherized feeling power extracted out of the feelings, emotions, needs, longings, sympathies and antipathies, liberated from the transformed MECM, and coupled with the lessons of death gained in the transformation of thinking, allow us to consistently actualize the solid astral foundations that are absolutely vital to the etheric individuation in the etheric world.

Building a Home

Setting out to accomplish our self-chosen spiritual initiative and task in the etheric world, first of all we have to 'build a house', an etheric dwelling, for which we must choose a proper 'location', qualitatively speaking of course, a well-known, cultivated, fertile and protected, piece of etheric ground. This 'location', that is, creative spiritual activity, is that etheric process and becoming, now a piece of objective human-world reality in the making, which above we referred to as the human-world mutual fertilization, conception and birth of the new etheric body. Here we start our work, which consists in consciously 'making a clearance' in the densely populated etheric woods. As with the building of a physical house on a chosen piece of physical land, so also here — qualitatively speaking — we must learn to deforest, limit and fence out a selected portion of this new, living cosmic life from its cosmic environment. Then we must contract and harden, differentiate and individuate it in order to give it independent existence and life. In short, we have to actualize the whole cycle of birth, growth, death and rebirth in full consciousness which happens on the earth completely unconsciously. However, the etheric work that we cultivate and transform now is not an external world, that exist simply outside of our being. We are already one with this world, and this oneness is most intimate on all the levels of our spiritual existence. Etheric individuation begins when we are ready to consciously kill the intimate, self-produced, new life-stream of becoming that we have created in partnership with the etheric world through the above described cognitive yoga practice. The problem is that we enjoy this new life tremendously outside of our body and could desire to indulge in this bliss forever. This bliss can be intensified a thousand fold in the etheric world (in which all self-enjoyments and pleasures, indulgences and desires can be cosmically magnified thanks to Lucifer and his hosts). The only source of moral certainty and the courage to transform this tempting cosmic self-indulgence is the real knowledge gained in the cognitive yoga practice about the cosmic meaning and future tasks of individuation. The true, Christened Spirit Self is the future beacon of human self-conscious co-creation with the hierarchies and the beings of nature. Its fire and light, kindled and empowered on the earth through the Consciousness Soul, can burn far and bright in the spiritual worlds. But this is the crux of the matter, indeed its cross, because the earthly born stream of new Christ life that we conceived with the etheric world is the very lifeblood of our most intimately shared being and becoming with the cosmic etheric world. It has also become our own most intimate, world imbued, soul- and spirit-life. It is our world-human being. If we are now to individuate part of it, as we chose to do in the etheric world, it means separating and isolating it after we have previously integrated ourselves intimately with this life world. Therefore, we have to separate what we have inwardly connected and merged with all the living fibres of our etheric being and becoming, and kill what we have resurrected from earthly bodily death. In the etheric world of infinite life and abundance of becoming, we have truly become one with our world. And therefore, everything we do to this world, we do to our own Spirit Self, because our Spirit Self *is* the world. Therefore, we have to demonstrate the capacity to dismember our won world-self consciously and volitionally in order to locate, separate, and individuate— inside this world-human Self—a 'private' etheric territory, a self-created etheric location that will serve us as the secure ground on which to build a home identity and selfhood. This is the only possible means of gaining self- and world-knowledge and finding orientation in the infinite cosmic expanses.

The Wound

This means: our spirit individuality is born and comes to real etheric life in the etheric world only to the extent that we can consciously separate a part of our shared human-cosmic life and give it the stamp of individual life of its own. We individualize it and give it birth as a localized separated Self. This is our entry into the real cosmic community, and it is actualized by means of a sacred self-world, world-self, death & birth ceremony. This is an etheric individual ritual of death and rebirth, held in the company of all our beloved spiritual teachers and angelic companions. In other words, we must be able to cut ourselves loose from our innermost cosmic surrounding, inflicting this death and birth wound on our own world-self, and it is this self-world, world-self, wounding and healing, scar-building process, that becomes the signature and mark that distinguishes true from false (luciferic and ahrimanic) 'individualism' on the etheric plane. Etheric individuation is a continuously living, substantial, wounding and healing process, marked and scarred in our own world-human etheric body in the etheric world. And we recognize each other out there as belonging to the same cosmic order when we demonstrate to each other and identify ourselves by the marks of our self-created wounds and healing processes, and this mark is the truthful mark of all the beings who serve the good evolutionary stream of humanity. Once we have engraved it in our own being we will always recognize it, when it appears through infinite variations, in cosmic events and beings that belong to this stream of human and cosmic evolution. Giving birth to our own Spirit Self in the etheric world in this way is a new art of spiritual self-procreation and propagation.

Spiritual Propagation

We have no examples of spiritual self-propagation and multiplication in the human physical world. Only among the lower animals and plants and on the cellular level do we still find primitive forms of asexual division and multiplication today. Paradoxically, the lower strategies of propagation are more similar to the higher spiritual propagation because both are asexual, that is, instead of the 'other sex' we have a holistic fertilization between the organism and the whole cosmos. (Only materialist illusion will believe that the lower organism propagates itself purely out of its separated physical existence. In reality, the whole cosmos fertilizes each single cell when it divides and multiplies.) This means that the specific manner of human spiritual 'self-propagation' described here has both aspects united and transformed in a higher synthesis. It is individualized because our 'I' has gone through physical human incarnation based on sexual differences and carries the spiritualized power of the 'I' to the supersensible world, but once it is one with supersensible life and existence, it will 'propagate' itself in post-sexual ways that will look more similar to the non- and pre-sexual propagation of lower organisms.

If we continue to stretch the limits of such comparisons, and if our reader keeps this clearly in her mind, we can say that, on the one hand, etheric birth can be compared to physical human birth, because it is our soul that goes through individual experiences of travail, wounding and wonder as a mother does in physical birth, yet on the other hand, the comparison with lower life suggests itself when we realize that it is in reality a virgin conception and birth, in which the whole cosmos replaces the other sex. And the whole cosmos is indeed the Holy Spirit. Furthermore, unlike human birth, the newborn child is also a new 'I' being in our expanding multiple stream of world-human becoming. But the expression 'the whole cosmos replaces the other sex' once again demonstrates the limitation of our common language and imagi-nation, because our real spiritual being in the etheric world *is one with* the whole cosmos. Therefore, we can just as well say that we fructify ourselves or that we are fertilized by the whole cosmos (this is actually what takes place in primitive organisms, but with-out the individual conscious participation of the organisms them-selves). Well then, as beings of Spirit Self in the etheric world, we are the whole holy family in oneness, 'mother', 'child', 'father' and 'holy spirit' all at once, because our real being is the cosmos in which we are fully and continually embedded. Therefore, we must learn how to actualize the *whole* process from beginning to end on our world-self. Our 'mother' being is that aspect of our Spirit Self that is at one with the whole spiritual world and remains one with it, while our 'father' being is the 'I' activity created on the earth in overcoming the death forces in ordinary cognition ('death is the new life-giving Father' as Rudolf Steiner says).* In addition, the 'child' is really our own future being that undergoes a process for which we really lack any physical comparison. No comparison can adequately describe a process by means of which our innermost essence must be *consciously* dismembered, by really cutting it off and separating it from that part of the 'mother' aspect of our self. But it is *we* ourselves, the whole spiritual family and growing community, who do this 'inside' our 'external' world-self (and there are also grandpa and grandma and all the uncles and aunts and many other members in this extended spiritual-cosmic family that we become, because the more we grow into the higher spiritual worlds, the more all the forces and members of our bodies, soul and spirit become independent beings).†

But now let us focus our attention on only the first and founding death and birth event in our new etheric family, in its coming into being in the supersensible worlds: it is the newborn independent spiritual baby that emerges into the light of the etheric world. And once more using these inadequate comparisons, the baby's etheric 'umbilical cord' must also be severed from the life-giving etheric circulation of his spiritual world-mother in order to become an independently embodied personality in the etheric world. That is, the 'father' in us must 'wound' the 'mother' in us, and then separate, isolate, and hence also 'kill' our newly gained cosmic existence and becoming, because we have to do consciously what in physical life occurs naturally, when a child is born. This is the only way to develop the capacity to self-actualize oneself in order to become a free, creative and contributing spiritual individuality, embodied and operative as an etheric agent in the open supersensible cosmos.

---

* The Gospel of St John in Relation to the Other Gospels, GA 112.

† Describing the more advanced stages of spiritual scientific Initiation, Rudolf Steiner speaks in *Occult Science* about the separation and individuation of the three soul forces, each of which unites with its cosmic counterparts to create a sixfold family, that together with the 'I' becomes sevenfold. And the same process of separation and individuation extends to the bodies, on the one hand, and to still higher spiritual potentials, on the other, all of which become individual spiritual beings, making up an ever expanding and diversifying community of our own cosmic being.

Etheric birth in fire

Now in the etheric world, the process that takes place when we consciously sever, separate and isolate something from its living roots, webs and streams of lifeblood, can only be compared to burning fire. When the cut is inflicted and the etheric lifeblood is flowing out of the cosmic-self wound, an all-consuming firestorm arises; and in this fire we—as a newborn—are consumed. What is consumed, is the isolated piece of the world's living substance that we severed from the cosmic body, in order to transform it into our own etheric self-substance. In the physical world a limb or organ disconnected from the whole living body must die and perish. In the etheric world death itself is alive, and what is isolated remains part of life. This is what is meant by the spiritual death in fire. This kind of death in cosmic fire (there are many different kinds of cosmic fire), however, rather demonstrates the fact that in this world no true isolation can prevail at all, not even for a millisecond. Anything isolated is immediately transformed simply by the basic law of life in this world, in which no absolute death and separation is possible. Yet, on the other hand, unlike earthly individuation, which really separates and isolates our consciousness from the universe, etheric world death, separation and individuation, again paradoxically speaking, forges the deepest link with the world, because this death is incredibly living, absolutely and consciously real.

When we accomplish this process, we undergo the following two experiences, which are two sides of the same process of the etheric individuation of Spirit Self and its etheric body. As self-separating and self-isolating, individuating world substance, process and becoming, we are truly burned down to our nothingness, to etherized ashes, in full consciousness. These ashes are world-self ashes; they are produced in fire, because their substance has been cut and isolated from the whole. But they are and remain the *ashes of the living etheric whole*. But what in reality are 'etheric ashes'? They are actually the seeds of resurrection of the kind of etheric body that can embody a being of the rank of Spirit Self. This body will be substantiated, to begin with, purely by the substances and forces of these cosmic seed ashes. And they are our own innermost ashes as well, because we have become this separating process and separated substance ourselves, have caused, internalized and assimilated its death, and have become the destroyers of cosmic life at its essence and source. And through this death in fire, becoming cosmic ashes, we have experienced for the first time substantial and solid existence as an independent Spirit Self, embodied as an etheric individuality in the cosmos. The new human-world stream of becoming described above, conceived and born on the earth must be consciously dismembered and led through fire, to die and become, develop, and then grow up in the etheric cosmos. This child, let us be reminded, is conceived and nourished through the purest spiritual earthly forces derived from the overcoming of physical and soul death by means of the etherization of perception and thinking, after their liberation from the clutches of Ahriman in the physical brain and body. And then both streams unite themselves with the corresponding purest etheric forces in the etheric world and the human body to bring about the birth of a new human-world etheric body. Now this newborn etheric body, the gift of humanity and the earth to the universe, is consciously led through cosmic fire and individuated in the etheric world. It must therefore first be consciously killed in order to become etherically individualized, free and creative. And this means also to set ablaze the spirit core of our 'I' on the stake of this burning severance, to burn in the world's flames of your own world individuation. And this is what you know when you are spiritually reborn out of this fire and your new etheric body is resurrected out of the world's ashes: the capacity to accomplish the whole process *is* your etherically embodied Spirit Self. This is what the newborn Higher Self is becoming in all eternity as the 'first born' earthly-human fruit. For the real human spiritual 'I' this self-caused fire is indeed spiritual death in cosmic fire; and it is also rebirth, growing up, maturing, and a spiritual *steeling* process (experienced through the feelings and steeled in the fiery core of the will).

Between the spiritualized and resurrected death in physical cognition, described above, and the birth in fire of the etheric individuality, a fully conscious bridge is thus created. This is the bridge of the continuation of consciousness between our common physical cognition and our new etheric imaginative cognition. This spiritualized activity is the continuous, unbroken, ever wakeful, transformation of the Ego to Spirit Self and back as *one* process of mutual essence exchange. Through the mastery of the forces of etheric breathing, *we* become a perpetual metamorphosis that transforms earthly death into eternal life and individualizes eternal life through self-conscious death in the spiritual worlds. It allows us to have an unbroken, unforgettable, spiritual experience of the continuous and eternally living and productive 'I' in our ordinary consciousness, and at the same time to create self-consciousness in the purely spiritual worlds. It makes us conscious of our eternal spiritual being in daily life and it makes self-consciousness possible in spiritual life.

In my book, *The New Experience of the Supersensible*, the same process was described, from a different point of view, as a first, etheric, stage in building the bridge of the continuation of super-sensible consciousness over the abyss of spirit forgetfulness:

> When we are securely grounded in our meditation so far, we can begin the actual 'heart confrontation' with the inner ahrimanic forces dwelling in the force-dynamic of the thought process which we have worked through. This confrontation is brought about through the most intensive condensation of the freezing-cold atmosphere that emanates from the forces released in the meditation described above, extracted from a thoroughly assimilated materialistic thought dynamic. Man gathers and guides all the sub-earthly head forces, which assume in the larynx region a darkening arrow or spear form, and then — being morally and cognitively permeated with the Christ-impulse — condenses its cold spirit-like metal further still and thereby also sharpens its cutting astral edge. He thrusts it consciously into his warm, luminous heart centre until it begins to bleed etherically. Imaginatively speaking, the drops of blood freeze in bleeding and are transformed into the shining pearls and diamonds on which the bridge is constructed. When this process begins to ray itself in pictures back to the head centre — circulating backwards and upwards in the consciously transformed and thereby closed etheric circuit — it becomes imaginatively visible.
>
> In the backward radiating inner imaginative pictures we perceive now the etheric bridge of remembrance arched majestically over the abyss of time's annihilation stream, shining with pure spirit light in

the Ahrimanic night of our age. This imaginative faculty is achieved as the result of the transformation process of the world intelligence that fell into the claws of Ahriman, now returned to its source as fully humanized Michaelic intelligence. *This faculty is the Michael sword,* and the process described above is the inner work of its conscious spiritual-scientific steeling. As we saw above, its metallic substantiality was won for the Michaelic forces in the inner fight with the materialistic and intellectual Ahrimanic forces that control the modern human brain. It was then etherically transfigured and steeled in the fire of the human Christ-permeated heart. This sword is the power that serves both to perceive and to overcome Ahriman's presence in the physical-etheric subterranean world, where he unfolds his mightiest power as the guardian and lord of all elemental intellectuality that is immersed and externalized in objectivity, far from its original source in the macrocosmic heart centre.

The process described above is precisely that to which Rudolf Steiner referred in the moment when he fierily exclaimed [to his young listeners]: 'We must find the possibility to turn to our supersensible heart!' [GA 217a, 20 July, 1924]

Man thus repeats microcosmically, freely and out of his fully conscious knowledge drama of the Second Coming, Christ's macrocosmic sacrificial deed for modern humanity. Man has, consciously, killed a part of his lifetime, assimilating his death livingly into himself, mastering his death and preserving the capacity of living death preservation self-consciously intact in the stream of spirit-forgetfulness. Rudolf Steiner described this macrocosmic process, the first aspect of the Second Mystery of Golgotha, as follows:

'That which will be gradually revealed to human beings is a memory or recapitulation of what St Paul experienced at Damascus. He saw the etheric form of Christ. But that it shall be visible for us now is based on the fact that in the etheric world a new Mystery of Golgotha took place ... the Second Mystery of Golgotha taking place now in the etheric world. And through this dying, this second death of Christ [in the etheric world], it was made possible that we shall see His etheric body. *This condensation, this dead part of the etheric body of Christ Jesus human beings shall see'.* [GA 265, 8 February 1913, my italics]*

---

* *The New Experience of the Supersensible,* Chapter 5: The knowledge drama of the Second Coming; the construction of the bridge p. 100–101.

At first this newly born, etherically embodied Spirit Self, *consists* solely in the capacity to separate and isolate, kill and wound, burn to ashes and rise again. It is a being that can enact this process again and again in an eternal repetition of self-world death and resurrection as the essence of spiritual metamorphosis, which is a continuous etheric reincarnation in and through cosmic fire. This newborn being can be conscious of having an 'I' only to the extent that it repeatedly actualizes this process of etheric individuation in and through fire, in a continuous cyclic process of dying and becoming, of self-immortalizing, self-actualizing metamorphosis of the Entelechy.

At this stage we learn to experience firsthand the truth inherent in the various legends about the phoenix and the order of the phoenix. It is a fact that in the spiritual worlds we recognize our teachers, colleagues and friends in the first place because, as purely spiritual beings, they carry the etherically inscribed mark of this process of fiery death and rebirth. We strive to become like them as infants, children, and adults during our cosmic individuation. Throughout eternity they serve as our loving and curative midwives and nurses and as our spiritual teachers from kindergarten on up.

After we have completed the birth through fire and have gained the first solid basis of self-conscious cosmic individuality, we now proceed to endow it with its first, elementary faculties and forces of body and soul. It also needs 'etheric clothing' as it cannot remain wholly naked in the etheric world. The naked, freshly fire-hatched phoenix must learn how to produce its own skin, feathers, and wings. This process takes place from birth on, and it is especially intense during the first 3–4 'years' of etheric life (to use again an altogether unfitting earthly comparison) in which we also learn to 'think', 'talk', 'stand up' and condense a firm etheric body and ground as fully embodied, that is, independent, etheric individualities.

9. Early childhood of an etheric individuality

It is just as if the Christ had said: 'I will be such an ideal for you human beings that, when it is raised to a spiritual level, you will be shown that which is fulfilled in each human body [in childhood].' In his early childhood man learns from the spirit to walk, to find 'the way'; he learns to present 'truth' through his physical organism; and he learns to bring 'life' from the spirit to expression in his body. No more significant interpretation seems possible of the words 'Except ye become as little children ye cannot enter into the kingdom of heaven'. And momentous is that saying in which the ego-being of the Christ comes into expression thus, 'I am the Way, the Truth, and the Life'. Just as, unknown to a child, the higher spirit-forces ... of man, through being interpenetrated with the Christ, gradually becomes the conscious vehicle of the way, the truth, and the life. He is thereby making himself, in the course of his earthly development, into that force which bears sway within him as a child, when he is not consciously its vehicle.

(*Spiritual Guidance of Mankind*, Lecture I, GA 15)

The new-born ego may now be trained to perceive within the spiritual world. There may be developed in this ego what, for the spiritual world, has the same significance that the sense organs possess for the sensory-physical world. If this development has advanced to the necessary stage, then the human being will not only feel himself as a new-born ego, but he will now perceive spiritual facts and spiritual beings in his environment, just as he perceives the physical world through the physical senses.

(*An Outline of Occult Science*, chapter 5, 'Cognition of the Higher Worlds. Initiation')

In describing the first steps of the development of the etheric individuality, I will use an analogy taken from earthly childhood, especially in connection with the first three formative years. However, such comparisons can be misleading because we must remember that we use them to describe a purely spiritual process. The education of the Spirit Self in the etheric world is taking place through mature and spiritualized earthly self-consciousness, which is a 'spiritual baby' at the same time. We are both the baby and the parent at the same time, on two different levels, that unite and work together, as we shall describe below. So, if we say that in the early years of earthly childhood, our growth in body and soul requires the appropriate nourishment, as well as effectively imitating the example of our elders, we must not forget that in the spiritual world all these processes depend on our own spiritually free initiative. Furthermore, in each of the steps described below, such as the development of thinking, speaking, standing and walking in the etheric world, do not forget that we ourselves are setting these goals, seeking out the teachers, and we alone determine the way we learn and grow. So while we are using these earthly childhood analogies, we must transform them to represent, however inadequately, completely different conditions.

Reversed incarnation

The newborn Spirit Self is an active force and agent of creative life, steeled in cosmic fire and composed through the cosmic operations described above. It is designed and produced for actualizing creative spiritual tasks and operations in the etheric world. However, it must first grow for itself a proper individualized etheric body, and then incarnate itself consciously in this body, in order to become an independent cosmic agent. This etheric body is created out of the forces that the newborn spirit individuality will have to produce by its own creative efforts.[*]

Now it is essential to realize that our etheric embodiment (or incarnation) takes place in reversed order if we compare it with the incarnation processes of the human being in the physical world. *It proceeds from above downward.* What we described above as the birth of the 'I' in fire, is the equivalent of the child's experience of his or her first rudimentary self-consciousness around the 3rd year of life.

---

[*] The new etheric body developed through our cognitive yoga activity on the earth, through the mutual fructification between the etheric body and the etheric world, described in Chapter 7, serves as the template and scaffolding, so to speak, for this fully independent etheric body. However, this body must be built anew from substances and forces taken only from the etheric world and actualized by our free spiritual activity in the etheric world alone.

After first becoming etherically self-conscious, our next infant creative task will be to individualize cosmic thinking to fit our individual capacities, then to learn to 'speak' a new spiritual language, while also learning to properly balance ourselves and 'stand-down-right' (as opposed to standing 'upright') in the etheric world. By this we will gradually learn how to walk, which means to eventually fly more or less freely in the etheric world. Then, as it develops and absorbs the lessons of childhood, the spirit individuality will freely choose its first mature task, which is to serve as an etheric vehicle and chalice that can meet the cosmic source of life, and be fertilized by its essence in order to transport and incarnate its grace on the earth. It will become, as shall be described below in Chapter 10, an etheric avatar through which humanity's cosmic source of life can incorporate itself, and through which it will humbly carry the gifts of this source to the earth.

That is, through our self-conscious creative activity in the etheric world, cosmic thinking must be gathered and hardened etherically, in order to become embodied. The same applies to our new etheric 'language', or spiritual speaking abilities; and only then can we learn to stand 'down-right', which entails overcoming the etheric levity in the right way through an individualized etheric sense of balance. However, here again earthly analogies must confront an inherent limit, because in the etheric world we must speak about a 'fourth' year or stage of etheric embodiment, which demands that we actually learn to co-create the very substance of our etheric body as well as the forces of 'etheric gravity'. And indeed we must also co-create an 'etheric ground' on which we will 'stand', which is really more like crawling and swimming combined with primitive flying. This means that there is no given etheric air, water, or ground for us to swim-fly and stand upon in order to support our positioning and movement in the etheric world. What is more, the reversed incarnation of the etheric body is not really an incarnation in a body that is offered to us ready-made by spiritual beings and their spiritual-physical forces. For in reality, strange as it may sound to earthly ears, we must co-create the very etheric matter that will fill this body and in addition, we will also create and condense, through the use of this body, the etheric medium through which it can swim or fly, and on which it can 'stand'. It is only the well-balanced and embodied etheric individuality that can become the chalice that will be able to meet and receive the future life forces from the spiritual source of universal life, and implement them on the physical earth.

A brief comparison with physical incarnation and the embodiment of a child in the first three years will nevertheless help us in our efforts to understand the process of etheric embodiment. After birth in the physical world, the child learns, by imitating the adults around him, how to stand up and walk in the first year, speak his mother tongue in the second, and begin to think in the third, thereby experiencing the first spark of ego-consciousness. But in physical life, the baby's first lesson is to come to terms with a body that is subjected to physical gravity. It will learn to master the elementary sensory-motor bodily functions hand in hand with learning how to grapple with gravity. Eventually, by the end of the first year of its earthly life, the child will have learned how to overcome the power of gravity, reverse its position and stand up. It finds its balance in space while lifting the head (the heaviest and biggest part of the body) and the whole body upward, freeing the feet, hands, speech organs and brain to support human upright walking, speaking and thinking in the coming second and third years. This sublime feat takes place in deep cosmic-spiritual unconsciousness, in which the baby's being is still immersed in the first three years of its life. Also, in the physical world the nourishment for the child's physical body is taken from the already prepared mother's milk and then from the fruits of Mother Earth, and the soul development during the first three years takes place through an unconscious imitation of grown-up humans.

As was already mentioned above, the essential difference between the two embodiments — the physical and etheric — is that in comparison with the baby's earthly embodiment, etheric embodiment is first of all fully individual and conscious, directed by a mature human individuality in the modern age of the consciousness soul and second, it progresses in a reversed order. The reason for this is that we come from 'above', so to speak, from a self-conscious spiritual birth in the etheric world, and we incarnate downward,

seeking our etheric embodiment in an etheric body and etheric
ground and gravity. Spiritual self-consciousness comes first in the
development of the spiritual individuality in the etheric world. In
contrast, on the earth, the newborn child receives a complete physical body and must learn — unconsciously — to overcome gravity
and to balance herself between earth and heaven, long *before* she
develops thinking and speaking and clear self-consciousness. Also,
while the earthly child is guided by the physical presence of mature
humans whom he unconsciously imitates, we must say that in the
spiritual world, our teachers 'imitate' us, which means that they
only instruct us in accordance with what we have initiated ourselves first, as a free impulse of becoming. In the spiritual worlds we
must first actualize these stages of bodily and soul development
through our own self-conscious spiritual efforts. And in the physical
world, our parents provide for our needs from the substance of the
earth, but the spiritual beings who both create nature and support
the life of the parents themselves remain invisible. But in the etheric
world, these spiritual beings move to the foreground and make up
our surrounding visible 'etheric garden'. And we ourselves, as
newborn spiritual children can learn from our kindergarten care-
takers and teachers how to become more and more independent co-
workers and gardeners in this Garden of Eden, the true paradise of
earthly-cosmic creation.

Into the kinder Garden

We must, pictorially speaking, first learn to 'crawl' to the cosmic
fields nearest to our place of birth in our new cosmic home. We have
to gather, process and consume some of its spiritual fruits, in order
to learn how to nourish ourselves in this new world. There we
wander breathtaken among the mighty everlasting trees with
magnificent flowers and fruits of eternal life and bountiful
meadows that flourish with indescribable radiant beauty and grace.
All creation freely offers its abundant life and fruitfulness in the
etheric world. But what we soon discover causes the greatest surprise and wonder of all: that everything we see, hear, touch, taste

and smell, is actually the spiritualized result of humanity's truthful creative productions on the earth in the sciences and philosophy, and in the arts, religions and moral-social life, from immemorial times. We realize that we enter the garden of spiritual earthly accomplishments, which the cosmic gardeners, the angels, tend and cultivate with infinite devotion, joy, love, and expertise. It is the first etheric land we enter and it is also the nearest garden to our place of spiritual birth and the spiritual region closest to the physical earth. As a matter of fact, we discover that we spiritually die and become right here, which means that we are born, etherically speaking, in the midst of this truly spiritual 'Garden of Eden'. 'Everything unfinished is here perfected' as Faust finds out when he arrives here after his death. Here we understand the consequences of our loving interest or cold indifference to humanity's truthful creations, because the love we invested in human creativity on the earth, becomes here the power to harvest and nourish ourselves by the cosmic fruits of this creativity.

This 'etheric milk' is the first vital nourishment for the infant Spirit Self in this vibrant spiritual garden made by humanity. And Faust's last recorded experience, 'the eternal feminine draws us on', becomes our first experience when we take our first baby steps in this etheric world. And this world is indeed 'feminine' in the sense that it is so abundantly angelic, that is, self-giving, nourishing and mothering, and this means that all newborn etheric individualities find here all they need in order to feed, process and sustain their new etheric life. This mothering process also allows the etheric individuality a time of healing after the above described travails of etheric death and rebirth. It can be most lovingly nourished and tended, as it grows its baby body and develops its infant spiritualized soul forces out of this lovingly spiritualized stream of human-cosmic curative nourishment.

What comes to life in the garden, flourishing with infinite cosmic beauty and truth, are not the finished works as we know them on earth. Rather we find everything that remained potential, young, flexible, and unfinished, even within the most 'perfect' earthly paintings, compositions, ideas and deeds. In fact, all of the unrealized life forces and youthful ideals of the living and the dead of all times and ages are abundantly sprouting here. Our bodily etheric organs, tissues and limbs are formed in the etheric world by means of spiritualized earthly creations and potentials. Each and every 'cell' of the etheric body in which the spiritual individuality is embodying itself is created through the human love of truth, beauty and goodness. All truly moral ideals and moral deeds, streaming from earthly human lives, flourish here with infinite spiritual splendour. Each good deed on the earth sends a stream of etherized and released life forces into the etheric world, and we learn to embody them as our own new etheric bodies (and later astral and spiritual bodies as well). Conversely, our work up there sends back new and enriched life potentials and seeds to those working on the earth, so that there is a perpetual life cycle circulating between the earth and the spiritual worlds, concerning which only very few incarnated humans are aware today.

Indeed, Paradise is that part of the etheric world where all truthful, fruit bearing earthly-human accomplishments grow and prosper. Only when we enter the garden and consciously experience the fruits of resurrected earthly life, do we begin to surmise the deeper meaning of human evolution and becoming for the whole spiritual universe.

Our infant spiritual development in the garden takes place, so to speak, in four locations:

Because humans are thinking truthful and idealistic thoughts, permeated by devotion to truth, the Spirit Self can develop its elementary cosmic thinking. In this location it learns how to individualize and embody cosmic thinking using the spiritualized earthly fruits of science and philosophy.

Because humans devote themselves to true beauty and have created works of art and all other creations of beauty in the physical world, the Spirit Self can develop the first rudiments of an individualized spiritual language. In this location we learn how to individualize and embody cosmic language as the result of the spiritualized creations of earthly art and beauty.

Because humans devote themselves with religious reverence to divine revelations, ceremonies and sacraments, the Spirit Self is able to learn to overcome the outward and upward pull of etheric levity to stand morally 'downright' (pictorially speaking, a reversed physical uprightness), and develop the ability to 'walk' (really to fly), achieving a true moral balance between levity and gravity in the etheric world. In this location we learn how to individualize the fruits of earthly religious life and actualize cosmic down-rightness and movement through its forces.

And because humans accomplish deeds of goodness, compassion and love to other humans and to the beings of nature, the Spirit Self is able to *produce* the very spiritual-moral substance and forces of 'etheric-moral gravity' in the etheric world. Thanks to the forces of spiritualized human deeds of love, it can build the solid moral-etheric ground under its 'feet' and condense the etheric atmosphere, or etheric 'air', 'water' and 'earth' needed for unfolding and using its individual etheric body, limbs and wings. In this location we learn how to individualize and embody the productive forces of etheric substance and ground, which sprout and flourish in the etheric world as the fruits of human morality.

Let us briefly describe some concrete aspects from this development during the first 'four years' of etheric life.

First year: learning cosmic thinking

In the centre of the evergreen gardens and forests of spiritualized earthly thinking, there grows and prospers a gigantic earthly-cosmic tree, the mighty world Oak or Ash. This is the Archetypal Tree of Life which in the Garden of Eden is one with the Tree of Knowledge. It is the spiritualized revelation of all truthful human thinking on the earth. Plato's tree of ancient life and Aristotle's tree of future knowledge are eternally one in the Garden, through the spiritualized, cosmic, results of *The Philosophy of Freedom*. Rudolf Steiner's work on the earth appears here also as the force that re-unites for the first time the two trees that were separated in the human being after the luciferic intervention and the outcast from Paradise. Now the two are merged into one eternal Tree of Life, rooted in the earth and bearing the most spiritual fruits in the heavens. We must understand that any foundational spiritual achievement of the great initiates of humanity becomes available in the spiritual world to all humans that walk loyally in their path. Rudolf Steiner's foundational deed, in conceiving and implementing *The Philosophy of Freedom* in the 90s of the nineteenth century, has become part of his eternally preserved etheric body which—united since the middle of the century with Christ's etheric forces—has become fully active and accessible a century later, since the 90s of the twentieth century. Therefore, when one ascends since the 90s of the last century to the etheric world through *The Philosophy of Freedom* and its intensification through the cognitive yoga breathing, one can experience how the two trees that became separated in Plato and Aristotle, become one again, through which all the great achievements of human thinking and science in the last 2500 years are gathered and spiritualized. (Rudolf Steiner demonstrated the essence of this gathering and spiritualization in his book, *The Riddles of Philosophy.*) But this is so only because the Christ forces flowing through *The Philosophy of Freedom* make all trees one again, as they were always preserved in their pristine unity in Paradise (in the pure etheric world), but outside of earthly human consciousness. Now for the first time they have become one in and through earthly self-conscious human creation. And in this spiritual scientific tree, knowledge *is* life, and life *is* knowledge, because Christ *is* this divine eternal tree. This etheric tree of self-renewing and self-metamorphosing life is also the one primeval tree of all creation, resurrected for the new cosmic age of light. Call it the Nordic Yggdrasil, or the Sephiroth tree, or whatever the name given to it in ancient traditions, it is rooted in the earth and flowering and producing magnificent fruits in the etheric world. And its fruits of life/knowledge can be accessed and processed through spiritual scientific activity and practice in the etheric world described here. These spiritualized fruits of Rudolf Steiner's epoch-making achievement become the seed of our own infant cosmic thinking, developed by the Spirit Self after it has consolidated its eternal spiritual 'I' through the fire of death and rebirth in the etheric world. Spirit Self can now begin to think cosmically in the etheric world, because it can eat, assimilate and use the richest fruits from the tree of creation, of life/knowledge, of the past, present and future evolution.*

Second year: learning cosmic language

We must use physical comparisons to describe, ever so remotely, the process through which cosmic self-consciousness, thinking, language, downrightness, movement and embodiment are actualized during the first stages of development of our spiritual infant life in the etheric world. When the harvest of the garden of spiritualized human creations is gathered, some of the flowers and fruits are consumed fresh and vibrant, as immediate nourishment, while others have to be dried and drained of their juicy cosmic stuff in order to extract their concentrated spiritual essences. The vital spiritual essences of each etheric leaf, flower and fruit, expressing a certain cosmically expanded and enriched earthly human creation, can be extracted, made into a condensed crystal, seed-like potency. This process must be added volitionally to what is happening naturally in the etheric world. Here everything earthly is infinitely expanded and enriched, and we can consume this already prepared etheric milk as our immediate etheric nourishment. But at the same time we may choose to be taught by our angelic teachers how to do what they do, to individuate it and use it in order to grow up and mature much faster. We learn indeed the whole art of spiritual cosmic-etheric biodynamic husbandry and agriculture. We can only offer single details from this sublime angelic practical spiritual art. For example, we have to learn how to transform and penetrate to the essence of a fruit of human creation on the earth. We learn to separate it from its unessential earthly envelopes and spiritualize its spiritual potential kernel. Only when we demonstrate the capacity to carefully and precisely separate the vital potential spiritual kernel

---

* I have demonstrated some aspects of this process applied to the thinking of the 2nd half of the twentieth century in my Colmar lecture: 'Anthroposophy and Contemporary Philosophy in Dialogue', published in my book: *Spiritual Science in the 21st Century*, and in the 3rd chapter, 'The Event in Philosophy', in my book, *The Event in Science, History, Philosophy & Art*.

from its more external earthly husks, can this fruit nourish the next stages of etheric development and maturity.

We discover during this work, often to our shame, precisely to what extent our interest in human life and creation is feeble and fleeting. We realize now that it is not at all about 'having an experience' of, say, Leonardo's *Last Supper* that counts (and even less so 'knowing' much about it), but only how deeply we have penetrated into its invisible core and essence, through our self-forgetting love and devotion and cognitive activity. Only what was truly firing our cognitive, aesthetic and moral activity on the earth is active and fruitful in us now. This painting, if taken together with its complementary companion, Raphael's *Sistine Madonna*, is one potent earthly-cosmic source of nourishment, body-building and language-forming activity. It seems as if it was produced specially to teach us the spiritual language and speaking capacity as newborn etheric individualities, because it radiates an intense aura of phoenix-like forces. What we achieved above, through all the stages of cognitive yoga work on the earth in connection with the trans-formation of the forces of birth and death, is now infinitely enhanced, through the etheric experience of the spiritualized fruits of these works of art (and you must imagine that in the etheric garden, *all* truthful works of the human arts through all ages and cultures are growing and thriving together). They are experienced as creative and formative, world creating and shaping forces that teach us our 'etheric mother tongue'. Their etherized spiritual potencies not only flow as life-giving nourishment into our newborn etheric bodies, but teach us how to individualize, hear and speak the local spiritual language. But how can we form a reasonable concept about this new spiritual language? What are the elementary forces of this language? How is it formed in the first and lowest super-sensible world and life?

The formative forces of this language are extracted when earthly death becomes cosmic life through the spiritualization of the potential earthly forces invested in the *Last Supper*. Through these forces the Christ united on earth with death (Judas's ahrimanic deed) and made death into a fountain of new life, transforming forever its innermost essence. The real accomplishment of Leonardo contains infinitely more spiritual potential than the actual physical painting reveals. These potentials flourish in the etheric world, and if we learn to cultivate and harvest them, we learn to speak the language of this world. And the forces of immaculate birth, the gate of the pure cosmic forces streaming into the earth, that death cannot touch, grow in us through processing the fruits of Raphael's *Madonna*. And this twofold stream that weaves earthly death and cosmic life with and through each other becomes an earthly-cosmic articulation that 'speaks' spiritually and teaches the vocabulary, grammar and syntax of this new language. Formative etheric forces invested through truthful love of beauty in earthly works of art, and spiritualized in the spiritual worlds, are the same forces that, on the one hand, are transformed into our new etheric bodily organs and limbs and, on the other, inform our individualized language and speaking. Language is bodily formative here, and hearing and speaking build etheric bodies and worlds. Speaking is also connected to the power of locomotion and movement (together with the already individualized capacity of thinking), through the essential unity of organ and limb formation, speech formation and movement. We 'speak ourselves and our world into being and becoming'. We can also say that learning to 'hear' spiritually means that we learn to harvest the extracted and spiritualized artistic forces, and we learn to 'speak' spiritually when, through hearing this language, we unite ourselves with it and begin to form and articulate ourselves and our immediate environment through its formative forces. In the etheric world to 'hear' and 'speak' means to be wholly permeated and transformed through spiritualized works of human art. Keeping to the example of the *Last Supper* and *Madonna*, we can say that we learn how to grow two 'wings' as our new etheric hearing-speaking-spoken limbs and movements. For when we 'hear' the forces extracted from the earthly painting, and 'speak out' (that is, to articulate and form the relevant etheric streams) the assimilated formative word movements, one wing will be formed that will lead us to eternal cosmic life through earthly death (the *Last Supper* Word stream). A second wing will be formed when we 'hear and speak' into etheric existence another eternal life stream which can be directed to flow back to the earth and help its etherisation processes (the *Madonna* Word stream), where birth will cease to be a death of cosmic life, but a continuation of eternal life in and through earthly embodiment.

Therefore, when the kernel of a spiritualized work of art becomes accessible as a vital stream of body-building and shaping nourishment, hearing, speaking and movement, we experience the bliss of learning, growing and becoming more fully human in the spiritual universe, because we begin to hear and speak the cosmic mother tongue and articulate our experiences through cosmic language. But as long as we have not achieved this, we suffer a kind of Tantalus' fate, reaching out to the sweetest fruits of the garden without being able to grasp and enjoy them. The sincerer, long lasting and intense our interest in human creativity on the earth, the more we can partake in its living etherized core and actualize this body and limb building as a formative language and speaking process, in fuller spiritual consciousness. And only through understanding and seeking the appropriate spiritual language do we grow inwardly to become one with the spiritual world.

In the limits of the present study, we can only indicate briefly the actual practical craft of assimilating, processing and producing this spiritual language in the etheric world. To do so we must continue to use physically derived images and words to describe it, because on the earth we don't yet possess the appropriate spiritual language. The practical work is accomplished when we learn how to penetrate to the artistic work's spiritual essence or seed, analyse its components, separate its etheric-force filaments and single them out. What otherwise takes place unconsciously in our digestive and growth processes in the physical body, transpires here consciously. To build consciously an etheric body means to build a living 'word body', a formation of spiritual language, based on hearing, assimilating, processing, and articulating, an individual body-word-language through our formative speech.

For example, each of the 12 disciples in the *Last Supper* constitutes a unique formative spiritual filament in the whole spiritual potential composition of the spiritual language we learn. In the above described process, we learn how to differentiate between them, assimilate each one of them, take them apart and put them together in ever varying combinations, and through this we come to know and use ever new aspects and constellations of this spiritual language. The *Last Supper* together with the *Madonna*, becomes our living, animated, language partiture, audio-visually articulated. Cosmically speaking, the more we can hear and speak this spiritual language, the closer we can come to deciphering and articulating the spiritual beings of the sun, planets and the 12 constellations of the zodiac, and their infinitely diverse spiritual connections to the earth.

All this of course will take us from the etheric 'kindergarten' to the etheric 'elementary school' in the etheric world, as we also learn to 'read and write' spiritually by individualizing the single spiritual 'concepts' (here concepts are streams of formative etheric forces) and the cosmic Sun Word or Logos, out of which the 'vowels' and 'consonants' are formed. These elements of the cosmic script are visible as our firmament now: the starry radiations filled with love and beauty are themselves the results of what humans have created through all ages consciously or unconsciously on earth in their creative thoughts, arts, religious sacraments and moral deeds. We must however learn to extract them ourselves if we are to learn to think and speak spiritually, to master this language in order to use it, as mature etheric beings, to co-create a new world with our spiritual teachers and colleagues.

All art on earth is transformed into our new spiritual language in the first supersensible world into which we enter. But as we emphasized above, this language and speaking ability must be actively created as are all other capacities in the supersensible world and existence. Nothing — absolutely nothing — is simply 'given' ready-made awaiting our passive imitation and handling of it. The spiritualized potencies extracted from all human creative works, constitute an operative and functional growing stream of nourishing forces that, once assimilated and properly digested, build our etheric body, limbs and empower the ability to think, speak and fly. To individualize cosmic thinking and then language means to create ourselves, our bodies, our soul faculties, again and again, continuously, and enhance our spiritual creativity as we grow more and more mature as etherically embodied spirit individualities in the etheric world. Therefore, increasingly, we join the work of our spiritual teachers, to the extent that we are ripe for this task, in the sublime art of cosmic creation. We learn to extract, combine and fuse as many of the extracted etheric potencies and forces that flow from the earth upwards through artistic human creations. The super-sensible world would have remained eternally silent *for us*, and we would have remained deaf, mute and wordless, if humans would have never created their works of art and beauty on earth through the millennia.

Third year: embodying cosmic down-rightness

At the same time, it is not only the forces extracted from the earthly sciences, philosophy and the arts that become formative etheric forces. For the more substantial body and limb formation, on the one hand, and the ability to descend, stand and walk downright, we need to extract forces that come from the spiritualized fruits of all truthfully devoted religious life, prayers, rituals and sacraments. What on earth strives ardently towards the ethereal heights becomes here the most substantial etheric body-building power. In the etheric world you learn to weave and substantiate a body that is growing, as it were, from above downwards. You weave a body by the same etheric activity that you use to learn how to 'stand down' and walk when you find the etheric sense of balance. As you resist the one-sided cosmic forces of infinite lightness and levity and remain true to the earth, you substantiate a body with the spiri-tualized forces streaming out from the earth as the fruits of religious devotion to God. In the earthly sacrament the formative forces of wine and bread (the forces that condense the physical and etheric kingdoms of nature and our bodies out of the spiritual), are spiri-tualized again; and the spiritualized fruits of all transubstantiations become in the spiritual worlds the forces that let us substantiate and condense sustainable etheric matter, body and life. Transubstan-tiation on earth becomes Etheric-Substantiation in the etheric world. Precisely because these forces were first materialized and then transubstantiated on the earth, their spiritualized etheric extracts have such a powerful spiritual force of etheric substantiation. The spiritual fruits of the earthly sacrament allow our growing etheric body to be filled with robust etheric substance and to be embodied down-right, to achieve the right moral balance between the infinite etheric levity that would estrange us from our earthly life and mission, and the ahrimanic death forces of earthly gravity. The moral balance that we need must first be produced and condensed as solid etheric counterweight to Lucifer and counter light to Ahriman. And only the spiritualized formative forces, extracted from all truthful religious life on the earth, potentized by means of the earthly sacrament, allow us to accomplish this in the etheric world.

The phoenix's new feathers

While the spiritual fruits of religious life are indispensable for etheric substantiation and balance, locomotion and flight, they are also the source of the etheric creations of the wings themselves. Wings are truly one of the most remarkable world creations in the physical world and yet they cannot begin to be compared with their spiritual archetypes. All the extracted and transformed fruits and seeds of human creativity not only in religion, but also in the sciences, arts and moral-social life are purified, refined and gathered together in this marvelous divine creation. Here the finest fruits of human creativity on the earth, spiritualized and infinitely enhanced by the gods, become the most purified and refined formative forces. These finest etheric forces substantiate and shape the etheric wing and feathers and the nascent spiritual plumage that begins to cover our still largely naked etheric individuality and form, gradually hardening the budding wings to support their unfolding.

Again, earthly comparisons and pictures that represent sensory things are inadequate to represent even remotely these 'wings'. Earthly wings are indeed highly sensitive and wisdom-filled organs of flight, and in this respect they are somewhat reminiscent of spiritual 'wings'. But spiritual wings serve other functions as well beside flight. We will understand this better if we visit again the workshop in which, especially in the reversed '3rd year', our individual etheric body is formed in the etheric world. And this is the fundamental difference between the body and soul faculties in the physical and etheric world. What is separated and distributed in the physical body between different organs and functions, flows together, in and through each other in the etheric world and in the independent etheric body. For example, we discover that in the etheric world, hearing and speaking and the articulated words are also truly 'wings' — indeed, 'hearing', 'speaking', 'seeing' and 'flying' flow together through one and the same bodily organ and functional operation. Furthermore, you *become*, bodily speaking, exactly what your speaking and hearing means. Every experience is a bodily formative power here. Therefore, both hearing and speaking shape your whole body and being, since the etheric body assumes a form corresponding to what the soul is experiencing. When you hear and speak, you become what you 'mean' and what you are 'meant' and you become what you see and intend. At the same time, you see, touch, taste, and smell your becoming and you fly on the wings of the words that are spoken or heard. Now also what we mean by 'flying' here is difficult to imagine, because spiritually speaking, you don't fly to 'where' you want to fly to, like travelling from your present location to your chosen destination in physical space. Instead you fly 'to' *what you become*, and this 'what' is the 'where', because what you are becoming *is* your flight and your destination, and you come to what/where you become, what you hear, speak, see and desire. And this is also the reason why these wings are truly 'full of eyes' as the scripture rightly says.[*] We know this fact now because we partake consciously in the making of these wonderful organs. Because each spiritual seed-crystal (extracted from the fruits in the garden of earthly-cosmic creation), is composed of varied and multiple etheric strands, woven and combined from countless human creations, spiritual wings can also be compared to a 'composite fly's eye' (and also ears and other senses), adapted for a multiplicity of active, operative cosmic vision. Each

---

[*] Ezekiel 1:18; 10:13; Revelation 4:6; 4:8.

combined extract of human creations is a budding, germinating sensory and motor organ in the etheric body. Larynx, ears, eyes, and wings compose one extended etheric-spiritual organ in which hearing-speaking, seeing, sensing, perceiving, are one and the same function as locomotion (flight). These are remarkable composite 'eyed-eared-larynxed wings'. By means of these 'magical wings' we learn to stand up (that is, stand down), move around and eventually fly with balance in the etheric and spiritual worlds. So to 'speak' is to activate bodily self-transformation, vision and flight at the same time, and to 'see' something is to become that thing and then you 'fly toward this thing' but the 'place' you arrive at is the present stage of your etheric becoming.

The more we learn how to compose our bodies and develop our spiritual faculties of thinking, speaking and moving in the etheric world from the spiritualized fruits of human creation on the earth, the more mature and free we become in the spiritual worlds.

Fourth year: producing moral gravity and ground

In a world of absolute anti-gravity and infinite acceleration of light and levity, generated by the etheric-cosmic forces flowing from the etheric sun (to which, as was mentioned above, the un-Christened etheric body feels irresistible attraction), everything depends on consciously developing the force of etheric gravity, because it is nowhere given. On the earth we are weighed down by physical gravity and tied to our bodies through their physical mass attracted by the whole physical body of the earth. In the etheric world, we are given one-sidedly to the infinite levitational attraction of the cosmic etheric forces of light. This is the reason why more or less three days after death the human etheric body expands and dissolves in the whole etheric universe. But in properly undertaken spiritual scientific development, we want to be able to create and maintain, actively, a balanced and poised position in the etheric world, without being involuntarily dispersed and assimilated by the forces of this world. But in the etheric world the only force that can create gravity is the spiritual essence of what on earth is true morality.

Moral gravity is absolutely needed as a basis for balanced down-rightness and walking-flying in the etheric fields irradiated by intensely dispersing and expanding cosmic light. This levity, necessary and beneficial as the force that leads us upward through the spiritual worlds in the life between death and rebirth, is extra-ordinarily tempting when we enter this world voluntarily and must rely solely on our individual capacity to form and condense forces of moral balance. There is no moment, nay second, out there in which the temptation is not strongly felt, to abandon oneself to the infinite bliss of merging with the streams of cosmic light and to forget all about the hardships and challenges of modern earthly life. That is, we must find the moral forces to create and ground etheric moral 'matter', 'earth' and 'heaviness', to form a basis from which we will be able to return to the physical earth in a healthy way. As was shown above, we could overcome the materializing, intellec-tualizing, brain-binding ahrimanic death forces in the physical world through the moral forces motivating the cognitive yoga practice. This allowed us to enter in full consciousness into the etheric world. And if we want to be properly embodied in the etheric world as truly balanced etherically embodied spirit indi-vidualities, and also re-enter physical and social life on the earth in the right way, we must gain the necessary moral weight to counteract again and again the Luciferic forces in the etheric world.

But what is 'gravity' in the etheric world of infinite levity, and how it is produced? Above (in Chapter 8) we described the steeling process of an independent Spirit Self through voluntarily actualized etheric death and becoming in the etheric world. Now, in order to understand what is involved in an etheric embodiment and the creation of the moral gravity and ground needed for this embodi-ment, we will have to search and find the needed nourishment and teaching for this task. Only in the etheric garden of all truthful human creative accomplishments can we find the forces we need. These forces grow, flourish and give forth the most nourishing fruit through the spiritualized results of humanity's moral accomplish-ments.

There, in the middle of the garden, stands the sun temple of the earth and humanity and in the middle of the temple the holy of holies as its innermost spiritual core. Here we find the spiritualized flowers, fruits and seeds of all truthfully motivated deeds of love, compassion and sacrifice through the ages. The spiritualized essence of all these deeds is also contained and preserved in the purest extracts of human etheric bodies, planted and fostered in the garden. These are wonderfully shining, immortalized, fruits and seeds of love and new life left here by the passing human souls after death that have individualized Christ's life and love during the last 2000 years and made his life a permanent part of their individual life bodies.* They are gathered and enhanced and developed further by the higher hierarchies in the earthly-sun temple. And we will need these forces for substantiating our etheric body, condensing the forces of its embodiment and consolidating the moral-etheric ground in which it can be embodied and embedded. This ground can only be created as part of the 'earthly-human sun' sphere in and around the earth. Only there can conscious etheric embodiment take place in our time.

And there, searching for the power needed to create an individualized 'piece of land' that will serve as the suitable moral ground for our etheric embodiment, we search, in the middle of this earthly-human sun temple, for its pulsating spiritual heart. This is the place in which the most precious moral accomplishments of humanity through the ages are cultivated and spiritualized. This is one of the main tasks of all the beings, human and angelic, that participate actively in the work in the supersensible Michael school since the middle of the twentieth century.[†]

To this place we are led in the search for the suitable nourishment and substantiation of an independent etheric body for our Spirit Self and to create the suitable ground for this embodiment in the etheric world. Only there can we co-produce and co-substantiate the

---

*See Rudolf Steiner's description of this process above in Chapter 1, regarding the Christ permeated 'etheric ring' around the earth.

[†] I described this decisive planetary, cosmic spiritual Event of humanity and the earth as a whole, which began during the founding 12 years, 1933–1945, in my book, *The Spiritual Event of the 20th Century*. I could research this event after completing the spiritual-scientific individuation of the meeting with the etheric Christ described in my book, *The New Event of the Supersensible*.

needed moral gravity and substance. This work is accomplished together with our human colleagues that work there in their life between death and rebirth and the high Michaelic beings under the direct guidance of Michael himself, around the being of the Christ in his etheric appearance. And the work consists in this: the participants capable of this conscious sacrifice, descend from the etheric heavens of the earth, into the core of modern human evil, produced during the last century. In our time only very few human souls can participate in this divine Michaelic, sacred work of redemption. They must be so strong and dedicated, to breathe this most radical human evil in, and bring it as their individualized wound to the altar found in the holy of holies of the earthly-sun temple. There a perpetual ritual is enacted, of purification, redemption and spiritualization of evil into a future potential of the highest good. Here, through human deeds of greatest love and sacrifice we find the centre of etheric moral gravity, the centre of the new human-cosmic creation, called the 'earthly-human sun' germinating in the etheric world of the earth since 1933–1945. This substance becomes the seed that draws around it the moral-spiritual forces and materials that fill and form the consciously individualized etheric body. And in and through this body these life forces substantiate and condense the new etheric earth, ground and soil. We already walk today, unknowingly, on an etheric earth founded on this love, becoming the seed of a new cosmos of love. On this foundation the new etheric body of humanity and the earth — the earthly-sun temple — is built in our age. In this temple, each human deed of love becomes a cornerstone and part of the power that erects morally balanced etheric ground and pillars, above which gradually the dome of the temple in the centre of the new earthly-sun, the New Jerusalem, begins to be securely arched.

In my book, *The Spiritual Event of the 20th Century*, I described a decisive moment in this process as follows:

> Now at the very moment when this truth [about the split of humanity and the earth in two wholly opposite parts] was perceived above [in the etheric world], a new embryonic heart organ for the future unity of divided humanity had to be created. It was now the task of the

Michael school, by making the destiny of divided humanity into its own destiny, to shape this future embryonic heart centre of humanity out of its own life-substance. An etheric heart organ of the future Michael-Christ humanity was now created, in place of the ancient, dying heart organ, prefiguring for all ages to come the higher unity of humanity, through which evil shall gradually be transformed into the highest good. And this new embryonic heart, stretching from above downward, bridged the abyss between the two separated parts of humanity and the Earth. What humanity failed to achieve through conscious anthroposophical work on the Earth in the first third of the twentieth century was now prefigured spiritually in the etheric world *after* the great apocalyptic division of humanity and the Earth. And only when this new bridging heart organ was Michaelically established could the Christ Himself join the work of redemption with His renewed sacrifice.

Then the Michael pupils could see how, out of the innermost core of the temple of the Earthly-Human Sun, a Being comes forth, no longer only an embryo of future evolution. Nurtured and matured through human acts of sacrifice, He made His way from the heights of His Revelation downward, crossing the Michael bridge from Heaven to Hell. As his pathway He used the etherized bloodstreams that ascended, spiritualized in the new heart centre of humanity, from the evil abyss below. They could follow Him with their spirit gaze. He descended ever deeper, until He merged Himself completely with the evil being of humanity in the abyss, blending His downpouring life, soul and spirit forces with that being. In their upward striving sacrifice, carrying to Him the etherized pain of the nations of the world, they beheld Him sinking ever deeper into the core of burning human evil, uniting Himself with it and dying livingly into the densest point of its being. They witnessed thus the culmination of the second Mystery of Golgotha at the moment of its happening.*

In the fully conscious participation in this perpetual human-divine sacrament through which evil is assimilated by the spiritual forces that guide and protect humanity, culminates the fourth stage of our etheric childhood in the etheric world. It gives us the forces of spiritual maturity, by means of which we can gradually learn, in the

---

* *The Spiritual Event of the 20th Century – an Imagination*, Temple Lodge, London, 1996, Chapter 3: 'The Imagination of the century's event', p. 42–43.

next stages, how to turn our adult, individualized etheric being to the earthly-human sun being. This is the universal, cosmic heart and source of all our human, planetary and cosmic existence. We have already drawn near to its presence and now we may prepare ourselves to approach the source as mature and independent human beings in the universe. And all the real spiritual schooling in the etheric world (be it consciously during physical life, as described here, or after death for the prepared souls) is directed above all to this sacred goal: to meet face to face, unite with and also individualize the Higher Self of humanity and the earth, the infinite love- and light-giving, Christ being. This is our etheric ritual of maturity, our acceptance to the Michaelic supersensible community as mature, self-conscious spiritual beings. As such beings we can re-enter our physical bodies and daily consciousness and tasks and implement the life forces received from the universal source of all life. Back in our human life on the earth, we will search for a suitable place and a path, knowing ourselves as the humblest beginners in the gradual and demanding becoming of our true humanity on the earth. This process—insofar as it can be described at all in ordinary human words today—will be indicated in the final chapter.

10. Essence exchange with the Cosmic Source

Might it not then also be possible today that something of infinite importance is taking place and that human beings are not taking it into their consciousness? Could it not be that something tremendously important is taking place in the world, taking place right now, of which our own contemporaries have no presentiment? This is indeed so. Something highly important is taking place that is perceptible, however, only to spiritual vision.

We thus comprehend spiritual science in a completely different sense. We learn that it imposes a tremendous responsibility upon us, since it is a preparation for the concrete occurrence of the reappearance of Christ. Christ will reappear because human beings will be raising themselves toward Him in etheric vision. When we grasp this, spiritual science appears to us as the preparation of human beings for the return of Christ, so that they will not have the misfortune to overlook this great event but will be ripe to seize the great moment that we may describe as the second coming of Christ. Man will be capable of seeing etheric bodies, and among these etheric bodies he will also be able to see the etheric body of Christ; that is, he will grow into a world in which the Christ will be visible to his newly awakened faculties.

Let us use spiritual science so that it may serve not merely to satisfy our curiosity but in such a way that it will prepare us for the great tasks, the great missions of the human race for which we must grow ever more mature.

(25 January, 1910, GA 118)

When the Spirit Self is fully embodied in an independent etheric body, developed the phoenix-like spiritual self-consciousness, and learned to 'think', 'speak', and 'stand-down' and move more or less freely in the etheric world, it can experience itself as a mature individuality in the etheric world. And when this four staged elementary education is complete, the etheric individuality, like a plant whose spiritual roots are rooted in the spiritual worlds above, can begin to grow its stem and branches and unfold its leaves and flower downward towards the warmth, light and life-giving earthly-human sun. While earthly plants grow upward towards the external sunlight, in the etheric world the human souls, who remain loyal to the true meaning of earthly evolution, grow towards the middle of the earthly-human sun. In its pulsating middle sphere they perceive the newborn, vibrant, Christ permeated etherized earth and its circling, breathing, etheric atmosphere and planetary etheric ring. The more we grow into this spiritual reality and the more we feel ourselves to be human co-creators of this new earthly-human sun, the more we feel also that the search for its pulsating middle is at the same time the search for our own human-spiritual sun being and becoming. Humanity's Higher Self is our most individual as well as universally shared Higher Self. It is the sun and light through which our lower, that is, our earthly grown self, is growing, thriving and maturing. And when we search for its most spiritual core we are searching at the same time deeper into our own spiritualized hearts. There we find the source of etheric light, love and life, from which the new earth and the new heaven receive their cosmic sustenance and substance. And our young cosmic wings of becoming, thinking-speaking-hearing and seeing, carry us gradually downwards towards the middle of the already clearly sensed pulsating life source of the new earthly-human sun seed, the germinating seed of a new universe.

This source is after all the primordial, original spiritual source of all human cognitive, aesthetic, and moral creativity on the earth, and its spiritualized and ennobled fruits point us in its direction. Let us be reminded that our newly formed etheric body is embodied and substantiated through humanity's deeds of love and sacrifice. This body becomes a spiritual body of evolutionary and historical conscience; it remembers the plight of the earth and humanity, keeps the moral pathway open, and secures the bridge that leads back and forth between the earthly-human sun and the physical and sub-physical life on the earth. This is the breathing, rhythmic inhalation and exhalation process that constitutes the life circulation connecting the earth and heaven of the earthly-human sun, the future heavenly Jerusalem.

The historical time of decision and crisis is well underway, and during the next 2500 years (until the middle of the 6th cultural epoch) a small but selflessly dedicated group of people will learn to co-create this bridge and draw near to its source, which indeed, is our own innermost Spirit Self, Christ's being and becoming through

humanity. And our becoming will speak and see, hear and articulate, orienting our flight along the meridians drawn by the intensities of the earthly-human sun. All true Christ-permeated life-
streams will increasingly gather around the 'I AM', the alpha and
omega of earthly-cosmic convergence, and merge with the vibrating, rhythmically circulating and pulsating sun becoming of
humanity and earth.

Mutual Essence Exchange

This event is the most intimate soul experience in the etheric world,
and we would have naturally shied away from any wish to describe
it in ordinary language. We do it only because we were convinced
that it is the expressed wish of the source being itself, that this
experience should be shared publicly in our time to awaken as
many people as possible. This is the sole reason for its communication in such an imperfect form and medium, and it is trusted to
the reader in this spirit.

Our etherically embodied spiritual individuality carries the purest
extract of the whole cognitive yoga process described above as it
approaches this source. It feels itself to be a humble emissary of the
whole earth and humanity. It is embodied in the etheric 'flesh and
blood' substantiated by the earthly fruits of humanity's truthful
creation and deeply marked by humanity's and the earth's spiritualized wounds. One comes to offer the spiritual fruits of the earth to
the source from which they originally came, to fulfil and enhance the
circle of spiritual receiving and giving. However, approaching the
source and middle of the earthly-human sun in this way, we realize
that the most essential characteristic of this meeting — this cannot be
described otherwise — is that it becomes a *mutual* meeting. Lacking a
better terminology, the only concept that can be used is once more
'mutual essence exchange' (which was used above to describe the
essence of the cognitive yoga's etheric breathing). It turns out that
this meeting is really mutual, contrary to what may be the common
earthly representation of such meeting. If we would have described
this meeting to the unprepared modern person, he would in all

probability be greatly surprised both in regard to what we give and to what we receive in this exchange. First, he would be surprised by the fact that the human contribution is accepted with such festivity and joy by the cosmic source. This really far exceeds his ordinary estimations of its objective value. And his second surprise would be that in face of his expectations from the divine source of infinite divine might, beauty and wisdom, the gift that we receive will appear to him rather insignificant. But inwardly, in reality, the true spiritual meaning of this meeting far exceeds anything we could have imagined, provided that we approach in the right way.

Indeed, one must say that it infinitely confirms and enhances everything experienced above concerning the meaning of individuation and the importance of the contribution of the earthly and human stream of evolution in the cosmos. Through this meeting we become finally reassured that though our human efforts are, cosmically and quantitatively compared, humble indeed, they carry with them something else, whose intrinsic cosmic value doesn't exhaust itself in such external cosmic comparisons.

When we approach the source of all our human and spiritual striving, we bring as an offer all our best human achievements, everything that we improved and developed in our thinking, feeling and deeds, everything we spiritualized from our daily, social and spiritual experiences on the earth and in the etheric world. We bring ourselves as a whole, as what we are becoming through our earthly evolution. And we say to the Higher Self of the earth and humanity, the Christ, 'I have accomplished all this thanks to your forces in me. It is truly not "I" as "I" would exist without you, that offers you these fruits, but everything is yours—your activity, your productivity, your love and grace, that I was allowed to actualize in my earthly life'. And we know full well— because we directly experience this Higher Self and can compare our best achievement to his true spiritual stature, that everything we may hope to offer, even the best fruit we have produced, is still only an outgrowth of our earthly self. And then we 'see' (let us be reminded that seeing is becoming and becoming is seeing in the spiritual worlds) in a real Imagination, how the I AM being, our Higher Self, the earthly-sun being, takes in our human offer and makes it part of his Self. We see how our lower self is taken into the heart, actually breathed in by the Higher Self, and we feel that our offer has been accepted. We experience the most noble bliss, free from false pride and carried by innermost gratitude, that this grace is given to us, to be able to offer something that is accepted as valuable by the Higher Self, and that He affirms that we have used His forces in a way that He can gracefully breathe them into his sun being and spiritualize them with his own infinite love. We give him a tiniest seed, but we see how in him it is transformed, purified, and becomes in all eternity a life-giving spiritual tree. Then we can say, for the first time in our lifetime, 'I offer the gifts, but in reality it is not "I" who is giving, nor is this "I" the source of my gifts, but it is the I AM, the Christ, that lives, works, moves, and offers in me'. This increasingly becomes an honest experience, one that we can face while we stand face to face with the being of our innermost spiritual conscience.

And then, if we feel inspired to become creative, morally speaking, by the example of the Higher Self, we may articulate ourselves and shape our offer into cosmic Word. Since we have meditated and assimilated many inspired passages and mantras from the Holy Scriptures and spiritual science, it is handy, spiritually speaking, to use a meditation that has become so intimately part of ourselves, that in its spiritualized form, it can be articulated and spoken in the etheric world.

Let us say that we have meditated and assimilated so intimately for decades a mantra such as the one below given by Mabel Collins in her book, *Light on the Path*. This requires, naturally, that it first became alive, repeatedly and intimately, in our human heart, in which we focused the activity of our 'I' and astral body, and then, to the extent that it was growing ever more potent, it was inscribed and embodied deeply in our etheric body. When this body was released from the physical (see Chapter 7 above) it served as an etheric template or scaffold, that helped to shape and consolidate an independent etheric body in which our spirit individuality could be embodied in the etheric world. Now, the real spiritual force extracted from such an etherized mantra, comes to our help spontaneously and we are able to let it speak us into expression in the etheric world, shape us through its spiritual power of articulation, with the outermost devotion and surrender.

On the earth we have mediated devotedly:

More radiant than the sun
Purer than the snow
Finer than the ether,
Is the Self
The spirit in my heart.
I am this Self,
This Self Am I.

However, before we continue to describe how we articulate this mantra in the meeting, we must first struggle to understand what is really meant by 'spiritual speaking' and 'communication' in supersensible reality. The other being is actually inside us, and we are already inside the other. Communication is here communion, not as a mere phrase but in all concrete reality. It means mutual essence exchange and mutual enhancement of the one, in and through the other. But what is the essence that is 'exchanged'? It is your essence in me, when I become conscious of your being and becoming in and through me. This is 'my' essence (we realize soon enough that all the possessive words and expressions, even more than all other earthly words, lose all meaning in the spiritual worlds, and furthermore, are the most misleading because we must use them if we want to communicate spiritual processes in ordinary language). But in the spiritual world we can only articulate something if we first con-sciously become this something that we want to 'say' to another being. Therefore, we must become the other in us in order to express to the other his being and becoming through us. We must become the Word that we want to 'communicate'; it is 'self-wording' of our own becoming, because *we are the other – and our becoming the other is the content of our message to the other.* Now when you stand imaginatively 'face to face' with the Higher Self (and only in the cognitive stage of Imagination we can still speak – only to begin with – about 'standing face to face', because in the more inspired and intuited imaginative stages these spatial concepts lose any meaning), you can only strive to become the humblest affirmation of what He is; but you can only become what He is if he gives you first these forces of becoming, that can only flow from His innermost spiritual heart. He *is* pure, absolute Being; and His beingness inspires the forces of becoming true Being. Therefore, we can only articulate — that is become — a word, nay, a syllable, or rather utter a single movement, after we first received the 'invitation' to do so, in the form of the forces needed to articulate them. They must be awaited; we cannot 'decide' that we 'want' to 'say' something to the Higher Self. The necessary forces to become what the Higher Self is are given to us through grace, and only then can we become what they mean. And what they mean is, to begin with, as we said above, the one and only possible affirmation of Being: 'Thou Art'. And only after this act of becoming can 'we' add (in reality, it is our Angel, who is one with our Spirit Self, who speaks with us, in unison with our heart) the interpretation: 'Not "I" but Thou, the Other — the Higher Self — in me'. This assimilation and self-transformation, this becoming in the inward likeness of the Imagi-nation of the source *is* the essence of spiritual communication-communion. This is the ABC of any true spiritual conversation. The forces of becoming-other, of metamorphosis, flow into us from the being of the Christ and we can only speak and articulate ourselves in so far as He supports our becoming-transforming us into the likeness of His Imagination. Therefore, the humble recognition and re-identification, expressed through the declaration: 'Thou Art' is articulated very slowly, because it must first become self-articulation and self-becoming, articulated according to the Imagination of the Higher Self, which we must first assimilate and become with all the fibres of our etheric body and spiritual being. And the next word we become must therefore express that through the 'Thou Art' we become the becoming of the 'Thou Art'. It expresses the fact that we are becoming the likeness of the Imagination of the essence of 'Thou Art', becoming, for example, 'more radiant then the sun' which again, is expressed very slowly, because we must first really become this radiance, this light and this sun ourselves. We are giving back — this is the meaning of the concept of 'essence exchange' experienced from our side — what we received: the power to become, that is, the force of eternal becoming, the gift of the eternal being of the Christ to the earth and humanity in our age.

On the earth we meditated it devotedly and now it lights up in us with all its precious, fresh, spiritual potency:

More radiant than the sun
Purer than the snow
Finer than the ether,
Is the Self
The spirit in my heart.
I am this Self,
This Self Am I.

Now in the etheric world, standing face to face with the Higher Self, we pronounce repeatedly, before each new approach, the heartfelt, devoted, 'Thou Art', which is the inner spiritual equivalent of heartfelt physical kneeling, while experiencing the true spiritual being of the Higher Self. And His true being is becoming and His gift to us is the gift of becoming.

We can only aspire to become His becoming:

Thou art,
My 'I' becomes more radiant than the Sun
Thou art,
My 'I' becomes purer than the snow,
Thou art,
My 'I' becomes finer than the ether:
Thou art,
My 'I' becomes the Self
Thou art,
The Spirit in my heart.

and now, embodying, becoming the power of becoming, experiencing the being of the Higher Sun-Like Self as our innermost self, we articulate ourselves as the metamorphosis of the lower self into the Higher Self:

I am becoming this Self;
This Self becomes my 'I'.

We feel honestly that through the Imagination of the Christ in our 'I', the 'I AM' becomes in us the becoming of new sun life, light and love. And we offer this essence to the being of the Christ as the fruit of His sacrificial life, planted gracefully in our earthly-human life and becoming.

And then — here ordinary words are less appropriate then ever — we experience how the Christ takes into Himself our lower self, embodies Himself in our lower self, and transforms His self into each and all aspects and forces of our earthly, lower, human being. We experience that He becomes our lower self and in so doing penetrates and redeems all our human forces, and that through Him there is nothing in us — even our most base, repugnant and evil vices and tendencies — that cannot become through His forces, in the future, His seeds of new sun life. He, the cosmic and all human Higher Self being, incorporates himself in our individual, personal, lower self and demonstrates in us that all lower life is the finest fertile earthly seed of His future sun life. We are His soil and compost and He is the spiritual gardener that plants in us His future sun seeds, and through Him our lower self will bring forth increasing streams of higher life, abundant fruits of goodness beauty and truth, if we follow His way and example planted and demonstrated in our lower self.

And then He offers us His exemplary deed as an answer to our offer of our highest life in Him. As we offered Him our highest life that He created in us, so now He offers us His life as a working, transforming, power inside our lowest life. And He may use, if He so chooses, the same words of becoming that we used to articulate our becoming, returning to us the fruits of the spiritual language that we became, to answer our upward offer by the downward pouring of His grace. He may then speak to us the reversed mantra, and exchange its essence with our human essence. We experience how He, the highest, is bowing down to embrace and purify the feet of our lowest self, and how He speaks to the lowest as we would have aspired to speak before to the highest:

I AM becoming darker than the earth
I AM becoming more tainted than the mud
I AM becoming coarser than matter
Your lower self

The spirit in my heart
I AM this self:
This self is I AM.

When the Higher Self becomes the lower self, and the lower self becomes the becoming forces of the Higher Self, the two selves merge and exchange each other in and through each other in an etheric breathing and circulation. Gradually this mutual essence exchange becomes a perpetual, repeated, lemniscate stream of metamorphosis. Thus we humbly learn the modern *Imitatio Christi*, individualizing Christ's eternal example in us, demonstrating in us the renewal and resurrection of all life in creation. And in this new life cycle, humanity and the earth become co-creative partners with the highest gods, who serve the divine source of all creation.

In the etheric world we use the forces of this mutual essence exchange to become, etherically speaking, an etheric earthly chalice that would contain the purest sun extract of the gift that we become. And now we turn back to our physical bodies and physical life on the earth. We may now return to our earthly life and its responsibilities and tasks with a potent seed of hope, love and faith. And we pray that we may become worthy to cultivate it rightly in our human hearts, minds and deeds, becoming a fertile human soil, compost and gardeners of the new sun seed in the smallest and greatest tasks of humanity in our age.

> *Might it not then also be possible today that something of infinite importance is taking place and that human beings are not taking it into their consciousness? Could it not be that something tremendously important is taking place in the world, taking place right now, of which our own contemporaries have no presentiment? This is indeed so. Something highly important is taking place that is perceptible, however, only to spiritual vision.*
>
> *We thus comprehend spiritual science in a completely different sense. We learn that it imposes a tremendous responsibility upon us, since it is a preparation for the concrete occurrence of the reappearance of Christ. Christ will reappear because human beings will be raising themselves toward Him in etheric vision. When we grasp this, spiritual science appears to us as the preparation of human beings for the return of Christ, so that they will not have the misfortune to overlook this great event but will be ripe to seize the great moment that we may describe as the second coming of Christ. Man will*

be capable of seeing etheric bodies, and among these etheric bodies he will also be able to see the etheric body of Christ; that is, he will grow into a world in which the Christ will be visible to his newly awakened faculties.

Let us use spiritual science so that it may serve not merely to satisfy our curiosity but in such a way that it will prepare us for the great tasks, the great missions of the human race for which we must grow ever more mature.

(25 January, 1910, GA 118)